NEGOTIATING A GOOD OLD AGE

NEGOTIATING
A GOOD OLD AGE

Challenges of
Residential Living in Late Life

MARY GWYNNE SCHMIDT

Jossey-Bass Publishers
San Francisco • Oxford • 1990

NEGOTIATING A GOOD OLD AGE
Challenges of Residential Living in Late Life
by Mary Gwynne Schmidt

Copyright © 1990 by: Jossey-Bass Inc., Publishers
350 Sansome Street
San Francisco, California 94104
&
Jossey-Bass Limited
Headington Hill Hall
Oxford OX3 0BW

Library of Congress Cataloging-in-Publication Data

Schmidt, Mary Gwynne.
    Negotiating a good old age : challenges of residential living in
late life / Mary Gwynne Schmidt. — 1st ed.
        p.   cm.—(The Jossey-Bass social and behavioral science
series) (The Jossey-Bass health series)
    Includes bibliographical references and index.
    ISBN 1-55542-293-4 (alk. paper)
    1. Old age homes—United States—Case studies.   2. Long-term care
facilities—United States—Case studies.   3. Aged—Institutional
care—United States—Case studies.   I. Title.   II. Series.
III. Series: The Jossey-Bass health series.
HV1454.2.U6S36   1990
362.6'1'0973—dc20   90-38688
                                                              CIP

Manufactured in the United States of America

The paper in this book meets the guidelines for
permanence and durability of the Committee on
Production Guidelines for Book Longevity of the
Council on Library Resources.

JACKET DESIGN BY WILLI BAUM

FIRST EDITION

Code 9096

A joint publication in
The Jossey-Bass Social and Behavioral Science Series
and
The Jossey-Bass Health Series

Contents

Preface

Negotiating a Good Old Age contains material that is critical to all of us, for both individual and institutional reasons. On an existential level, it answers "Where am I going and what will I become?"; on an institutional plane, it addresses the question "What is the emerging shape of long-term care?" Above all, this book covers the meeting ground of these concerns as it describes patterns of interaction between residents, staff, and setting in two homes for the very old, homes that were themselves in the process of change.

These issues gain their urgency from demographic changes that have generated a growing sense that familiar economic forces have slipped out of control. The ensuing uneasiness is expressed by such concerns as the right-to-die movement. Aging individuals look at patients in nursing homes and ask, "Must we live and die like this?" Passive euthanasia draws much of its support from the middle-aged and old. For its part, society examines the bill for long-term care, shakes its head, and says, "We can't afford it."

The attention now focused on issues of aging is but one part of a general concern about being human in a crowded world. Both the corrections and mental health fields deal with some individuals who appear to be unable to use the community alternatives our society is willing to fund. As their absolute numbers grow, increasing interest in settings of close containment will follow. Professionals will be forced to consider how these troublesome or needful people can be handled efficiently when care must be delivered within walls; those who are thoughtful will also begin to think about how individuality can be maintained under such circumstances. As these issues come into focus, we need to learn more about how people negotiate relationships in closed and semiclosed environments.

By describing the experiences of 116 residents in two homes for the aged over a fifteen-year period, this book examines negotiation about status and relationships and how individuals seek to maintain an acceptable self. Far from accepting the "elderly mystique" with its low goals and self-expectations (Cohen, 1988), these residents jousted with peers, attempted to control staff, and tried to make good lives and deaths for themselves in settings that some chose and others did not.

Each home offered two levels of care and control. Most residents liked the boarding units but waged lonely battles to stave off patienthood. In describing similar struggles in a retirement complex, David Morgan (1982) points out that when persons entered they shed their burdens, but when they became patients they lost their independence. Some won their fight to remain boarders to the end; more did not. Like the residents, staff members also aged and left, while the homes themselves changed under the impact of economic, regulatory, and population factors.

The homes were in flux. They were transforming themselves in order to survive. At the study's start, the dichotomy was clear-cut: one home was proprietary, the other sectarian. Each typified its kind. Seventeen years later, the two homes have become more like each other. Both are like small ships tossed on the same sea of regulation that has accomplished some professionalization but has failed to make most facilities for the elderly decent places to live and die.

Background Information

This book is based on a longitudinal study I conducted in the 1970s and 1980s. Instruments measuring social resources, norm conformity, and morale were administered to a cohort of residents in

1973 to 1974 and again to the survivors in 1978, 1979, 1980, 1981, 1982, 1983, and 1984. By the last year, the number of subjects had shrunk from the original 116 to 10. At the present writing, one survivor remains. In-depth interviews centering around the Philadelphia Geriatric Morale Scale provided a rich flow of qualitative data that reflected changes over time. (See Resource A for attrition and Resource B for all of the instruments except the Philadelphia Geriatric Morale Scale, which is available in Lawton's [1973] chapter of a book edited by Brantl and Brown.)

In this book, I use material about residents anecdotally but also follow some persons throughout the narrative in order to illustrate changes in status and in the management of self over time. *Negotiating a Good Old Age* stays with individuals, settings, and staff long enough to find out "how it all came out."

Because of my personal relationship with each of the subjects, a word of explanation is in order. While I was engaged in doctoral studies, I provided social services at Mountainside, a sectarian home for the aged. Theories relating to deviance, control, and social resources came alive as I observed daily exchange in the setting. When I came to do research for my dissertation, I found that these well-educated residents were happier to have me as a researcher than as a social worker: They wanted to contribute to knowledge; they were not sure they needed social services.

To expand my sample into numbers I could work with, I added Countryside, a proprietary facility. I spent several months getting acquainted with its residents before I began administering tests, and from 1973 to 1974, I gathered data. My role at Countryside was purely that of researcher, but again I found myself drawn to the residents and the staff.

Eventually I completed my dissertation and set off for Australia; but I was hooked, and I corresponded with people in the two homes. From afar, I watched the small dramas, the deaths, and the sudden turns of fortune.

When I returned to the United States in 1978, I went back to the homes and administered tests to the survivors. Thereafter, I returned each summer, interviewed those who remained, did in-service training for the staff, and observed the changes in the settings. By 1984, only ten of the original subjects remained. Three were lost to the study and the others were dead, so that year I tested for the last time. In December 1984, the last members of the original cohort at Countryside died and I ceased my visits there, but I continued to go to Mountainside. At this writing, one Mountainside resident from the original group remains in the nursing unit, and we stay in touch. As an old friend might, I have come to feel a sense of personal loss at each resident's passing and also to experience vicarious release when I knew the person was praying for death.

The study's strength lies in its longitudinal perspective. The people, the buildings, and even the neighborhoods change over time. Peer leaders rise and fall and many individuals snatch small victories and die good deaths. Administrators despair but keep going.

The study's limitations have positive features. On the one hand, because it was not tightly planned as a longitudinal study, the point of view shifted to take into account larger structural features: Over time I became aware that the ship was moving as well as its passengers. On the other hand, the instruments were frozen into place, although some might not be chosen today. Because of the age of the residents, time eventually reduced their numbers below statistical convenience. Finally, the two homes were atypical in at least two respects: Neither belonged to one of the big national chains that have come to dominate the long-term care "industry," and most of the residents were middle class. The two homes experienced the constraints of smaller size and state regulation, but their independence of distant management may have made them more responsive to individuals and to intrasystemic pressures. In addition, the absence of the poor and minorities meant that findings were not complicated by the problems of lifetimes of deprivation and struggle. Life had been relatively kind to these people, and what happened to them at Countryside and Mountainside reflected the experience of old age and institutionalization relatively uncontaminated by past or current social injustice.

For Whom Is This Book Intended?

For various readers, the book offers special features and attempts to answer certain questions.

For readers in general, there are the portraits of the residents.

How does one preserve something of one's self when others control so much of one's life at the end, when the biological assault seems so inexorable? What happens when children grow old and friends die? Can others take their place? How, at the end of life, can one live so close to so many others?

For the sociologist, the social psychologist, and the anthropologist, there are the two settings, each offering two levels of care and control, each level with its own roles, statuses, norms, and sanctions and with residents moving between them. Is transfer between boarding and nursing units determined solely by medical criteria? And if not, what other factors enter into the decision? Who is able to fend off transfer, and how? How do different ground rules constrain the individual's ability to bargain for status and to resist demands? When staff's expectations compete with those of peers, which prevail? Do "conformers" conform to everything or do they choose their areas of conformity? What is lost and what is retained when most familiar statuses are stripped away?

For the planner, the applied sociologist, and the administrator, there are the changes over time in the two settings. These homes serve similar clienteles and charge equivalent rates, but only the proprietary home makes a profit. Do nonprofit facilities provide more, or do they operate less efficiently? Do licensing requirements improve care, or do they result chiefly in the paper compliance that is easier to check than is the quality of service delivery? Can nonprofits remain service oriented in a climate of rising costs? How can the demands for affordable care be reconciled with the demands for individualization and self-determination?

For those professionals with patients and clients in old-age settings—physicians, nurses, psychologists, social workers, activities directors, administrators, and board members—there are the day-to-day and year-to-year observations in the two homes. Why does so much friction surround the interaction between staff members and the patient's spouse? Why are so few roommates friends? Why do some residents slip easily into the hierarchies of congregate living and others persistently court rejection? What happens to patient care plans when professionals must depend on paraprofessionals to implement them? Does the patient become their hostage? How can the arrival of a new director of nursing affect the incontinence level?

How do residents shape the behavior of staff? Does the resident's unhappiness over placement necessarily mean that he or she is dissatisfied with the home?

Above all, what happens to the inner self in the course of the moral career, when the challenges of institutional living reach from entry to the door of death? (See Resource C for waystations in the institutional career.)

Finally, for all readers as responsible members of society, there are the profound and sometimes costly changes that have taken place in both settings. How can an appropriate degree of consumer autonomy be engineered into a system already burdened with staff accountability and budgetary and licensing controls? Within the existing constraints, what can be done to support the elderly resident more and make the system better?

In dealing with these issues, *Negotiating a Good Old Age* employs a symbolic interactionist perspective to help the reader understand the interplay between resident and resident and between resident and staff, especially in status negotiation. It draws on the social exchange theory of Blau (1964), Emerson (1962), Rogers (1974), and Dowd (1980); Goffman's (1961) institutional totality; Roth's (1963) concept of the career; Lieberman and Tobin's (1983) work on institutions and identity; Litwak's (1985) exploration of the complementary roles of formal and informal systems; Strauss's (1978) examination of negotiation; and Glaser and Strauss's (1971) work on status passage.

Because of the rapidity of change, journal articles and demographics ground observed shifts within the two homes. Those emerging from the 1985 National Nursing Home survey (National Center for Health Statistics and Hing, Sekscenski, and Strahan, 1989; National Center for Health Statistics and Hing, 1987) are of special importance.

Overview of the Contents

The book describes the efforts of residents to negotiate acceptable selves as they move through the levels of care and the concurrent changes in the two homes themselves. These are discussed in three parts, each with its own introduction.

The first part, "The People, the Places, the Paths," describes the homes themselves, the roles and rules available to residents, and the way the elderly residents moved through them.

The five chapters in the second part, "What Actually Takes Place in Residential Settings?," examine the ways in which residents negotiated their statuses, the resources on which they drew, the shifting patterns of constraint, the support and power they encountered, and how their residential careers came to an end.

The final part, "Adaptations to a Changing Climate: Where We Are Now and What We Can Do," relates the two homes' adaptations to a changing political and demographic climate for long-term care and considers the three areas most deeply challenging to the preservation of self and most amenable to change: the management of incontinence, dementia, and staffing. The section closes with concrete steps physicians, nurses, social workers, and families can take while waiting for larger-system change. Despair is immobilizing; action is liberating.

Acknowledgments

Because all names have been changed to protect people's anonymity, I cannot thank as I would like to the wonderful residents and staff members who helped me write this book. I can only say that I owe a good deal to them and to Ludwig Geismar, my mentor, and Albert Schmidt, my husband.

I would also like to thank reviewers of the manuscript, especially Carolyn Wiener and Rosalie Kane, who contributed to my thinking and made this a better book, as did my editor, Gracia A. Alkema. I was never alone.

San Diego, California   Mary Gwynne Schmidt
September 1990

The Author

Mary Gwynne Schmidt is professor of social work at San Diego State University. She received her B.A. degree (1943) from the University of North Carolina, Chapel Hill, in American History; her M.A. degree (1958) from Teachers College, Columbia University, in the teaching of social studies in secondary school; and both her M.S.W. degree (1964) and her Ph.D. degree (1975) from Rutgers, the State University of New Jersey, in social work.

Schmidt's published papers have appeared in *Health & Social Work, Nursing and Health Care, The International Journal of Aging and Human Development,* the *Journal of Gerontological Social Work, Hospital & Community Psychiatry,* and *The Gerontologist,* and she serves on the latter publication's editorial board. She contributed a chapter in Irene Burnside's *Working with the Elderly: Group Process and Technique* (1984).

Schmidt previously taught at the Flinders University of South Australia. She presently serves on the faculties of the San Diego State University School of Social Work and the San Diego Geriatric Education Center, a partnership between the University of California San Diego School of Medicine and San Diego State University's Center on Aging. All of her consultation and most of her teaching have been in the field of aging, with special attention to long-term residential care.

Key Characters

Because this book deals with change over time, certain individuals appear more than once. To avoid having to reintroduce them and to aid the reader, some are listed below with a few words of introduction. These are not their real names, nor are Mountainside and Countryside the names of the two facilities.

Mountainside was a sectarian home in an urban setting. *Barbara Archer* was its administrator and *Beth McGann* its second director of nursing.

The *Santa Claus Society* helped educated persons maintain their lifestyle when their means were straitened because they had lived lives of service.

Characters

Evan Brewster fought an eight-year battle with cancer while living in the mansion he had admired as a boy. He was a table host, belonged to the Old Guard, and continued to drive his car.

Agnes Chase, a physical education teacher, entered Mountainside at seventy-five because she had only English cousins as her family. She brought much energy to her crusades for social justice.

Sarah Coleman, ninety-three, worried about rising costs and her fixed income. As she neared one hundred, she said, "I wish this wouldn't go on so long." She chose Mountainside in order to be close to her church and her friends.

Ramona Everly was a handsome, strong-minded woman, alert and mentally engaged, but she was very, very weary at the end. Like Sarah Penfield, she was an early peer leader.

Robert Farmer entered as a patient and later transferred to the boarding unit, where he became the unofficial organizer of games. His social resources included two physician sons.

Miss Godfrey, as a child, had romped with the children who lived at Mountainside when it was a family estate; in her nineties, she returned as a patient. A stockbroker's daughter, she retained her social connections.

Henry Hobart, legally blind, composed poetry on the typewriter to two loves. When the first died, he commented sadly, "Our children did not want us to marry."

John McGreevy, a Catholic, tweaked the blue noses in this nest of Protestants but basked in the affection of his family and his community and treasured his special telephone.

Dr. Ernest Magyar entered Mountainside at sixty-three with multiple sclerosis. When *Dr. Maria Magyar* came to visit her husband in the home, she deflected staff anger from him with her many demands.

Elka Miller was European in outlook and never quite at home at Mountainside, but she held on. Henry Hobart wrote poems to her.

John and Sarah Penfield had been active in Mountainside's founding and were respected peer leaders.

Elizabeth Reynolds had visited her church's home as a girl and knew "when the time had come." She carefully maintained her boarder status.

Margaret Wesley was pushed into the patient role when she entered the nursing unit as her husband's roommate. *John Wesley* had advanced Parkinson's disease but survived his wife.

Marcy Mae White was an English kindergarten teacher with a following of former pupils. She entered the nursing home rather than the boarding home because she was ninety-four.

Rachel Windsor, sixty-three, was Mountainside's youngest boarder.

Despite stroke-impaired speech and gait, she functioned well and had great symbolic importance for the group.

Countryside was a proprietary home in a rural setting. Most of its owners were physicians. At the study's start, *Ernest Miller* was its administrator and *Winnie Mason* its director of nursing.

Characters

The Commander was a feisty old explorer whose athleticism posed a problem. Colorful and a celebrity, he was "homesick" for flying.

Dorothy Dietrich, wealthy and unmarried, flourished with a private duty nurse while her ninety-year-old roommate, *Nellie Brown,* was often physically restrained and helpless.

Gretchen Elder alienated peers with her lamentations and staff with her rigidities. She spoke of her son's suicide with envy. She was a reliable informant.

Mrs. Flowers was unhappy in the home but fearful of leaving it because of her memories of lying helpless in her big house, waiting for her housekeeper to come. She had an attentive daughter.

Grace Gladwin, once head of a nursing agency, was a colorful, flamboyant figure whose descent into confusion troubled those who had known her.

Greta Hansen was taken from her husband's funeral straight to Countryside. She was cheerful and friendly but confused.

John McDevitt never ceased to complain about the "conspiracy" between physician and family that brought him to Countryside, where he was a peer leader in the boarding unit.

William McGillacudhy, a city politician, came to Countryside to be close to his daughter. A stroke sent him on a downward course. He and John McDevitt were Countryside's two Irishmen, but they were not friends.

Mamie Slocum tyrannized her fellow boarders. Among her prey was the sad widow she labeled "the Creep." Like Napoleon at Elba, she was angry at the cancer that cut short her late-life career and divorced her from her troops.

NEGOTIATING A GOOD OLD AGE

Part One

THE PEOPLE, THE PLACES, THE PATHS

> This is a more important place than the hospital. The hospital is for short danger, but this is for your finish. . . . I'm here for life.
>
> William McGillacudhy, age 84,
> Countryside boarder

Most elderly persons entering a home for the aged view this move as their last one. But whatever sense of loss they may feel, they are concerned also with the life they can make there. Thus, homes for the aged become little laboratories of human behavior as residents deal with change on a scale for which their previous lives have not prepared them.

The two homes described in this book serve as particularly good laboratories because each offers two clear-cut roles with associated statuses: boarder and patient. Negotiating over these roles is part of residents' efforts to control their own last years. It is also their defense of self. The way residents in the homes coped with these transitions reveals something about the way people everywhere deal with issues of autonomy and control.

The initial reluctance to enter homes for the aging is hardly surprising. Robert Kleemeier (1963) observed that old people dislike the special settings society provides for them in proportion to just how congregate, segregate, and institutional they are—that is, to the degree that they mandate group living with its diminished opportunities for privacy, reduce interaction with other age groups, and exercise strong behavioral control. Kleemeier said entrance into

1

these settings forced a break with past concepts of self, in part because the elderly themselves recognized and possibly shared society's negative attitudes. He added that if their need to conserve energy was great, they would put up with the setting's restrictions.

Kleemeier's congregate, segregate, and institutional setting was congruent with Irving Goffman's (1961) total institution, which applies bureaucratic principles to the processing and management of people. All the residents' living takes place in a single setting under the direction of one authority. A caste-like division exists between inmates and staff. Unlike staff members, residents of total institutions have few community contacts and are deprived of normal family life.

Subsequent literature has emphasized the variations in institutional totality, a point that Goffman himself made but that has tended to get lost in the starkness of the mental hospitals, prisons, and concentration camps he described. Some total institutions are benign (Bennett, 1963; Wolins and Wozner, 1982; Jones and Fowles, 1984). These would include nunneries, institutions for the blind, and homes for the elderly, but even these standardize their human material in the interest of more efficient processing. Because standardization makes deviance stand out, it enables a small staff to manage a larger number of people, which explains the continued existence of the total institution in a century that has seen its full potential for evil. Civilized society is willing to tolerate the depersonalization of prisoners and patients because the most expensive feature in people processing is staffing. Standardization makes it possible to keep this cost down.

Some uniformity is necessary wherever people are being served in groups. The level of institutional totality tends to be particularly high in nursing homes despite their benevolent intent because the need for hands-on labor is great and cost is a pressing concern. These issues affect the definition of residents.

The "batching" principle—handling numbers of people together in the same way at the same time—was integrated into the moral order of the nursing units by the use of status generalization. As Webster and Driskell (1985) have remarked, it is not necessary for a status characteristic to be relevant in order to shape the immediate interaction. The designation as patient in and of itself discounts the individual's capacity for decision making and thus makes it possible to simplify the planning process by not taking the affected person's preferences into account.

The three chapters in this section deal with these issues: They introduce the two roles available to residents, the homes themselves, and four common pathways through them. The first chapter compares the experiences of patients and boarders, the differential impact of staff and peer norms in the boarding and nursing units, and the burden of accountability that shaped the staff's actions.

Chapter Two contrasts Mountainside with Countryside. Although they served similar populations, they differed in character because of sponsorship. Countryside was proprietary and emphasized medical leadership and private enterprise; Mountainside was sectarian, with strongly held values about propriety, activity, and service. The two homes differed also because Countryside was rural and Mountainside was urban and because the personal philosophies of their administrators were not the same.

The longer third chapter presents the career as a common path with a series of transition points and ongoing negotiations surrounding them (Roth, 1963). The chapter and the section close with descriptions of the four common residential careers in these two-step settings: boarding-unit-based careers, symmetrical careers, nursing-home-based careers, and careers ending in exile.

CHAPTER ONE

Roles for the Elderly:
Boarders and Patients

Robert Farmer approached Mountainside's ordained roles in a deviant sequence and thus his experience made plain how differently its occupants were perceived.

While awaiting a room in Mountainside's boarding unit, Robert Farmer, then eighty-two, suffered a small stroke. Instead of entering as a boarder as he had planned, he therefore came in as a patient.

He had been looking forward to Mountainside. He was a lifelong member of the sponsoring Protestant sect and many of his old friends lived in the home. Instead of joining them, he found himself on the same grounds in a stigmatized and segregated status. He wore a wristband lest he wander and need to be returned. His activities were closely supervised; he had no privacy and little meaningful companionship.

The effects of the stroke had been transitory; his speech was clear and his hand was steady. He was restless and depressed and passed his days doing crossword puzzles, reading to a fellow patient, and trying to get himself transferred to the boarding unit. He protested that he needed more exercise—and was promptly scheduled for walks under the supervision

5

of a uniformed aide. Officially, he was a stroke patient inappropriately trying to become a boarder.

The staff charted everything he did as evidence that he should remain a patient. His depression was recorded without attention to antecedent events: Within ten months, he had lost his wife, his home, his car, and his freedom. Tears came to his eyes when he spoke of family deaths, which the staff cited as evidence of "emotional lability." The aide who escorted him on his walks reported that when he was out of sight of the home, he became disoriented. When the social worker observed that his recall for past and recent events seemed good, that he was neither concrete nor tangential, that he displayed a clear grasp of his situation and feelings, that he dressed and shaved himself, and that he did not seem in need of so much supervision, she was confronted with the nursing notes. It looked as if he would remain a patient forever.

Then five weeks after he entered the nursing unit, he became a boarder. He tactfully assured the administrator he would speak with her before setting off on any independent projects. Next he began to organize the play life of the boarding unit: He introduced an ongoing game of scrabble, and bridge games began to take place regularly. He went with the other men from the home to the weekly meeting of the Old Guard where, as one man primly reported, he was not at all interested in the business meeting but just wanted to play bridge and have fun. He had grown up in a large family and he appeared to slip comfortably into the life of the home, happy to have so many age peers and to be on an equal footing.

Mountainside and Countryside offered their residents two formal roles: boarder and patient. As Robert Farmer quickly found out, the differences were great. Boarders were asked; patients were told. Boarders were addressed by title; patients were often called by their first names. Patients were put to bed; boarders retired when they were ready. The incompetence of patients was taken for granted; anyone questioning the competence of a boarder bore the burden of proof.

The staff viewed everything Robert Farmer did in the patient role in the context of his stroke-patient status. Thus they overlooked his recent losses and his depression, which they attributed to his "organicity." That he wanted to become a boarder was cited as evidence of his poor judgment. The facts that he was shaving, feeding, and dressing himself, that he was solving doublecrostics in ink, that he was reading to another patient and that he was experiencing no difficulty with recall were ignored while his behavior was scrutinized for evidences of aberration. One was found: A nurse discovered him sitting on the cool tiles of his bathroom floor working a crossword puzzle. When she suggested that he would be more comfortable seated at a desk, he invited her to join him, and she charted this behavior.

Each role carried with it a packet of behavioral prescriptions, and each status had a bundle of duties and rights. Robert Farmer's status gave him his ranking in the system: It told him to whom he owed deference and from whom he could expect it. Patienthood overrode all his other statuses: While Mountainside's administrator and professional nurses were meticulous about calling the elderly patients "Mr." or "Mrs.," the nursing assistants were not; they called him "Robert."

Boarders were socialized to their new roles principally by their peers; patients were taught role expectations by staff. This was understandable because boarders had an investment in the behavior of their fellows while nursing personnel were held accountable for the acts of their patients.

Residents encountered both staff and peer norms. Staff norms were rules for residents that made it easier for employees to process and protect them. Peer norms kept the social climate comfortable and projected a positive image of the group. The elderly residents wanted to be identified as members of a presentable group, a collective facade that is important to individuals who live in an institutional setting. Part of patients' distress, on the other hand, comes from the fear that they will be clumped with the demented persons around them.

Behavioral prescriptions for patients implied passivity; those for boarders implied prudent activity. The most important patient norms facilitated staff work and promoted safety by calling for the patient to cooperate with staff efforts and not to demand too much staff time. Examples included taking medicine promptly without argument and not resisting the bath. Not demanding too much attention was a peer norm that served staff interests as well, because the resident who got too much attention upset her fellow patients, who immediately presented nurses with competing needs of their own. A Mountainside nurse said of a pair of rivalrous roommates, "I don't dare go in with meds for one if I don't have meds for the other."

The demand for passivity reflects the Parsonian dilemma of the nursing home patient. Parsons held that it is all right to be ill if you can't help it, if you don't like it, and if you cooperate with professionals in an effort to get well (Parsons, 1970). Unfortunately, few nursing home patients can expect to recover and therefore they face the prospect of cooperating with professionals the rest of their lives. The dilemma, then, is that they must want to get well while knowing they never can.

Boarders were viewed as quite capable of planning their own activities as long as those activities did not interfere with staff routines. When they did, there might be some question about the residents' judgment and eligibility to remain boarders. Most staff norms for boarders involved doing something, such as signing out when they left the facility or keeping their own rooms picked up so they would not require more than their share of maid service. Initiative was not encouraged in the nursing units; within bounds, it was rewarded in the boarding section as long as it did not entail "pushing oneself forward"—that is, competing with established peer leaders or upsetting staff. As will be seen, Mountainside, the sectarian home, encouraged more independence than Countryside, the proprietary facility, where an aura of patienthood hung over the entire home because of the dominance of its nursing unit.

Mountainside boarders were willing to cede some freedom and

privacy when safety was at stake. After one woman fell in her room and remained on the floor for hours, the staff convened an emergency meeting. Boarders agreed to a proposal advanced by staff and even helped to develop the details. When they retired, they would leave their doors partially open on long hooks. Twice each night a trusted nurse or aide would walk through the boarding unit, checking to see that each person was all right. A few late readers looked forward to the rounds: One gallant Irishman kept a peppermint for the young woman who came around. In a world these residents perceived as increasingly dangerous, security was one of the things they had come for.

In the same spirit, they did not resist the sign-in, sign-out provision, although they took it less seriously and, not infrequently, they would do both on their return. One afternoon I found Robert Farmer recording his morning trip to town; he confided that he had forgotten about it and did not want to upset the administrator.

The boarders at Mountainside themselves introduced the plan of having day hosts and hostesses after they read about theft in the changing town. The entrance had always been kept open until the door was locked for the night, but now one of the duties of the host or hostess was to unlock the door to admit guests or returnees and to greet them.

Countryside boarders not only manifested less concern about city crime than their Mountainside counterparts, but their norms differed also. For example, one rule prescribed that Countryside boarders bathe only with an aide present. Although they were not immune to falls, Mountainside boarders would have rejected such a norm out of hand. These differences in boarder norms are reflected in the two versions of norm conformity tests that appear in Resource B. If rules for the two homes' boarders differed, however, those for their patients did not.

In the nursing units of both homes, even peer norms served the interests of staff. One related to making a "decent" appearance—that is, if you were a woman in a wheelchair, you kept your knees covered; if you were a man, you made sure your trousers were zipped. Failing to do so hurt the image of the group, but it reflected on staff as well, since it was assumed patients "didn't know" and staff should be "responsible."

Because they were less likely to be judged by the behavior of boarders, staff members invested less in their indoctrination: They put out written rules relating to payment and safety and posted typed notices about signing in and missing meals. On the other hand, the rules relating to group life were more crucial to residents in the boarding units and these were communicated to new members informally but emphatically by their peers rather than by staff.

At Mountainside, many of these rules related to demeanor or dress and its reflection on the image of the group. When describing her first days at Mountainside, for example, Elizabeth Reynolds spoke with gratitude about her neighbor, Miss Pierce. "She taught me the ropes. I had assumed that I could wear morning dresses to breakfast and lunch and good dresses for supper. She explained that this wouldn't do and so I wore two or three dresses again and again until my daughter could come to go shopping with me."

When the summers were warm, protocol relaxed a little: Men could come to the dining room without their jackets as long as they wore ties. Mr. McGreevy related, "I met Mr. Hobart in the hall. He asked me where I was going. I said, 'To lunch.' 'Not in those suspenders,' he said. I went back and got a belt." This was Mr. McGreevy's account. A fellow boarder told it differently, "We were disturbed about the way Mr. McGreevy came to lunch and finally we asked Mr. Hobart to speak to him." Her version suggests group concern and group action.

For patients, it was quite different. Mountainside's original director of nursing said, "When I'm helping them get settled, I explain their opportunities." The "opportunities" included the fact that a relative ("responsible person") might select a physician and a pharmacy for them. Although some rules were discussed, patients appeared to learn others, especially those setting the boundaries, by violating them and being corrected. Small children are taught this way, but for adults the process is painful and indelible. The method seemed to reflect staff's embarrassment at telling new patients just how much of their adulthood they had forfeited. One such patient was Margaret Wesley, who, like Robert Farmer, was atypical. Her experience sums up how the nursing unit's socialization processes worked.

> At seventy-seven, Margaret Wesley entered the nursing unit at Mountainside to be a roommate to her husband, who had Parkinson's disease. They had been together since college. She was mentally alert and physically healthy but, by virtue of her rooming arrangements, she became a patient with a band around her wrist.
>
> The morning after her arrival, she started toward the door, and the director of nursing promptly asked her where she was going. She indicated the public library across the street. The nurse explained that she could not leave the unit unless she was accompanied by a "responsible" person.
>
> Shortly afterward she made plans to go to church with one of the boarders who had a car. When she appeared, dressed and ready, she was told that she could not go, that she should attend services in the nursing unit. When she replied that she had better tell her friend, she was informed that the other woman had already been told. Later it was explained that she could not leave the grounds without her family's (that is, her son's) consent.
>
> In the same way, she discovered the limits of the garden: She could go there only within sight of the staff. After she was invited to join the bridge game in the boarding unit, she was escorted by an aide—the administrator expressed the fear that she might get lost, although the boarding unit was under the same roof.
>
> At night, her boundaries narrowed still further. She had a bed rail, which made her bed crib-like and meant she had to ring for a nurse if she wanted to go

to the bathroom. She was allowed to shower by herself but only with a nurse or an aide nearby.

Initially, she was very unhappy: Staff members reported that one day as she sat at lunch, tears ran down her cheeks, and, as with Robert Farmer, this was cited as evidence of incapacity. Eventually Margaret Wesley came to terms with the constant supervision, but she never forgave Ann Hartpence, then Mountainside's director of nursing, for her loss of freedom.

CHAPTER TWO

Mountainside and Countryside: Two Very Different Homes

Like Robert Farmer, William McGillacudhy was a widower who entered long-term care in his early eighties. In other respects, however, the two men were very different and so were their surroundings. Mr. Farmer had spent his life in the country before coming to Mountainside as a patient; Mr. McGillacudhy had spent fifty-four years in the city as a Republican politician before entering Countryside as a boarder.

Mr. McGillacudhy was well pleased with Countryside and he accepted the finality of the move. When he praised the home, he added, "I have no choice—I'm here for life." (This was a phrase I was to hear many times.)

After the death of his wife of fifty-five years, Mr. McGillacudhy had moved to an apartment near the affluent community where his daughter lived. When he began experiencing transient periods of confusion, she arranged his move to Countryside.

There he puffed on his cigar and reviewed his current situation and the life that preceded it. He said he had attended every Republican convention through the one that nominated Thomas Dewey, and he displayed with pride his metal admissions card for the

1940 convention in Philadelphia. He looked back on his career with satisfaction. ("I was always my own boss.") He described his daughter as the source of his present comfort ("She's keeping me here"), and she took him home for mass and dinner every Sunday.

The setting met all his other needs. It provided him with diversions and with age mates, including a rival, John McDevitt. While others cringed before Mamie Slocum, the tyrant of the boarding unit, he withstood that sharp-tongued widow by ignoring her. When he came upon a bingo game in Countryside's dining room, he asked how much it cost. When told it was free, he observed that the house would lose money, and he quickly settled down to win a board and the nominal prize that went with it.

Slightly more than a year and a half after his arrival, Mr. McGillacudhy's contentment came to an end when he suffered a stroke. He was hospitalized, then transferred to that hospital's own convalescent center and finally back to Countryside, but this time he entered its nursing unit. His daughter said she would never again let him go to the hospital, where they gave him tests and otherwise left him alone all day. She said he experienced similar neglect at the hospital's convalescent center, which she described with distaste as having vermin on the floor.

He was eager to return to Countryside, but he came back incontinent and unsteady and found himself tied in a wheelchair. His old rival, Mr. McDevitt, reported cheerfully that when Mr. McGillacudhy's daughter came, he basked in her attention, but otherwise he spent the day asking people to help him get out of his wheelchair. Once he mistook one of the nurses for his daughter and beamingly held out his arms. After eight months, he was transferred to a Medicaid home, where he died within two weeks.

Mr. McGillacudhy would never have found a bingo game at Mountainside, the sectarian home. He might

have missed also the loose, comfortable warmth of
Countryside, where an aide and a maid were assigned
to "take care of" the fifteen boarders and where his
earlier episodes of confusion and unsteadiness had
been acceptable as long as they were transient.

Mountainside and Countryside were chosen for the study because
of the similarity of their populations and the difference in their
sponsorship. Their populations were broadly alike, as both were
white and middle class. The educational level at Mountainside was
slightly higher and the income level a little lower, but the two
homes numbered among their residents attorneys, engineers,
teachers, nurses, business persons, dentists, and physicians. Countryside's residents were drawn from a slightly more varied pool,
ranging from secretaries and farmers' widows to corporation exec-
utives and the aging members of a yacht club set. Mr. McGillacudhy
appears to have spent his working life as a wardheeler, but he was
a wardheeler with an affluent daughter and he viewed his life's
achievements with complacence. Generally, when a widow entered
Countryside, a house had been sold and the proceeds were paying
for her care. The middle-class character of both homes came from
the fact that neither accepted Medicaid patients. In this respect, both
homes were atypical, since nationally 40 percent of nursing home
patients are dependent on public assistance the first month they
enter residential care (National Center for Health Statistics and
Hing, 1987), and almost all become dependent on assistance if they
live long enough.

Although the two homes served the same socioeconomic class,
they differed in history, culture, and geography. The greatest difference lay not between the two homes themselves, however, but
within each home, between their own boarding and nursing units.

The differences in their development reflect the respective histories of sectarian and proprietary homes generally. Over time, Mountainside and Countryside became more like each other, but in 1974,
when this study began, there were striking differences engendered
by their sponsorship. For example, although their rates were similar, Countryside, the for-profit home, paid its owners a steady re-

turn; Mountainside considered it a good year when it nearly broke even.

Proprietary and Nonprofit Facilities

Historically, for-profit and not-for-profit homes grew in different directions. Proprietary facilities began as nursing homes and added lesser levels of care—the path that Countryside took. Voluntary facilities began as homes for the aged and built infirmaries when their residents grew older—the course followed by Mountainside.

Traditionally, voluntary homes for the aged were sponsored by religious, fraternal, or immigrant-aid societies. Mountainside's sponsors belonged to a liberal Protestant sect. At a time when they were becoming concerned about living arrangements for their older members, they were given an urban estate by a donor who did not belong to that religious body but was well aware of its works. He and members of his family took a continuing interest in Mountainside's progress, and when the nursing wing was needed, they supported it generously.

Mountainside was a Victorian mansion that occupied a block in a town on a commuter line. Some of its large rooms were cut up to make smaller bedrooms and extra bathrooms were added, but great changes were not needed. The elderly residents loved the sweeping stairs, the Tiffany glass, and the high ceilings, to say nothing of the great trees and the garden. They gathered in the fine old library to glance at the newspapers before breakfast. They took pride in the paintings, some left by the owner and others given by members of the sect. A few enjoyed gardening, perhaps tending a small bed of flowers or herbs or helping with the watering in summer. Henry Hobart, who had left his own garden with reluctance, pruned the dogwood trees. All liked to walk the paths. The toolhouse had once been the stable, and near it stone slabs marked the graves of beloved family dogs.

Many of the residents remembered the house in its days of local grandeur. Miss Godfrey, for example, a broker's daughter, had romped with the children who lived at Mountainside when it was a family estate. The donor had been one of those children and he, too, was very old and frail, but he came occasionally to visit the home. He always looked up Miss Godfrey, and on these occasions her already high status rose higher. Miss Godfrey, now in her nineties, was a graduate of a famous women's college, class of 1902, and an early career woman.

A Mountainside boarder recalled the deliveries he had made to the estate when he worked as the pharmacist's boy. In the years between, he became a successful manufacturer. He said he had never dreamed that someday he might live in that big house. Memories like these gave the old estate a special prestige.

Local residents liked the home for another reason as well—they could live there and continue with their clubs and churches. These pleasant features of life at Mountainside, however, did not solve the problem of what to do when residents grew ill or frail. They had given up their homes and come as a "last move," not taking into account the inexorable course of aging. About this time, state regulations began to dictate who might remain in such a facility. Canes were permitted but walkers and wheelchairs were banned, and anyone needing real and prolonged nursing care had to move out. To be forced to leave when support was most needed was distressing to the individual and frightening to the bystanders.

With Hill-Burton funds from the government and help from the original donor, a nursing wing was added. The house was Victorian, but the nursing wing was built to the minihospital specifications Public Health Service standards required. Vladeck (1980) has suggested that these specifications have given the U.S. nursing home its institutional air. The boarding unit had twenty-five beds and the nursing unit matched it with twenty-five more. One bed was set aside for boarders with transitory illnesses. Boarders who needed long-term nursing care took precedence over outsiders, but sometimes residents required care the home could not offer.

Countryside also had previously been an old estate, but it had served as a group setting before its physician-owners bought it. Two wealthy sisters gave their home as a vacation retreat for the young women whose labors in the sweatshops had made the sisters' fortune. Times changed and so did the young women, so that the day came when one young woman suffered a "sickness" that proved to be pregnancy. The persons running the home for working girls arranged for physicians from a local hospital to provide health care for the city visitors, but by this time, two well-chaperoned weeks in the country had lost some of their appeal.

Sometime later, the administrator of the hospital learned that Countryside would soon come on the market and he quickly rounded up partners—an accountant, an attorney, and a number of physicians—who wished to make an investment. All were familiar with the property and saw its potential as a nursing home, recognizing its usefulness for patients they wanted to discharge from the hospital. In addition, they believed it would fill a need for many elderly persons marooned without relatives in a changing world. As one remarked, "These old people become the prisoners of their servants." Miss Dietrich, wealthy and without kinsmen, fit the picture.

> Dorothy Dietrich found herself increasingly alone during her last years in the community. She had always been provided for by others and at eighty-four she was not equipped to care for herself. She had had a good deal of jewelry: Some disappeared—given away, lost, or stolen. A "friend" had some pieces "reset" for her and apparently replaced the stones.
>
> Miss Dietrich's trustee placed her at Countryside and saw that she had a private duty nurse to tend to her grooming and act as a daytime companion. She spent the last three years of her life as she had the first eighty-four, tended by others.

The initial conversion of Countryside was relatively easy. There were some small, individual rooms on the first floor and upstairs there were more rooms and a large cheerful sunroom, where patients could spend the day. In time, fire regulations became stricter, and Countryside's owners were told that they could no longer keep nonambulatory residents on the second floor. They resolved this by adding a large modern wing for patients and using the second floor for sheltered care, with beds for twelve boarders and forty-five patients.

To be a boarder at Countryside, applicants had to pass the "stairs test" to demonstrate that they could manage the steps. One frightened woman, with so many dollars at stake and so many persons watching, was unable to do so, but five months later she succeeded—and effected substantial savings.

Each home was influenced by its developmental sequence. At Mountainside, the boarders continued to set the tone even though there were now an equal number of patients. At Countryside, the nursing unit remained dominant, not solely because its patients outnumbered its boarders by almost four to one but also because nursing care was perceived by its owners as the home's primary business. Other differences also distinguished the two homes, including differing administrative styles, cultural differences that arose from sponsorship, and differences caused by location.

Differences in Administrative Styles

The hospital administrator who had assembled Countryside's physician-buyers managed the home from the start. He and his director of nursing determined its character: He brought the hospital connection and a style of outreach that had worked well there; she supplied a commonsense warmth that kept things going.

The hospital to which Ernest Miller had devoted his life began as a converted residence and grew into a multistructured community medical center, and he grew with it. By the time he left, grateful donors had dedicated a Miller pavilion in his honor. He began in the nonprofessional period of hospital administration and gathered credentials and offices in the state association as the field developed. He never swerved in his unquestioning loyalty to his physicians, and he always viewed his task as one of serving them.

The hospital's expansion owed much to the devotion Ernest Miller was able to marshal for it among the laity. The hospital served what was initially a rural fishing resort area with summer visitors. From the beginning, he visited every single patient every day, attentive to the needs of the community's wealthy summer residents who, in turn, made large bequests. He remained grateful long after the gifts had been given.

Something of these relationships showed in his continuing support for Marie Walters, whose mother had been one of the hospital's largest donors.

Before her stroke, Mrs. Walters had been an active member of the hospital auxiliary. She served more hours than any other volunteer in its gift shop, where a large oil portrait of her hung. She introduced the administrator to her friends, who also became donors.

In her early seventies, Mrs. Walters suffered a crippling stroke that left her unable to speak. She had private duty nurses around the clock and refused to leave the hospital. After three years, even the physicians were demanding her discharge. Her family also felt she should leave, but Mrs. Walters communicated by shakes of her head her extreme opposition to going. Mr. Miller defended her against expulsion even as he tried to persuade her to accept other arrangements.

Mr. Miller had been providing the part-time management Countryside originally required while continuing as hospital administrator, but the job was getting bigger. In 1971, he retired from the hospital and devoted himself to the nursing home. When he explained to Mrs. Walters that he now would be at Countryside every day, she consented to the transfer, bringing her nurses with her, one of whom remained till her death. Mr. Miller stopped in to see her daily, an attentive and reassuring presence.

Sheltered by his interest, Mrs. Walters spent her last years well. Although she was totally dependent on the care provided by others, she was much more active than initially seemed possible. My first notes read, "Mrs. Walters is a tall, slender, beautifully tended and attending . . . figure . . . unmoving but benign." She had a small cancerous lesion on her forehead that from time to time required the services of the dermatologist. She did not speak but nodded or shook her head. In the protective climate he had created, she was like a goddess, enshrined in plaster and surrounded by

votive figures. That she was responsive became abun-
dantly clear when she encountered some of her old
friends, now patients like herself at Countryside.
When I took one of them, Mrs. Flowers, on a wheelchair walk, Mrs. Walters reached out and detained her.
The unspoken communication seemed spontaneous
and meaningful. Mrs. Walter's face lit up with pleasure at the sight of welcome visitors. She spent her
afternoons watching baseball games on TV and appeared to follow them with interest.

The protectiveness of her nurse proved an obstacle
to serious interviewing. The nurse agreed that I might
administer the Philadelphia Geriatric Morale Scale
but reserved the right to censor the "sad" questions.
To make matters worse, as the patient nodded or
shook her head, the nurse intervened to urge positive
responses, but fortunately, Mrs. Walters stood her
ground with clear negatives. This still left three questions I was not allowed to ask because the nurse
thought they were "too depressing." (Sample: "As I
get older, things are better, worse, or the same as I
thought they would be.") Almost two months later, I
finally found Mrs. Walters alone and told her I
thought she could handle the "tough" questions, too.
She nodded her willingness and we went back over the
items I had not been allowed to ask. When we came
to "things are better, worse, or the same," her gesture
on the *worse* was unequivocal, giving credibility to
her more positive replies. Her morale score, at the bottom of the middle range, was not bad for a woman
spending years in a wheelchair when she had expected
to spend them on the beach instead. She died of a
stroke shortly before her eighty-first birthday, still attended by her private duty nurse and still visited daily
by Mr. Miller. He had repaid her mother's gift to the
hospital a hundredfold through care he had given her
daughter.

While Countryside's administrator dispensed status and recognition to residents, its director of nursing gave them comfort care and warmth. Winnie Mason was a mature blonde, vigorous, decisive, and overworked, who was realistic about what could be changed and what could not. Her robust sense of humor steadied her through the unending demands.

Miss Mason derived her philosophy of gerontological nursing from her experience with rehabilitation's failures. These were patients who arrived at Countryside when Medicare refused to pay any longer for their care in convalescent facilities. Even Countryside's own patients were recycled through these treatment centers when a fall or an illness took them back through the hospital. Because Medicare would pay only for rehabilitation—and neither Countryside nor Mountainside was certified to provide it—these residents went to Medicare homes from the hospital and returned to Countryside only when Medicare payment stopped, which was as soon as they ceased to appear to be making "progress." They often came back from the Medicare homes confused and functioning at a lower level than before, or, at the least, badly shaken—a predictable response of the very old to so many transfers and so much rejection. Generally their relatives complained that these older patients had been neglected in the rehabilitation facilities. Since their slower progress frustrated rehabilitation workers who found it more rewarding to deal with young accident victims, it appeared that many had received only token treatment and had been quickly relegated to the limbo reserved for the "unmotivated" (Becker and Kaufman, 1988). Their relatives' complaints were therefore not without substance.

All of this reinforced Miss Mason's view that what the very old wanted was to be kept clean and comfortable and well fed. She contended that methods developed to restore the young old—those in their sixties and seventies—to independent functioning after an illness or accident were poorly suited to the old old with their low energy levels and their multiple disabilities. Too often the vigorous and sometimes painful interventions served only to unbalance a generalized slowing-down process and to save the victim from one system failure so that he or she might survive to die of another.

Her views were congruent with Cumming and Henry's (1961) disengagement theory, which held that there was a natural, mutual, and universal process of disengagement that caused distress only when society and the aging individual did not withdraw from one another at the same rate. Opponents criticized disengagement theory on logical, methodological, and humanistic grounds (Neugarten and Havighurst, 1969; Cath, 1975; Gordon, 1975; Hochschild, 1975; Markson, 1975; Spence, 1975) and Cumming (1975) herself deplored its misuse to justify neglect of the elderly in nursing homes.

For her part, Miss Mason decried activities programs for the institutionalized elderly. She expressed the view that these existed chiefly to salve the feelings of families and staff, while the very old themselves wished only to be left alone. She appreciated the value of routine and called attention to the low energy level of the residents. Nevertheless, she good-temperedly supported a Fourth of July picnic, even though holiday absenteeism by the aide staff greatly increased her difficulties.

At this period also there were small bursts of entertainment and Mountainside's residents embraced them hungrily. Two daughters of patients organized an occasional bingo game, music, or a travel slide show, and once a retirees' square dance group appeared and performed. The same general dearth of activities applied to organized religion. Although the elderly residents came from a churched generation, they received little attention from the local clergy. The Catholics at Countryside watched mass on TV; the others attended religious services only if their relatives took them. Then Father Cohen appeared—an Episcopal curate dispatched by the local canon to visit a parishioner. The young clergyman stepped into the home wearing his clerical collar and was promptly swamped by eager elders. That day, every resident who could use a walker or manipulate a wheelchair greeted me with the news: Father Cohen had been there. The young man continued his visits during the remainder of his summer in the parish.

Miss Mason noted the residents' response with a lively eye, since many of them, such as Mrs. Florentine, were Roman Catholics. As she got into the Episcopalian communion line, Mrs. Florentine asked, "What will Luigi think?" (Luigi was Mrs. Florentine's son.) Miss Mason assured her Luigi would probably not mind too much.

Ernest Miller continued his visits to residents, always with a special word for Mrs. Walters, and Winnie Mason worked side by side with her nurses. A new regime would meet transforming demands for professionalism, but, in the meantime, these two were setting the tone for what Countryside did best: providing warmth and a standard of cleanliness and care that patients' relatives generally applauded.

Ernest Miller approached long-term care both as an investor-owner and as an experienced hospital administrator. His counterpart at Mountainside, Barbara Archer, was a member of the sponsoring sect and an experienced daughter. Their respective backgrounds served them well. Part of his strength lay in his commitment to the viewpoint of the physicians who had invested in Countryside; part of hers lay in sharing the values of the Mountainside residents themselves.

When her husband's death made it impossible for Barbara Archer to take care of her mother while continuing to commute, she was offered the post at Mountainside with the inducement that she might bring the older woman as a patient. She secured her professional education as administrator but in many ways related to the residents as she had to her mother and her mother-in-law: She coaxed, scolded and worried over them with vigor.

Barbara Archer was bred on a brand of Protestantism that dwelled on God's justice and converted to another that emphasized His mercy, but she encountered many persons, especially nursing assistants, who struck her as deserving neither. She held strong convictions about the association between cleanliness and godliness and about the merits of hard work. She approached the job with her whole being.

She lived in the home, swept her eye around the breakfast tables each morning to make sure all the boarders were well, conferred with the director of nursing, drove patients to the physician, picked up supplies and groceries, hired and fired, and worked in her office long after most of the residents had turned off their lights. During dry spells, she watered the flowers. Living in the home, she heard the murmur of pleasure that greeted a favored menu and saw the collective shudder that followed each increase in rates.

Even in the heyday of disengagement theory, its opponents espoused activity theory, which held that older people were happier when they were involved. Unlike Countryside's director of nursing, Barbara Archer favored activity, especially for the boarders. When there was a local concert, she marshaled volunteers and board members to see that the boarders got there, that no one fell, and that each sat where he or she could hear. She saw that there were teas with crystal and flowers and china in the boarding unit and weekly entertainments in the nursing unit. She invested much effort in the annual open house, held each year when spring met summer and the peonies were in bloom. She cultivated local pastors, priests, and rabbis, getting them to come for Sunday afternoon worship services.

Residents who were interested in gardening or flower arranging were encouraged to continue. In the boarding unit, each table had its host or hostess, who made the breakfast toast and saw that table conversation steered clear of forbidden topics like poor health. Tasks existed for any who wished to undertake them.

Barbara Archer brought the same energy to bear on the monthly fire drill, which was unannounced. Stopwatch in hand, she checked the whereabouts of each resident: patients were wheeled to fire-safe areas; boarders were herded out of doors regardless of hour or weather. There were no exceptions. Her expectations seemed so reasonable to her that she was scarcely aware of there being norms at all. Therefore she suffered considerable frustration when John McGreevy terminated their exchanges about his behavior with the statement, "I obey all rules." "We have no rules," she protested. "I obey all rules," he repeated with a smile. Goaded by Mr. McGreevy's bland rejoinder, she turned to a trusted elder, John Penfield, a former chairman of the board, now a resident. His first reaction was like hers, "There are very few rules," but when the two began to compile a list of all they had read, heard, sensed, or remembered, they were astonished at its length. The norms were invisible, not only because they seemed perfectly natural to her but also because they roused little protest. This made Mr. McGreevy's watching a ball game with a beer can in his hand seem like an offense against nature; it could not help but inspire her indignation.

She listened to residents, especially those like John Penfield and his wife, who were part of the history of the home. They were elder members of her religious group and this gave a parental weighting to their views, and their likes and dislikes influenced her own.

She was a "good soldier." She would dutifully carry out a decision of the board even when the responding rage was sure to be directed at her head. For example, when the board told her that a long-time resident had to go—he was a forgetful smoker and they feared fire—she protested in the meeting but braved his family's wrath. In return, the board often supported her simply because she asked it to.

The collective character of the administrative style at Mountainside thus reflected its sectarian sponsorship.

Cultural Differences Arising from Sponsorship

Each home's sponsorship influenced its culture: the values espoused, the way residents were perceived, and the norms that governed behavior. At Countryside, the ethos was medical and entrepreneurial; at Mountainside it was Protestant.

Most of Countryside's investor-owners were physicians in private practice, and those who were not, like Ernest Miller, were hospital connected. They favored private enterprise and professional hegemony. Residents were perceived as both patients and consumers. The resulting ambiguities were illustrated in Countryside's dealings with its boarders: although they were called "guests," an aide was assigned to provide care and tactful supervision. By definition, boarders were supposed to be able to take care of themselves and manage their own medication, but many of them forgot it, so the aide resolved the problem by keeping it for them and reminding them to request it. Some residents, like Mr. McGillacudhy, suffered occasional bouts of unsteadiness and confusion, and needed more careful watching.

Resistance surrounded the bath. Fearing falls, the home required the aide to be at hand when anyone bathed or showered. Some boarders did not want to bathe at all and had to be persuaded—for example, Mr. Post, who suffered from shortness of breath and avoided exertion. Some objected to supervision, and they needed to be persuaded also. Feeling it was improper for the aide to see him naked, Mr. McDevitt asked her to buy him an athletic supporter.

The "guests" were not given keys to their rooms lest they lose them, but when they went away for several days, the doors were locked to protect their belongings against theft and the home against accusations. Countryside accepted human frailty as long as it did not cost money and as long as a physician endorsed it. This was especially plain in relation to liquor and tobacco. At Countryside, many of the hardships of patienthood were mitigated when the nurses dispensed prescribed doses of spirits shortly before supper. Kate Briggs, a patient too confused to realize she was in a nursing home, nevertheless showed an uncanny sense of when it was time for the nurse to get out the bottles of Scotch and the paper cups.

> Another example was Mrs. Shannon. There was an impromptu conference at the nursing station: Mrs. Shannon wasn't eating. One nurse pointed out that Mrs. Shannon would drink anything she was offered, but that her family had said her liquor should be discontinued. The nurse was reluctant to override the family members who, after all, were buying her beer. Winnie Mason, the director of nursing, replied that the patient's happiness should be considered and that she would like to conduct a little experiment. She settled Mrs. Shannon before a baseball game on TV with a can of beer and a bowl of crackers. Soon she was munching and cheering.

No effort was made to check smoking as long as it did not constitute a fire hazard: One boarder's cigarettes were kept for her by the aide because she was forgetful and likely to leave one burning.

Enforcement of the rule about bed rails was equally flexible. For continent patients, for example, no matter how confused, the rail was likely to be down if a physician ordered it.

What the resident could pay for, he or she enjoyed. Permission was most likely to be denied on economic grounds: "I can't spare an aide to . . ." For example, a feisty old explorer and ancient athlete, the Commander, was restive in confinement and campaigned to walk on the grounds. When his brother, who was also his physician, urged the director of nursing to let him go, she responded that she could not spare an aide to accompany him. When the Commander's brother said he would take responsibility and wrote the order, the Commander was allowed to wander the grounds at will and life became easier for the staff.

At Countryside, five residents had private duty nurses. At Mountainside, this was forbidden, implicitly because all souls were equal in the sight of God and it was questioned whether anyone should be advantaged in the purchase of an essential service. These policies had implications for cost and control.

Initially, Countryside's private duty nurses were registered nurses, but with rising costs, more were licensed practical nurses, finally nursing assistants and, in the end, there was a tendency to dismiss or not to replace them. Although most of them took care of their own patients only, they nevertheless eased the work of the staff because they served on the daytime shift when the needs and demands of the patients were greatest. They were accountable to the employing family, responsible for their patient, and dependent on the physician. They were operating on Miss Mason's territory, but they were not under her direct command. Because most of the physicians attending most of the patients at Countryside were investor-owners—or, at the least, members of the local hospital staff—there was a network of control that could have addressed major discord. None was observed. The system was not one the home was likely to disrupt.

Mountainside staff nurses provided all the care for patients in its nursing unit, and every nurse and nursing assistant was directly accountable to the director of nursing. Many of the private duty nurses at Countryside were conscientious about trying to stimulate their patients and provide special care, but it must be conceded that much of their time was spent grooming and sitting while the floor nurses and aides scurried to finish their work.

In contrast to Countryside's pragmatic laissez-faire, Mountainside seemed strongly governed by rules. The puritanical character of those rules was not a problem because most of the residents shared the values they reflected. Only a third of the residents belonged to the sponsoring sect, but most were members of mainline Protestant churches with conservative rules of conduct.

Practical reasons were often given for rules that appeared to have moralistic roots. Smoking, for example, was confined to a very small area in the nursing unit and any boarder or patient who wished to smoke had to step outside or go to the home's single ashtray near the nursing station. Historically, the sponsoring sect had deplored tobacco because of its association with slavery, but the official explanation was fire safety. The sect also frowned upon alcohol. Therefore, when an obliging physician did prescribe spirits for two residents, the sherry was dispensed by the nurse and sipped under her supervision. A prescription was a prescription, not a cocktail hour.

The philosophy of the sponsoring sect pressed for activity, equality, and order. Respected boarders were busy boarders who contributed to the life of the group. Residents took responsibility for making announcements, selecting puzzles, and locking up. They read to patients and once a week, a sewing group met to stitch, knit, and embroider crib blankets and small garments for the sect's charity. Statuses were reaffirmed on these occasions and judgments passed. Nursing unit staff responded to the same call for activity and order. While many of Countryside's feeblest and most confused patients often appeared in dressing gowns, every Mountainside patient was dressed in street clothes unless comatose or otherwise bed-bound.

One aspect of the leveling tendency at Mountainside was the exclusion of private duty nurses in the nursing unit. Another was the "Don't-push-yourself-forward" norm that was manifested most concretely in the seating at the weekly entertainment. No resident would brave the censure of the group by sitting in the first row: The administrator learned to place a few decoy chairs in front so the residents could begin seating themselves right behind them. A third example was criticism of Miss White, a patient who appeared to be taking over a staff role.

> When Miss Marcie Mae White, an English woman, entered the nursing unit, she was in good health and of clear mind, but she was nearing her ninety-fourth

birthday and her friends—all of them her former kindergarten pupils—felt she wasn't eating properly in
her own home. She grasped their concerns perfectly:
"After you're ninety, they get worried about your living alone."

With cheerful pedagogical command, she managed
the staff. Each day she walked twice around the block
that encircled Mountainside, without the escorting
aide assigned to Robert Farmer. When they wished to
enter her room, nurses knocked. As one commented,
"I walked right in one day and you should have seen
the glare!"

For the most part, she was sunny, alert, and active. At
the music hour, she recalled hearing Paderewski with
his great mane of golden hair; she spoke of her Edward-
ian girlhood and of the waving white handkerchiefs that
greeted the Salvation Army's General Booth. She soon
displayed a welcome skill: Like any good kindergarten
teacher, she played the piano with a clear thumping
rhythm and a melody line any child could follow.

About this time, Barbara Archer arranged for a
physiotherapist to lead exercises for the boarders. Each
week Miss White went to the boarding unit to play the
piano during the exercises; she took notes and introduced the exercises, modified for the wheelchair-
bound, in the nursing unit. She ran the group crisply
but with a noticeable lack of backup from the nursing
assistants. (One of their number had previously conducted wheelchair exercises from time to time.)

Chief among her critics was John Wesley. He expressed the view that so much activity was unseemly
and should be left to staff. Margaret Wesley, his wife,
had been forbidden to cross the street and now this
ninety-four-year-old Mary Poppins was allowed to
prance around the block!

Mountainside's sectarian sponsorship provided an essence to
which its residents could relate. Even when they disagreed with its

views, the existence of that corpus lent coherence to their lives in the home.

On one level, there was the religious organization itself, to which the administrator, most of the board, and about a third of the residents belonged, which gave a sense of mutual accountability and entitlement. On a more intimate scale, a network of long-standing associations and kinships existed—board members and volunteers could hardly be detached when friends and relatives were among the residents. Informal contacts broke the *cordon sanitaire* that staff members usually interpose between boards of managers and the persons they serve. Board members and their spouses hung bird feeders outside patients' windows, drove the boarders to the concerts, shopped for residents, showed slides at the entertainments, and led craft groups. As a further incentive, board members could envision themselves as future Mountainside residents.

Just as Countryside residents were consumer-patients, Mountainside boarders and patients were members of what the administrator called the "Mountainside family." This is not to say that all members of the Mountainside family were equally esteemed, got along equally well, or agreed with the tenets of the sponsoring sect, but only that there was a sense of belonging to a larger whole. This explains the force of the Mountainside norms designed to protect the home's public face as a collectivity from the perspective of residents and as an institution from the viewpoint of staff. All drew some of their own status from the reputation of the group. This is why Mr. McGreevy was censured for coming to lunch with his suspenders in plain view: Residents felt his behavior affected their public image as well as his own. Countryside could afford to be more laissez-faire because within its private enterprise environment residents might be fellow passengers on a ship but they were not members of a timeless group. A group implies some sense of common investment.

Differences Arising from Location

Another source of difference between the two homes was geography. Countryside was approached by a road that wound through green acres. There were houses now where once there had been

farms, but a sense of country remained. Mountainside had gardens
and great ancient trees, but it was bounded by a city block and an
older neighborhood surrounded it. Countryside's handsome but remote setting made its residents prisoners of distance, while Mountainside's urban location empowered its boarders and may have
helped it hold its staff.

Several residents showed how geography affects freedom and
choice. Few residents left Countryside successfully without a con-
federate. From time to time, a boarder appeared to have been over-
persuaded by physician and family to "give it a try." Some of these
tries were short-lived, but even in these cases, the erstwhile resident
needed the help of others. Mrs. Frances illustrates such a departure.

> Mrs. Frances, a handsome eighty-seven-year-old
> woman, came with a fine fur piece and a self-assured
> manner. While everyone else was impressed with the
> new arrival, one patient watched with quiet interest
> and did not comment. This was Clarissa Bennett,
> eighty-six, her opposite number; Mrs. Bennett's son
> was married to Mrs. Frances' daughter. The two
> women spent little time together because Mrs. Frances
> lived "upstairs" and enjoyed the status of boarder,
> while Mrs. Bennett remained downstairs as a patient.
>
> A few weeks later, I learned that Mrs. Frances had
> gone to lunch with friends and telephoned the staff
> that she would not be returning. Curious, I checked
> with Mrs. Bennett.
>
> Mrs. Bennett said she had known from the start that
> Mrs. Frances did not intend to stay: She had brought
> a minimum amount of clothing and had left her TV
> at home. She believed that Mrs. Frances wanted to
> dispose of her own belongings and perhaps sell her
> house herself; then she would move to a retirement
> hotel but not to a nursing home, as it did not suit her.

Mrs. Frances did not say that she was leaving. Instead, she found
it necessary to decamp. She telephoned to say that she was not
coming back from her friend's home rather than informing the staff

in person. Had she announced her intention earlier, family and staff would have joined forces to dissuade her. But plainly she had made up her mind.

No Countryside resident still drove, but some Mountainside boarders kept their cars. Others walked to town or caught a bus to the metropolis. One Mountainside boarder commuted regularly to take an art course.

On the other hand, Countryside residents needed family or friends with a car or to have someone order a taxi for them because there were no shops, libraries, or entertainment within walking distance. This relative isolation made Countryside more self-contained and raised the level of staff control. Access to the outside was mainly through family and staff members, the very persons who might be expected to want the resident to remain in the setting.

Mountainside's urban setting provided more choice, including the ability to shop for another residence.

> Lacking kindred and feeling alone, Elka Miller left the large city where she lived and entered a home in town run by nuns. Once there she found herself mismatched: life was regimented because the facility was geared to impaired residents. She secured permission to leave the grounds for her daily walks, including trips to the library, where she was befriended by the librarian. When she poured out her unhappiness, the librarian called her attention to Mountainside, just across the street. Miss Miller went to Mountainside and arranged her own transfer, thus illustrating the ultimate freedom of the institutionalized: freedom to leave.

On a more daily basis, Mountainside's urban setting made it possible for boarders to sally out for supplies and to avoid or delay uncomfortable confrontations.

> Henry Hobart was an old journalist and an incurable romantic. ("My daughter asks, 'Daddy, aren't you ever going to grow up?' ") Although legally blind, he was

able to compose poems and notes on the typewriter. When his first love at Mountainside was transferred to the nursing unit, he walked to town each day to purchase her a small treat, such as a candy bar, and he brought back tales of adventure.

A period of intense grief followed her death and then, life being short when one is in the late eighties, he fell in love again. On one occasion, he inadvertently agreed to meet two women at the same hour. Fearing a confrontation, he fled to lunch in town so he would not have to spend an uncomfortable half-hour sitting between them.

The increased accessibility of town was of little use to patients, however, whose wandering was a source of concern and immediate staff action. The most resolute wanderer lived at Countryside, but she would have confronted Mountainside staff with similar problems of retrieval, the difference being that in the urban setting there were neighbors to phone the home and police to return the stray patient. At Countryside, Ernest Miller himself and a nurse had to scour the roads and lanes to the highway.

Bernadette O'Neil had handsome dark eyes, a spray of white hair, and a touch of Irish in her talk. She reported that she had been born and bred in the west of Ireland and had come to this country by herself at nineteen. This was the truth, but she was a less reliable reporter on more recent matters.

Mrs. O'Neil had lived with her nephew until his adolescent children got tired of retrieving her. She next went to a boarding home that demanded her removal because of her running away. From there she was dispatched to Countryside as a patient, not for health care but for supervision.

She was confused about where she was but manifestly contented. She explained that she hadn't really intended to take this "situation" but talked it over with her family and decided to do so. She quickly

found a friend as confused as herself and the two
women spent hours watching the other residents and
gossiping. Within the month, however, this eighty-
seven-year-old woman set off on foot and was found
near a furniture store on the highway a number of
miles away.

After that, the staff sedated her and she drowsed in
a chair, no longer gossiping with her friend.

Mrs. O'Neil belonged to an interesting class of wanderers. She
did not know where she was but she clearly affirmed that she had
chosen Countryside. She did not appear to be seeking a "lost"
mother or a vanished home. Rather, she seemed to be engaging in
a flight into activity, much as a housewife might have baked bread
when she felt restive (Snyder and others, 1978). A recommended
strategy for managing such wanderers is more exercise rather than
physically and chemically enforced inactivity (Cherry and Rafkin,
1988).

Three things make running away difficult for patients: the frailty
that makes it hard for them to deal with doors, the surveillance that
stops them at the exit, and the wristband that identifies them as
patients and ensures their return. State troopers, policepersons,
first-aid squads, physicians, and family members return the elderly
runaway without hesitation.

An urban setting not only expands the choices for elderly
boarders but makes it easier for staff members to get to work. Mountainside aides were able to use public transportation or walk to work
if necessary. Countryside nurses needed independent and dependable transportation, and if a Countryside aide's car broke down or
someone failed to get home in time to give her a ride, she had only
two choices: She could call a taxi or she could phone in sick. Mountainside aides were able to use public transportation if necessary.

Differences in Staff Turnover

In 1974, a questionnaire was administered to a convenience sample of employees in both homes, that is, to those available on the
day shift. In 1978, 63 percent of Mountainside employees and 29

percent of those from Countryside were still there. By 1979, this had dropped to 56 percent and 24 percent, respectively; in 1980, the numbers still employed were 41 percent and 14 percent. By 1982, of the Countryside employees interviewed in 1974, only the cook remained. This survey of original interviewees, however, must be viewed with reservations. The first interviews had never been intended as a census and did not include those on days off or the night shift. Some nurses remained. Nevertheless, it does suggest that Countryside had a somewhat greater staff turnover.

This picture of staff change is in keeping with observations elsewhere (Stannard, 1973; Garabaldi, Brodine, and Matsumiya, 1981; Waxman, Carner, and Berkenstock, 1984; Cohen-Mansfield, 1988). In the seven proprietary facilities Waxman and his associates (1984) studied, 37 percent of the nursing assistants had been in their present jobs less than a year and only 10 percent had been there five years. Garibaldi, Brodine, and Matsumiya (1981) found that seven Salt Lake City nursing homes had had almost a 100 percent turnover of nursing assistants and about 30 percent of licensed nurses during the preceding three months. Cohen-Mansfield (1988) reports that professional staff has less turnover than aides.

At both Mountainside and Countryside, aides earned substantially less than nurses, but policies at the proprietary facility may have underscored this. Winnie Mason informed an experienced applicant that she could hire her only at beginner's wages, while Barbara Archer increased the salaries of the nursing assistants each time the minimum wages of the tray girls went up in order to preserve the clear differential that marked the difference in their skills and performance. Countryside aides had more trouble getting to work than either their Mountainside counterparts or their own nurses because in the first instance, the distance was greater and, in the second, fewer of them had good cars. Finally, Countryside's larger size may have increased the sense of social distance; at Mountainside, nurse and aide were more likely to be working side by side. All of these factors may have contributed to the difference in work records between the two homes and between the nurses and nursing assistants, but there is a final consideration: The nursing assistants were holding a job; the nurses were practicing their profession.

At Mountainside and Countryside, several nurses died, one be-

came a nursing home patient herself, and some women moved away
with their husbands' jobs or retirement. The directors of nursing in
both homes left, but their successors were still in charge ten years
later. The second Countryside director of nursing, a staff member
in 1974, had grown in her role: At the study's end, she was engaged
in an off-campus degree program in nursing administration.

One Countryside nurse typified the aging-in-place of staff and its
effect on work patterns.

> About thirty years earlier, Mrs. Dwight's son received
> severe head injuries when he was vacationing in Ber-
> muda. The Dwights resolved to keep him at home as
> long as they could, and all of Mrs. Dwight's earnings
> went into a special account for his care "later."
>
> In 1974, she was working on a regular night shift.
> As she grew frailer, she reduced the number of nights
> per week, first to two and finally, she began to work
> only on call. By 1986, the Dwights had placed their
> son in a nursing home because they wanted him
> settled while they were still standing by to intervene
> if necessary. They chose another home in the area, one
> that would not put him out if his funds were ex-
> hausted, and he appeared to be enjoying the activities
> and the presence of other patients.
>
> They visited him often. When they could no longer
> manage, they planned to join him there. The years
> had taken a toll but they were pleased with the out-
> come. As this was being written, word came that Mrs.
> Dwight had died, leaving her husband and son.

Each of the homes had a distinct personality born of its history,
geography, sponsorship, and staff. By the end, they would have
many problems in common.

CHAPTER THREE

Choices and Challenges
of Residential Life

———————◆———————

Countryside's two old Irishmen had quite different experiences in the last years of their lives. Both entered Countryside in their early eighties. Mr. McDevitt came first and was the only male in the boarding unit when the Brooklyn-born Mr. McGillacudhy arrived. Mr. McDevitt, who had grown up in rural Ireland, did not warm to the newcomer. Both men avidly watched the St. Patrick's Day parade, but they did not watch it together. Mr. McDevitt lived longer and could be said to have had the happier time in the home although he was displeased with the circumstances that led to his coming.

John McDevitt at eighty-four was a tall, straight man with dark eyes and still-dark hair. He had been a policeman and a tavern keeper and he combined the easy but commanding manner of both. He was very neat, active, and independent.

He never tired of telling about the "plot" that brought him to Countryside: In his account, his daughter-in-law had all the qualities of Lear's bad daughters and his son was her innocent dupe. His physician had suggested his going to the hospital for a checkup. While he was there, his daughter-in-law asked if she could have his furniture and, thinking she meant after his death, he agreed. But when he was ready to leave the hospital, instead of taking him home the family drove him to Countryside, explaining he could not go home because the daughter-in-law had given away his furniture. His son was contrite at what his wife had done. "Tom was all broken up. He cried," Mr. McDevitt related.

Mr. McDevitt's wife had died the year before and he had had surgery, but he felt he was managing pretty well in his own home. Someone picked him up for mass and the local police gave him rides. He blamed his neighbors and the woman who cleaned for him for convincing his daughter-in-law that he was too old to live alone. Perhaps it is significant that the cleaning woman got the furniture.

His son and grandchildren lived near Countryside and were attentive. At the home, he was accorded respect in a setting where to be on one's feet and clear in one's head was a source of status outweighing previous occupation or wealth. Except for Mr. McGillacudhy, he reached out to other men who entered the home—a widower who came to convalesce from surgery because he lived alone, a "young" male patient, forty-seven with a spinal-cord injury—but always he kept something of himself to himself. Winnie Mason, the Countryside director of nursing, thought he avoided Mr. McGillacudhy because the old politician's gregariousness was too intrusive.

Underneath lurked a substratum of sadness that became plain when he took the Philadelphia Geriatric Center morale test. Not only the score, 9 out of a possible 21, but the flood of comments the test elicited revealed a loneliness for times gone by.

He talked of his youth in rural Ireland. He spoke with pride of his parents, who shared what they had, even lending a cow to a neighbor who had many children. He came to America to his sister's home

when he was sixteen but went back for a visit ten years
later. "I cried when I left Ireland that time because I
knew I wouldn't be coming back."

He missed the town where he had raised a family
on a policeman's pay, $2,000 most of the time, and the
second town where, after retirement, he had run a tavern. One day he reported with wonder and pride that
his granddaughter was marrying a young policeman
who earned $12,000. He missed the rich web of kins-
people, cronies, and organizations, and most of all he
missed going to mass, as his wife had done everyday
and he had, too, most of the time. Seeing it on TV was
no substitute. (In actuality, family members often
picked him up on Sundays and took him to church.)

He had his ups and downs. At eighty-five, he was
sick and spent a few days "downstairs" as a patient.
He returned to the boarding unit quickly but seemed
slow to recover his old vigor—he looked thinner and
occasionally he mixed recent dates. In a month or so
this passed and he was his old self, telling tales about
his days as a policeman, stories in which the heroes
and villains were clearly indicated. In one, the villain
was Welsh, the good servant girl was Irish, and he was
the rescuer.

Just before his eighty-sixth birthday, John McDevitt strolled over to visit an Irish friend from the town
where he had been on the force. The two old men
spent a pleasant evening and he died on the way
back—his body was found by the roadside. He had
remained a boarder to the end.

Mr. McDevitt and Mr. McGillacudhy illustrate two quite different residential "careers." Once they entered congregate living, they
experienced a series of events sandwiched between a beginning and
an end. What happened to each was as different as the two men
themselves.

Mr. McGillacudhy encountered more turning points: He entered
as a boarder, went to the hospital, returned as a patient, and ulti-

mately left Countryside to enter another facility as a Medicaid patient. His was a downward progression, which explains some of the unhappiness and neglect he suffered at the end.

Mr. McDevitt's course was horizontal: He began as a boarder and kept this favorable status except for brief bouts of illness. Although his culture made little provision for placing old people out of the home—he related keeping his own father-in-law with the family till he died—his greater sadness seemed a loneliness for people in times past. When answering the question on the morale scale, "How much do you feel lonely—not much or a lot?" he responded gravely, "Very much."

After defining careers and moral careers in general, this chapter will describe and illustrate some of the "good" and "bad" paths through the home and how individuals dealt with them.

The Career Concept

A career exists when enough people encounter the same sequence of events that generalizations can be made. Because each person brings a different self to the common course and because even the same careers are lived out in different settings and seasons, each individual's experience is also different.

The ultimate uniqueness results from the dynamic interplay among the times, personalities, individuals' responses to their experiences and to each other, social structure, and management. A circle appears: The way the career is defined affects the response of the human actors; their responses determine the way the career is defined. Altogether, these and other contingencies shape the career's trajectory (Corbin and Strauss, 1988).

The term *career* is most commonly applied to work, as in corporate career, medical career, military career, and artistic career. A young sociologist broadened the definition. When Julius Roth completed his doctorate, instead of being launched on his intended academic career, he ended up incarcerated in a TB sanitarium, where staff members viewed him not as a promising researcher but as a patient encasing an interesting set of lungs. While they tested him, treated him, and made decisions for him, he observed them and his fellow patients and perceived that staff and patients assigned quite different significance to the same events. He noticed also that there were typical routes through the TB hospital: people entered, got better, and left; or they got worse and died; or they remained seemingly forever. Throughout their stays, patients tried to negotiate good prognoses as quicker pathways to discharge.

When Roth had negotiated his own way out, he wrote a book about the career of the TB patient and called it *Timetables* (1963). He pointed out that patients and physicians read timetables differently: Patients interpreted every sign as calling for early discharge; doctors got into less trouble if they erred on the side of caution. Physicians and nurses tended the gates while their patients attempted to manipulate, bargain, or maneuver around them.

In all its uses, the word *career* describes a common human course with a beginning, an end, and customary turning points in between. For example, in writing about the "dying career" of the nursing home patient, Gustafson (1972) describes a progression from the patient's early struggles to redefine his or her condition to inevitable death itself. In many careers, the beginning and the end may not be equally obvious to all, but for those familiar with the course, both are clearly discernible, at least, in retrospect. There may be differential awareness along the dying trajectory (Glaser and Strauss, 1965), but at some point, all must acknowledge that the patient was terminally ill, if only at the funeral.

Ervin Goffman (1961) added another dimension when he wrote about the moral career of the mental patient. More recently, old age itself has come to be viewed as a moral career (Arling, 1979). *Moral career* includes both personal and public responses to an altered identity: There are changes in the perception of the person, both by himself and by others. Labeling theory would look on this as a socialization process that is complete when the individual accepts and has some degree of commitment to the new identity and its values, no matter how discreditable. The moral career begins with the new identity and ends when it is replaced by another. For example, at the other end of life, the delinquent career ends when the criminal career begins.

In a state hospital with both mentally retarded and mentally ill patients, the former described themselves as "MRs." They recognized that in the hospital's status system, they ranked below the

"MIs" and, in a dispute, they would fling "MR" at peers as a term of opprobrium. But they applied it to themselves as well—however unwelcome it had been, they accepted the assigned status.

Thus there is both a private and a public dimension to the moral career. There are no secret scarlet letters. Generally others recognize the new identity first, especially if it bears its own stigmata. A moral career need not involve status deescalation: A cardinal becoming a pope would integrate into his public and private selves the new identity and experience a series of turning points. A brotherhood of papal predecessors could have told him much about what he would encounter but part of the experience would be solely his own.

Some identities go deeper or are more indelible than others. Identity does not change drastically with membership in the ROTC because other more salient roles accompany the college career, but the recruit is seen very differently the moment he is sworn into the army. "Dogface" then becomes his dominant role, which changes the way he sees himself and others see him. Similarly, at Mountainside and Countryside the role of "patient" obscures all others. The term *boarder* is not so engulfing, especially for those mobile enough to retain a variety of other roles in the family and in the community.

The generic career deals with the typical developments, stages, and transitions that mark the road map of a role with its accompanying status; the moral career involves the public and personal perception of changed and changing identity and the way a workable self is crafted. As treated here, the residential career encompasses both aspects, although questions arise about what happens when the individual's understanding of what he is becoming is partial, autistic, or denied.

Residential Careers

The residential career begins the day the person moves into the home. Tobin and Lieberman (1976) have suggested, however, that its effects start sooner. In their study, they found that the greatest behavioral change occurred during the preadmission phase before their subjects actually entered the home. They concluded that good settings are unfairly blamed for emotional and cognitive constrictions that are really due to the trauma of abandonment that occurs when the decision for placement is made. Nevertheless, the act of entry marks the official change in public identity. This act launches the individual on a residential career that ends only with death or a return to noncongregate living, a return that is unlikely. A parallel transfer to another facility does not end the residential career but only changes its setting.

Staff members think of the newcomer as patient or boarder from the start. Friends and family may accept the full meaning of the new identity sooner than the resident, but in the end, the redefinition is general. The resident's peer group has no doubt about his or her new status.

Mountainside boarders sanctioned their deviant members strongly because they did not want the nonconformer to spoil their shared identity. They defined boarders as being like community residents except that they had made a decision to have certain services provided. Individually, they might add clauses about future need and independence from the family, but as a body they presented themselves as autonomous older persons who had elected the convenience of living with others. They socialized newcomers to that definition and frowned on public behavior that might undermine it. Patients also were aware of a shared identity but failed or were unable to mount a common defense.

Only psychosis protects the individual from knowledge of where he is and what he has become, a phenomenon illustrated by the patient who glanced around the dining hall at Countryside and explained, "This is a hunting lodge my father was fond of." The wide-windowed room with its expanse of countryside did indeed fit the description. Another explained, "This is a hotel we came to," and added, "It's rather common." An unmistakable lobby sustained her belief. Obviously neither of these women saw themselves as patients.

Individuals can be very confused, however, and at the same time grasp the general nature of the setting and the new relationships that exist there. This is true even when they cannot describe it clearly.

> Soon after she came to Mountainside, Margaret Goudie, eighty-two, indicated her fellow patients and con-

fided darkly, "Those people are crazy!" Two years
later, she declared, "The 'teachers' treat us differently
when the 'parents' come." She was now one of them.
She knew that she, like the others, was dependent on
local authority figures (nurses and aides) who expressed more concern for her when her other authority
figures (family members) were around. On other occasions, she referred to the nurses and aides also as "parents"—"parents" were people who took care of her
but did not consult her about her care. She had lost the
words but she grasped the power structure perfectly.

Thus the confused and the alert alike came to terms with the
implications of the setting, even if only in acknowledging it as a
place that provided services, such as meal preparation, that freed
one from dependence on one's family.

Precipitants of Placement

Many Mountainside residents explained that they wanted their
children's company but did not wish to be dependent on them for
care. Most of these old people were no more enamored with "role
reversal" than Margaret Blenkner (1965), who described it as "pathological," but they might have endorsed her view of the adult
child's "filial task" as seeing the parent as a separate adult and as
being dependable when needed. The residents not only experienced
the power shift that occurs when the flow of services becomes unidirectional (Barusch, 1987) but showed the strong value they placed
on independence (Troll, 1988). Many Mountainside residents saw
entry and care by paid strangers as a means of prolonging this
relative independence.

In each situation, the intrinsic and extrinsic factors that pushed
for placement—those that resided within the individual and those
in that person's social environment—could be either predisposing
or precipitating. The predisposing factors might be no longer driving a car or unsteadiness, with its threat of falls. A common pre-
cipitant was the death or departure of a supporting person. The mix

of intrinsic and extrinsic factors differed between patients and boarders.

With the passage of time, circumstances are reconstructed and residents change, making it difficult to determine what was most salient when placement was planned. Ill health and cognitive impairment cannot be viewed as sole determinants of placement because at least three million equally disabled persons still live in the community (U.S. Senate, Special Committee on Aging, 1988).

After reviewing eighteen studies, Wingard and her associates (1987) say that age, sex, caregiver availability, and functional status are commonly described as contributing to nursing home placement. They agree with those who contend that functional status is a better predictor than medical diagnosis because it reflects the impact of illness and the need for care.

A high prevalence of cognitive dysfunction is attributed to nursing home patients: 63 percent are estimated to be disoriented or have memory impaired to a serious extent (U.S. Senate, Special Committee on Aging and Vierck, 1990). When examining factors that put residents on one path or another, it is helpful to look for cognitive impairment at the point of entry: Time, illness, and other factors, including some intrinsic to the setting, may contribute to dysfunction later.

Among twenty-eight persons who initially entered Mountainside's nursing unit, 68 percent (nineteen) were alert at the point of entry, 29 percent (eight) were confused, and one was psychotic. Of forty-three persons who began as boarders, 93 percent (forty) were alert, 5 percent (two) presented acceptable social facades but retrospectively can be seen as moving toward confusion, and one had a hearing problem that makes it difficult to say, although he appears to have been alert. When cognitive impairment did exist, it often appeared to be only predisposing.

The loss of a significant other appears to have been primary. This was true for almost a third of the boarders (fourteen)—in nine cases, someone had died and in four others the supportive person moved away, although a responding behavior or incidental illness often figured in the explanation. For example, John McGreevy "holed up in his apartment" after the death of his wife. Mr. Brewster actively mourned his wife but hospitalization provided the occasion for his physician and nephew to decide that he should not go home alone. One boarder described herself as freed to make arrangements for herself after the death of a frail older sister: She herself was eighty-nine at that time. In the home, she became a peer leader. Two patients came because of deaths of persons they lived with and a third said she applied following the death of her brother. They had lived apart but his death increased her own sense of vulnerability. Five boarders and two patients entered because aging adult children were moving or making other late-life changes: In one case, a supportive former son-in-law was remarrying; in another, the adult children's retirement meant they would be adopting a more migratory lifestyle.

Thus, altogether, 33 percent of the boarders and 18 percent of the patients entered Mountainside because of a change in the status of another person on whom most were in some degree dependent. To these should be added Margaret Wesley, who had been her husband's caregiver and entered the nursing unit to be his roommate. She had been the supporting rather than the supported figure. This would change the patient proportion to 21 percent.

Four residents, three of whom were patients, were physically frail persons who had entered Mountainside only after efforts to live at home with paid help. To do this, it was almost essential to have a relative or reliable friend nearby, and even with such support, each had had bad experiences when the help failed to appear.

Twenty-three boarders and two patients entered because they were old and alone. These were not ill people. In several instances, they came as part of a later-life plan. What entry meant to them is indicated by Miss Mary Van Wyck, who elected to move into the nursing wing instead of the boarding unit, for which she was clearly eligible.

> She had been the youngest of a physician's five children, the one the others were admonished to protect. After the death of her brother, whose last year had been spent in a nursing home, she applied for admission herself. "After my brother died, I was the last one in the family—I was so alone," she confessed.
>
> Her blue eyes blinked nervously as she described the

fear she had felt of having a stroke when she was alone
in her apartment: She had seen two sisters and a
brother-in-law die after long periods of helpless
paralysis.

At eighty-five, she was somewhat unsteady on her
feet but otherwise in good health. She took her daily
walk and managed her own affairs. When asked why
she had elected the nursing unit rather than the boarding home, she spoke of the sadness of leaving her
apartment and said, "I never wanted to move again!"

But if Miss Van Wyck was relatively well, others were not. At
least fifteen patients came because of intrinsic incapacity—such as
that caused by blindness, Parkinson's disease, or confusion. Two
marginal boarders had been pushed by adult children more aware
of their growing incapacity than the individuals themselves.

With today's talk about "alternatives," it is fair to ask whether
better social provision in the form of home health care, shopping
services, meals-on-wheels, and outreach for the bereaved might have
obviated placement or whether vigorous rehabilitation could have
aborted it? In many cases, it might have bought delay, an important
consideration for the very old.

Points of Entry and Exit

There were two points of entry, the boarding and nursing units,
and two common exits, transfer or death. If a person went to
another facility, the residential career continued, but if the person
returned to community living, it was ended or suspended, perhaps
to be continued later.

Some Countryside residents went home. A few of these had come
merely to convalesce, and most were persons whose need for care
was marginal but whose living alone made family and physician
uneasy. Countryside's physician-owners were allied with the home
and liked its care, but the residents they persuaded to "give it a try"
were not always as enthusiastic.

Shortly after her eighty-second birthday, Grace Rogers
came to countryside as a boarder. She was a kinder-

garten teacher who had married her supervising principal, a widower with two daughters. "No one had
ever called me 'Mother,'" she said, relating how
pleased she had been when the daughters' children
had asked to call her "Grandma." By the time she
entered Countryside, she had been a widow living
alone for twenty-five years.

The stepdaughters were attentive but did not live
near enough to help on a regular basis. After she was
hospitalized, because she was sick and obviously careless about cooking for herself, her physician told the
daughters that she did not want to live alone. He suggested that she would get proper meals and company
at Countryside.

She was a tiny bird-like figure, with brown-dyed
hair and well-groomed nails. At Countryside, she was
strikingly active and quickly concluded she did not belong there with "them." The home was not unfamiliar
to her because she had visited friends there; now friends
came to visit her. Her bridge threesome brought their
cards. A member of her church taped their pastor's ser-
mon and sat by her side and played it. While enjoying
the support of her friends, she recoiled from the companions the physician had offered her. She ate in the
dining room once and quickly arranged to take her
meals upstairs thereafter. The wheelchairs depressed
her, and she commented on the people "with fine faces
and chaos behind them." She reassessed her physical
status: "Things wear out and you have to learn to live
with them." Two weeks after arrival, she left.

Six and a half years later, the local newspaper reported her death at Countryside. She had died so
quickly after reentry that when I inquired six months
later, none of the staff remembered her, and no one
remained who might have recalled her earlier stay.

The admission of boarders was more likely to have been voluntary than that of patients. Resisting placement is hard for frail el-

derly persons being discharged from acute care hospitals and fairly difficult for those so impaired that they have been living in a relative's home because that person is concerned about their safety. It is a good deal easier for those coming from their own houses or apartments to resist, especially if they are minimally dependent on others for help. Most boarders were therefore at least passively accepting.

Elaine Brody (1969) investigated a group of persons for whom inquiries had been made about admission to a home for the aged. Some followed through with an application and others did not. Whether or not the adult children pressed for placement, the decisive factor proved to be the attitudes of the old persons themselves. Some who refused were forced to enter other facilities within the year.

Some Mountainside and Countryside residents began their residential careers elsewhere. They transferred from other facilities because (1) Mountainside or Countryside had been their first choice and they were on its waiting list, (2) they wanted to be nearer a son or daughter, or (3) they were dissatisfied with the care they had been getting. Transfer is illustrated by Evan Brewster.

> Two months after his wife's death, Evan Brewster had his first cancer surgery. His nephew had him admitted to a nursing home near his own home in another state so he could watch over him. The nephew and his wife were attentive, but Mr. Brewster was unhappy in the cold, well-regulated facility. His nephew urged him to "adjust," but his nephew's wife followed up on his desire to transfer to Mountainside near his former home.
>
> The move was a good one because Mr. Brewster returned to familiar scenes. In his youth, the mansion that became Mountainside was the local exemplar of elegance, and now he lived there. He entered as a boarder and continued as one for the remaining eight years of his life except for brief stays in the infirmary after his recurrent trips to the hospital for treatment of his cancer.

Even when they were unhappy about placement, many boarders and patients viewed the current setting as the best option they had. They indicated this by their answers to a question in the version of the Philadelphia Geriatric Morale Scale employed in the study: "If you could live where you wanted, where would you live?" Only one answer was scored positively, "Right here." A remarkable number of respondents used just those words. On the first round of interviews, 38 percent of the seventy-three patients and 68 percent of the thirty-one boarders responding said, "Right here." Patients and boarders reversed positions on the "Not Right Here" replies.

The other answers appeared to be of two kinds—those expressing a desire to return to earlier and happier days (often the towns where they had raised their families) or reflecting armchair travel ("London," "Miami Beach," "Hawaii") and those that appeared to be a more direct rejection of present circumstances ("Heavens, I'd live in a home with a little H!" "Alone—or if I had just one friend, I'd prefer to live with her." The woman who said this was perceived as demented and treated accordingly, kindly but without much regard). Another woman replied, "In the apartment I lived in before I came here," but in response to another item, "I am afraid of a lot of things," she said, "I feel well protected here. I would be afraid if I were in my apartment." The pragmatic character of these responses is revealed by the fact that some persons who were truly unhappy nevertheless responded, "Right here." It was hardly surprising that Mrs. Bennett, with a high morale score (18) replied, "At my age and condition, right where I am," but Mrs. Flowers, with a low score (2) was equally adamant when she said, "Right here." Mrs. Flowers was not pleased with the options life was offering her, but she regarded Countryside as the best choice she had. At home, she had employed a series of housekeepers and had lain helpless whenever one of them had failed to appear.

Accepting a home for the aged as the best option does not mean that adapting to the residential role will be easy—individuals entering congregate living must always make some alteration in lifestyle and self-image. At best, they expand their identity by becoming a member of an acceptable group, a more likely resolution for boarders than patients. The concern then is to find one's niche.

Both Mountainside and Countryside were socially approved solutions; therefore, being a boarder in either implied no coming down in the world for entrants or their families. For the residents, however, there was also the message about not being able to manage alone. Mr. McDevitt, for example, not only experienced the insult implicit in others' deciding he was too old to live alone but also the hurt at not having been invited to join the household of his son. Those who had lived with their children were very explicit that they themselves made the decision to leave.

When residential status signals a point of no return, entry can become a painful acknowledgment of change in self. Even confused patients look at the physical and mental frailty around them and exclaim, "I don't belong here," or "I don't belong with them." Soon after her transfer to the nursing unit, for example, Mrs. Revere was asking for her suitcase: She wanted to leave. Like Alice trying to find her way out of the looking glass world, she searched for the door back to the boarding unit.

Alert patients shield themselves by cocooning in their rooms, an action that Senn and Steiner (1978–1979) interpret ethologically. Small animals in new places hole up and dart out occasionally to explore. Unlike the small animals, however, alert patients who cocooned showed little impulse to explore; they accepted the care but rejected the definition that went with it. Status generalization assumes that old persons who need physical care also need supervision and that those who need supervision also are physically frail— and that all are hard of hearing. These residents grasped the classificatory system perfectly.

The Shape of Residential Careers

The residential career of the elderly is marked by way stations. (See Resource C.) To the wary, each transition communicates change in status and self, and to the less alert, loss of certainty and control.

Those beginning at the boarding home level entered with misgivings and feelings of resentment, loss, and hope. Earlier experiences determined which was dominant.

> · Elizabeth Reynolds's youth prepared her to view a
> home for the aged as a proper conclusion. As a child,

she celebrated the harvest festival at her church's home with members of her Sunday School; as an older girl, she went to the home with groups to sing hymns; and, as a young woman, she visited a favorite aunt who lived in the home. When she began to feel, "Now is the time for me to make a permanent change," that church home, which still existed, came to mind, but the neighborhood around the quiet place had become an urban ghetto. Her children replied, "Not unless you wish us to visit you in a tank!" She then chose Mountainside, which was comfortably close to her son.

Some, like Mr. McDevitt, mourned a past to which there was no returning. If they were very old, ties had been thinning and placement did not so much create a break as resurrect the ghosts of separations past.

Acceptance was aided, however, if the new residents were well received by the peer group. For its part, the peer group was influenced by the newcomer's attitude. Two depressed old men at Mountainside, for example, elicited quite different responses.

Tears came to Mr. Brewster's eyes when anything reminded him of his wife—and a good deal did. The other old men, especially the widowers, rallied around him. They took him with them to the weekly meeting of the Old Guard and he plunged into its activities, and soon was elected as an officer.

Mr. Schmitt, on the other hand, came to Mountainside "for a month" when his daughter went to a large medical center for surgery. He anxiously awaited her phone calls. Her mother had died of cancer, and at first he was preoccupied with her survival, but when she returned home and he did not, he became restless. When it became plain that he was going to remain, he said, "I would like to go out. In a box."

The other residents were critical. In the beginning, Mr. Schmitt had made it plain he was not one of them, that he was only staying till his daughter got well. Afterward, their sympathies shifted to his daughter, who played Cordelia to his Lear. She brought cookies for him and the others, she took him home every Sunday, and she paid quick, frequent visits during the week. When she was out of town, a grandson visited and did his laundry. (Most of the boarders used the available washing machine to do their own.) When he complained that his daughter had abandoned him, their replies were terse.

In residential arrangements for the very old, the usual progression is unidirectional, with status falling as care levels rise. Sheltered apartments offer more privacy and less surveillance and therefore are a step above boarding homes. Intermediate care facilities are almost as stigmatizing as nursing homes because their purpose is to provide supervision, which therefore implies incapacity.

At Mountainside and Countryside, persons came to the nursing units from the community, the boarding unit, and the hospital. Those entering the nursing unit directly from the community were subject to the same sense of abandonment and loss as those who began their residential careers in the boarding unit except that the imputation of incapacity was greater and their ability to deal with it less because of illness, confusion, or both. The intrusiveness of the setting stripped those who had been shielding themselves at home by withdrawal.

Those coming to a nursing unit from the hospital often are given little explanation or choice in the decision. A study of forty consecutive hospital discharges led Coulton and her associates (1982) to conclude that twelve patients were substantially involved in the decision-making process and another eleven were partially involved, while seventeen had no voice at all. In a few instances, the family made a unilateral decision and requested that the patient not be told. Cognitively impaired patients usually had less say, but even some fully alert patients were excluded from the process. Minimal involvement was associated with subsequent dissatisfaction.

For Mountainside and Countryside residents, entering the nursing unit from community, boarding unit, or hospital usually meant they were not expected to get better. This sense of finality surrounds nursing homes even today and explains the reluctance of families and physicians to discuss placement with the persons most concerned.

Sometimes a stroke or a fracture precipitated abrupt transfer from boarding to nursing unit, but generally a protracted period of strain and anxiety ensued while the resident endeavored to conceal failing health or functioning and staff built a "case." They might or might not discuss the transfer openly, depending upon the resident's reputation for "reasonableness."

> Mrs. Gladwin had been the "Auntie Mame" at Countryside. A public health nurse who had once run an agency, she remained a colorful, dramatic figure. She and another boarder enjoyed a late-life romance: Till his death intervened, they passed their days together and took their meals at a table of their own.
>
> Now, at eight-six, she was becoming dangerously unsteady and forgetful. To move her to the nursing unit, the nursing assistant explained that they were going to paint her room and that the odor of the paint would make her ill. She helped her move her things, and Mrs. Gladwin accompanied her downstairs obligingly enough.
>
> Once in the nursing unit, she began to "give nursing care to my patient"—her half-crazed and frightened roommate. She wandered into the room across the hall and upset its articulate occupant. Soon she was tied like a runaway child.
>
> When the nursing assistant who had lured her downstairs returned to Countryside after her days off, she found Mrs. Gladwin among the demented patients ranged in restraining gerichairs around the nursing station. The erstwhile boarder looked at the nursing assistant reproachfully. "You let me down," she said. In relating the story, the aide concluded, sorrowfully, "Those words cut me worse than a knife!"

Mountainside provided its boarders with free infirmary services when they were sick, which carried neither threat nor added cost but was an accommodation geared to a short stay. When the allotted days were used up, the individual had to pay not only for the bed in the nursing unit but also for the room in the boarding unit if he or she wished to retain it. Giving up the latter signaled that the transfer was complete.

> Mrs. Windsor had defended her independence more resolutely than any other resident: Despite a stroke that scrambled her speech, despite cancer and a colostomy, and despite diabetes, she retained her boarder status and functioned well. Four years later, overwhelmed by illness, she entered the nursing unit but kept her room in the boarding area. A month passed and the dual charge began. No one wished to broach giving up her room, and, in the end, she relieved the tension. When her friend visited, she asked her to move her things to the nursing unit. Three days later she died.

Transitions did not end with the move to the nursing unit: Residents might die in the home, die in the hospital, or exhaust their funds and be sent to a Medicaid nursing home. The desired goal was to die in the home. Occasionally death came quickly while the resident was still in the boarding unit, but more often the person slipped away slowly in the nursing unit. Neither home was equipped with the high technology needed to drag out dying, so patients expired in the nursing units with comfort care. Those who went to the hospital, however, did not always fare as well. Miss Dietrich's regular physician was on his vacation when she was sent to the hospital. A colleague of his took over her medical management. According to the word that trickled back from her nurses, he managed to prolong her misery for fully a week.

Common Courses

Four common residential careers existed: boarding home–based, with brief terminal care in the nursing unit; symmetrical, with substantial stays in each, nursing home–based, and nursing home–based with transfer. Most residents following the latter were nursing home exiles.

The Boarding Home–Based Career. These residents retained boarder status until they became terminally ill. Their stays in the nursing unit could be measured in days or weeks and never exceeded two months. Mrs. Windsor at Mountainside illustrated this career, as described earlier.

The Symmetrical Career. These residents had substantial stays as boarders but transferred to the nursing units when their chronic illnesses required more care.

> When Sarah Coleman's husband died, she applied for admission to Mountainside. She had no close kinspeople, but she had lived in the area for sixty years and had both her church and many friends nearby. She was then eighty-six.
>
> She became a respected member of the peer group in the boarding unit and often acted as table hostess. During these years, her major concern was inflation: She feared the cost of a prolonged stay in the nursing unit. When she was ninety-four, her unsteadiness could no longer be denied and she transferred to the nursing unit, where she spent her days in a wheelchair. At ninety-eight, she described her own health as "good" and I agreed with her. She died quietly in the home two weeks before her hundredth birthday.

The Nursing Home–Based Career. These individuals began and ended their residential careers as patients.

> After many emergency trips to Bernard Pincus's seaside rooming house, his son felt that he needed more care and wanted him closer to the family. Mr. Pincus entered Mountainside's nursing unit at eighty-seven and remained until his death eleven years later.

Responding to the morale scale question, "If you could live wherever you wanted, where would you live?" Mr. Pincus replied, "Miami Beach." Nevertheless, Mountainside provided a snug harbor. His son visited daily, he passed his days reading his paper, occasionally he chanted a blessing over the meal, and he was careful not to eat meat and dairy together. At Passover, his family came and brought food for the Seder.

Near the end, he became quite hard of hearing. He withdrew increasingly, but his tenor remained quiet and equitable. Staff liked the pleasant old man.

The Nursing Home–Based Career with Transfer. Of the 116 persons in the study, 30 transferred. Seventeen were Medicaid exiles, who moved to facilities that would accept them at the public assistance rate. Thirteen other residents also departed, but these moved for disparate reasons, while the Medicaid exiles constituted a distinct group. As such, they were significant for three reasons.

First, their transfers posed an ethical dilemma for Mountainside. To ask these patients to leave was contrary to the sectarian home's service orientation, but if it kept nonpaying residents, it would have to raise the rates for the rest, hastening their impoverishment.

Second, Mountainside did not turn away all who had exhausted their funds, and it often made substantial efforts to keep others. Like the deviants in any system, the Medicaid exiles therefore laid bare its workings and raised questions about the social resources, the kind of negotiations, and the larger systems factors that determined who should stay and who should go.

Third, these departures had consequences for the system itself. In time, Medicaid transfers from Mountainside appeared to cease. Chapter Nine will speculate about how this change was achieved.

Greta Hansen's first days at Countryside were a burden only to the alert. She wandered into her roommate's wardrobe and struggled against the shower, but flashes of a cheerful, friendly personality shone through her confusion. She had a short, happy friendship with Countryside's prime wanderer, Bernadette O'Neil: The two women sat side by side, apparently commenting about the passers-by, making little sense but being pleasantly companionable.

In time, the confusion became encompassing. Eight years after admission, she was disheveled and toothless, confined in a gerichair near the nurse's station. Her speech was incomprehensible, but she made friendly noises in response to a greeting. By then, her funds were exhausted, and a Medicaid home was being sought for her. She moved to a County facility and died there shortly before her eight-second birthday.

Greta Hansen was more fortunate than many. Those who were alert saw the transfer coming and appeared to experience shame because no one seemed to care enough or to have money enough to save them. The pain of families was also apparent.

More recent studies of relocation have questioned the earlier contention that elderly residents forced to move die sooner (Aldrich and Mendkoff, 1968; Blenkner, 1967; Pablo, 1977; Coffman, 1981; Borup, 1983 and 1981; Horowitz and Schulz, 1983). At these two homes, there was no significant difference in the death ages of Medicaid exiles, those making other moves, and those who remained. Six did die within a three-month period, but, in view of their advanced ages, this was not remarkable. What was sometimes evident was the discomfort of staff. At Countryside, for example, staff members told patients only that Mr. Beasley was "going with his nephew," without adding that his nephew was driving him directly to a Medicaid home.

Some patients sought transfers to move closer to an adult child or to enter their own church home. For the Medicaid exiles, however, the transfer was for economic reasons: They had outlived their money.

The residential career at Mountainside and Countryside can be summed up succinctly: People entered, moved through one or more levels of care, and left or died. The plot of *Hamlet* also can be described in a sentence: It is the way you play the parts that counts.

Part Two

WHAT ACTUALLY TAKES PLACE
IN RESIDENTIAL SETTINGS?

At eighty-three, Mr. Schiller, a wheelchair-bound stroke patient at Mountainside, performed a remarkable feat of behavior modification. He trained the director of nursing so well that she fetched his breakfast tray herself and took it away the moment he had finished. Mr. Schiller liked to have his tray removed promptly and Mrs. Hartpence could not bear to see the old man's dangerous agitation whenever there was a moment's delay. It is possible that neither of them understood that Mr. Schiller had conditioned the nurse's behavioral response, but in this instance, he achieved his preferred pattern of care. Mr. Schiller was an active agent.

It is safe to say that any patient who was not comatose engaged every day in some piece of interaction designed to affect his or her situation and the persons involved in it. Those who were comatose had surrogates acting or attempting to act on their behalf. Their success or failure depended on many factors, including their personal, material, and social resources and the constraining or supporting structures within the home—its physical design, ground rules, and overriding values.

This section deals with processes of negotiation and control that occurred as the residents attempted to make acceptable lives for themselves. For most boarders, the major concern was to ward off transfer to the nursing unit, but all residents had other goals as well, such as establishing a proper persona, discrediting a rival, or asserting one's personhood by discomfiting a staff member. For a patient, these goals might include securing a longer soak in the tub of good, warm, pain-dispatching water. The list was endless. Comparing social resource and morale scores backed observations. Morale scores presumably reflected the residents' satisfaction with the general outcome of their transactions, and social resource scores reflected what they had to negotiate with. Observation supplied the process.

Chapter Four defines the counters in the contest and tells how they were employed. The counters are resources for social exchange, as described by Richard Emerson (1962) and Peter Blau (1964).

Chapter Five looks more closely at external resources—family and friends. Residents not only wished to use them in their ongoing transactions within the home but also had to negotiate with these human resources themselves to get them to intervene on their behalf. The still-married residents present particular problems to these settings because they are deviant to the system and because staff members generally prefer to deal with the adult children. The reasons for this are examined using Litwak's (1985) dichotomy of tasks that the formal and informal systems each do best.

Chapter Six begins with Goffman's (1961) paradigm of responses to institutional totality. It then turns to control processes and illustrates them as they were used against deviants who pushed the homes' tolerance too far. Difficult residents bare the jungle constraints buried deep in any social system. Goode (1972) once said that behind every open ward lay the threat of a closed one. These systems' extreme sanction for the boarder was transfer to the nursing unit and for the patient the ultimate penalty was expulsion, but a system cannot employ its extreme sanctions too freely without arousing protest from those beyond its control. Staff members were sensitive to this and when strong sanctions were employed, they reconstructed their definitions of events in the manner suggested by Robert Emerson and his associates in their treatment of the politics of trouble (Emerson and Messenger, 1977; Emerson and Warren, 1983).

Nothing remains the same, and Chapter Seven turns to the thinning social networks of the aging residents and their shifting sources of support. With the passage of time, more of this support lay within the system and less outside. The intrinsic sources of power also diminished. To what degree did social credit for past contributions and for simple survival take their place? Time tends to legitimate existing arrangements, which may erode more slowly than the conditions that called them into being. This chapter examines the changing status of residents over time.

The end of the residential career is as important as its beginning. Chapter Eight examines the good deaths, the proper exits, and the unhappy departures. At this point, it is possible to ask how well the personhood of residents was nurtured by others or maintained by the residents themselves. What combination of personal attributes, external resources, and social structure made for a good old age?

CHAPTER FOUR

Getting What One Wants: Resources and Obstacles

Nellie Brown lay so still that I thought she was comatose. I had been chatting with her roommate, Dorothy Dietrich. When Mrs. Brown unexpectedly stirred, I asked Miss Dietrich to introduce us. Miss Dietrich asked me my name; I repeated it and soon discovered that she did not know her neighbor's name either, although they had been sleeping side by side for almost a year.

"Girlie," she said to her neighbor, "This is Mrs. Gwynne." I went to Mrs. Brown's bedside and admired her afghan. She told me her daughter had made it. I said I understood she played the harmonica, and she told me she had learned it when she was a girl. She chatted pleasantly enough. At last, I asked her her name. She paused, and then, with some surprise, replied, "I don't remember." After a moment she added, "Just now."

At this point, Miss Dietrich, who had been following our conversation, suggested that I not keep her talking too long, but Mrs. Brown quickly volunteered that she was not tired.

After that, I stopped and talked with her whenever she seemed fairly alert. One day I found her lying there as usual, looking dead, but with her harmonica in her hand. She played it for me and we talked about the music she liked. I asked her to tell me her favorite hymn and, in an incredibly thin voice, fudging some of the words, she sang "Jesus, Lover of My Soul." The next time I played records for patients, I made sure she was included, and she raised her voice in "Home Sweet Home."

But when I visited her the next day, she was in distress, she wanted me to undo the leather wristlets that were confining her hands. Some days, I would find the harmonica placed beyond her reach or tucked in a drawer. On another occasion, I found Mrs. Brown spread-eagled and tied. She said things were not so good with her and asked me to untie her, which I couldn't do, but I asked how this thing had happened. She said she didn't know why. (Later the charge nurse reported that her hands were tied to keep her from getting them into feces.)

Recall is not required to complete the Philadelphia Geriatric Center Morale Scale: It is enough to know how one feels. On a day when Mrs. Brown was relatively clear, I administered the test. Her comments made it plain that she grasped the tenor of the questions; for example, she volunteered, "A lot of times I wish I was dead." Her score hit bottom: 3.

Her roommate's score, 13, was well within the average range for the setting. Mrs. Brown was ninety at the time and Miss Dietrich eighty-six. Both women were cognitively impaired, but the difference in their facades was striking. Miss Dietrich was a nice-looking grey-haired woman with glasses, well dressed and well groomed, who spent most of her day in her wheelchair or in an armchair by the window and made trips to the sunny dining room for ice cream. Mrs. Brown was a small figure in a nondescript gown, with her hair pulled back. She was generally in bed, although her attendance at the music program showed that staff could get her up if encouraged to do so.

The major difference between the two was that Miss Dietrich was a wealthy woman with a trustee who provided her with a private duty nurse. As Lawton has pointed out (1981 and 1985; Lawton and Nahemow, 1973), the less competent the individual, the more important the environment becomes for that person's well-being. Miss Dietrich enjoyed a good deal of environmental support although it could not protect her totally.

Miss Dietrich was victimized by the two men across the hall who relieved the monotony at night when her nurse was gone by playing a game of "setting her off." Because she was afraid, she often cried out, "I want somebody to feed me. I want somebody to feed me. I want . . . " A floor nurse marched down and told her to stop. As soon as the nurse retreated, the two men chorused, "Somebody come here. Somebody come here," starting her off again. Her cries brought irate staff members who sometimes punished her by pushing her wheelchair into the semidarkened hall, which frightened her even more.

In the end, her resources came to the rescue. The game stopped abruptly when the Countryside director of nursing suggested to the trustee that he add a private duty nurse for the evening shift.

Ironically, the second nurse came about the time I found Mrs. Brown spread-eagled. Miss Dietrich's private duty nurses did not help Mrs. Brown, they were chiefly concerned with seeing that she did not annoy their patient or themselves. It was they who put the harmonica out of reach when its rusty tones became too repetitious.

This profile points out that both women knew what they wanted but that Miss Dietrich was more successful in getting it, chiefly because she had people to fend for her. This is one source of power and an important one for those whose physical mobility and cognitive resources are failing.

There is a large literature about social exchange and power. In relation to aging, much of this literature is field based (Dowd, 1980; Dunkle, 1983; Gilford, 1984; Martin, 1971); elsewhere, it is often laboratory bound and number ridden or highly abstract and theoretical (Cook and Emerson, 1984; Cook, Emerson, Gillmore, and Yamagishi, 1983). For the purposes of this study, Richard Emerson (1962) and Peter Blau (1964) supply a useful body of concepts.

By creating a web of diffuse obligations, social exchanges provide much of the "glue" that binds people together. Individuals try to remain in relationships they find rewarding and, when they can, to withdraw from those that are not. Opportunities to secede from inimical relationships are limited in total institutions, which is one reason people dislike closed settings even when their purpose is benign. ("Why would she want to remain in her house when she could be taken care of in a nice home for the elderly?")

Social exchange differs from economic exchange in that the "price" is not clearly specified and a too-hasty or exact return is viewed as bad form. When Mrs. Jones buys rolls from the baker, for example, she pays promptly in cash. That she will do so is understood. When Mrs. Smith passes a plate of home-baked buns over the fence to her neighbor, Mrs. Jones does not reciprocate with an identical batch, which would be seen as competitive, or instantly reach for her purse, which would deny the friendly intent behind the gift. Even if they had a cash transaction between them (for example, if Mrs. Jones became Mrs. Smith's regular babysitter), it would first be phrased as a favor: They would agree that Mrs. Jones was accepting the money so Mrs. Smith could be comfortable about receiving the service. This would keep some part of the transaction on an informal basis and loosely defined. On the other hand, if Mrs. Smith is always doing for Mrs. Jones, giving her home-baked buns and little services, and Mrs. Jones never reciprocates by word or deed, Mrs. Smith is likely to reduce her investment in the relationship. The relationship would soon become formal or even nonexistent.

Exchange relationships are not always equal. When they are not, those with fewer resources must repay their more powerful partners with deference and compliance. The clergyman in Jane Austin's

Pride and Prejudice who spent his idle moments composing compliments to pay his patroness is a prime example. He was quite complaisant about this arrangement—and, indeed, his subservience was probably a fair exchange for her bounty. It never lessened his fatuous self-esteem. Outside of contractual arrangements like work, however, most people feel uncomfortable when the discrepancy is too great. Status differences arise from persistent patterns of unbalanced exchange.

Dunkle (1983) found that aging parents who moved in with their children were more depressed than those who lived alone. They were less distressed if they contributed to the household—for example, if they did the mending or helped with the grandchildren. This appeared to be because it represented an exchange, lessening the dependence they would incur as mere consumers.

In the nursing home, even the family paying a staggering bill for the care of its elderly member does not feel itself on a plane that permits it to complain forthrightly. The daughter advances the view that a nursing assistant is stealing from her mother with the diffidence of one complaining to a monarch about his lord high executioner. Her mother may be dependent on the same nursing assistant for an item as urgently required as a bedpan. The family believes it needs the nursing home more than the nursing home needs the family. The power differential lies between patient and staff.

Some patients are less disadvantaged than others. Miss Dietrich was able to get more of her needs met than Mrs. Brown, but even Miss Dietrich could not fire her nurse and she did not have a direct line that would enable her to ask her trustee to do so. He communicated with the director of nursing, her physician, and the nurse herself—and depended upon them for an interpretation of Miss Dietrich's needs and wishes.

> Miss Dietrich was enjoying her afternoon ice cream in the dining room while her private duty nurse regaled a small group with her adventures. At several points she said something self-derogatory ("Me and my big mouth!") and on each occasion, Miss Dietrich, ostensibly eating her ice cream, quietly chuckled. She

plainly took pleasure in the putdown of the powerful
nurse, even if the nurse did it herself.

Resources for Social Exchange

In line with the Emerson-Blau power strategies, a resource for
social exchange is anything that enables a person to reward a favor,
extort a service, secure other sources of supply, or do without what
the other has to offer (Blau, 1964; Emerson, 1962). What constitutes
a social resource depends on the setting and what is scarce.

A superior television that could be shared was a social asset at
both Mountainside and Countryside. So was an attentive daughter
who might include her mother's friends on an outing. This was one
of the social assets enjoyed by Mrs. Flowers, one she used to reward
those at Countryside she viewed as suitable companions.

> Mrs. Flowers' daughter was a resource in a second
> sense as well: She could be used to coerce. The daugh-
> ter generally appreciated staff's efforts to care for her
> mother but when she felt those efforts lagged, she had
> threat value. She was a long-time resident of a yacht-
> ing community that provided Countryside with many
> of its more affluent patients. If she felt her mother
> seriously abused, there was every reason to believe she
> would share her views widely. At the same time, there
> was a delicate balance: Both daughter and mother
> needed the home.
> Mrs. Flowers' Parkinson's disease made her de-
> pendent on staff, a dependence that rose sharply at
> night when she was tied in bed with the bed rail
> raised. She was terrified of fire. At night she wanted
> to keep the nurses and aides at hand and so she rang
> her bell for them to come until their patience was
> exhausted. It was only the night shift that engaged in
> reprisals: Her fears made her more vulnerable then
> and the night shift was the least likely to encounter
> her daughter or the administrator.

Miss Dietrich's private duty nurse demonstrated both the advantage of having an alternative source of supply and its limits. The private duty nurse made Miss Dietrich independent of the floor nurses during the daytime but left her at their mercy at night, and it was the night shift that pushed her wheelchair into the hall and left her alone with her terrors. Both Mrs. Flowers and Miss Dietrich became more restless and demanding at night, when their power to negotiate was the least, with predictable results: Staff disregard, patient demand escalation, and finally, staff reprisals.

Just as residents' needs left them at a disadvantage in their negotiations, so the opposite, the ability to do without, conferred a measure of invulnerability. Peers or staff could compel reluctant individuals to conform only if they were hungry for approval, if the group could reward them, or if the cost of resistance was high. This takes into account both the strength of resources to fend off sanctions and the inner resolve of the resident to do without.

The residents regarded as most deviant could be said to have renounced the rewards of pleasing and, to that degree, to have become untouchable. Many of these were patients. What was demanded of them, passive compliance, was little enough but their rewards for conformity were infinitesimal. Objective evidence supports this: Those residents with the lowest resource scores were also the lowest conformers (gamma 0.7). The residents with the highest resource scores were the most conforming: They received better rewards and, had they not, they could have left.

Patients were disadvantaged in their bargaining by the imposed conditions of patienthood and by their own lack of internal and external resources, while boarders had more alternatives. Elka Miller, for example, was able to leave a home she experienced as demeaning because she found another. Partly this was possible because of the urban setting, partly because of qualities within herself.

Resources and Negotiation

Some writers distinguish between negotiation and other means of getting things done, such as threatening, persuading, or appealing to authority (Strauss, 1978; Kuhn and Beam, 1982; Raven and Kruglanski, 1970), but in life the interplay is constant and much behavior, even behavior that leads directly to the actor's desired conclusion, is unconscious. In this analysis, negotiation is the interpersonal work that determines status and action. Sometimes negotiation meets obdurate social structure, that is, resistant processes that are slow to change. The resources for social exchange include everything the individual can bring to bear on negotiations. According to the Blau-Emerson paradigm, these would include the ability to reward a favor, extort a service, secure alternative sources of supply, or do without.

As Strauss (1978) points out, there are structural and climatic limitations to negotiation. We have already seen that at Mountainside and Countryside these included whether you were a patient or a boarder, whether the home was sectarian or entrepreneurial, and whether it was in the country or in town.

It is superficially simple to identify the powerful people in a setting because things happen in ways that serve their ends, just as it is possible to determine who is deviant by seeing who is being pressured to conform. Neither test is complete, however, because powerful deviants may escape sanction and persons of low status often get their needs met, albeit on others' terms or for others' purposes. Those who are powerful can generally deflect sanction or attenuate it. Those with few intrinsic resources may have at their command other inducements with which to motivate others to do their will, or there may be intervening structural factors or norms they can turn to their advantage. It is important, therefore, to look closely at what constitutes social resources in the particular setting.

Social resources at Mountainside and Countryside were measured by an inventory that took into account (1) residents' ability to do for themselves as opposed to their need for help from others, (2) other persons likely to come to their aid, (3) material resources at their command, and (4) certain special resources that varied somewhat between the two homes. The instrument is given in Resource B. A staff member who knew the individual well did the scoring. Of a possible 38 points, 24 could be scored under three categories of internal human resources. The first, cognitive and self-care skills, included being able to manage dressing, personal hygiene, food, and procurement. Today most of the cognitive and self-care skills would be subsumed under activities of daily living (ADLs) and instrumental activities of daily living (IADLs). This subcategory separated the patients from the boarders because it indicated the level of help required. For residents these scores fluctuated over time, and with them their patient-boarder status. These capacities determined that status and were influenced by it: Self-care skills erode when staff members find it quicker to do for residents than to permit them to do for themselves.

A second subcategory under internal human resources was social outreach, which included both outreach and particularization. Outreach was the individual's willingness or ability to engage with his or her social world, and particularization involved relating to persons in it as distinct individuals. Miss Dorrer, for example, called out, "Help me, help me . . . " all day long. She was appealing for a personal rescuer but addressing a vaguely generalized other. She neither particularized nor really reached out. Particularization was measured by scoring residents on whether they could name some of their fellow residents and the staff members who served them. Residents were asked, "Name five people who live here and three people who work here" and staff members were asked to name "three residents you would miss . . . " Between them, the two measures distinguished not only the residents' ability to particularize but also (in another part of the test) their salience for those around them.

The cognitive and self-care skills and the social outreach sections provided a welcome substitute for the Mental Status Questionnaire (MSQ) (Kane and Kane, 1981) that so distressed impaired residents that it was soon set aside. (Individuals struggling with memory loss are devastated when they find they cannot answer questions like "What is the name of the president?") Even very confused residents completed the Philadelphia Geriatric Center Morale Scale with support. Some quavered as they struggled through but, in the end, almost every respondent was smiling and triumphant: They knew how they felt and had been able to communicate it. When this was followed by the Mental Status Questionnaire, however, their faces often fell and their voices dropped. The alert, on the other hand, enjoyed the test, especially a former postman at Countryside who responded to "Where is this place?" with specific directions including the zip code; but for the marginally functioning, the MSQ, which uncovers organicity, was devastating. A score of 12–18 on this part of the social resource inventory painlessly separated the relatively alert from the less alert, without confronting anyone with failure.

The third subsection was health and physical mobility. Mrs. Flowers's fear of fire was fanned by her inability to get out of bed unaided or to escape without her wheelchair. A diabetic boarder who could manage his or her own insulin was relatively independent, but one who could not needed the nurses.

The second major category, external human resources, included both outside significant others (friends and relatives in the community) and inside significant others (residents and staff members). Although Mrs. Flowers depended on staff for help with the activities of daily living, her overall social resource score was in the middle range because of strength here: She was quite alert to the social setting and had an active daughter to do battle for her.

The third category moved directly to the control of resources that could be bestowed or withheld. The first subcategory, access to funds, took into account that it was possible to have money but not to control it while the second, facility, took cognizance of benefits that could be shared, such as excursions provided by family or friends or a color television. Miss Godfrey, for example, had a wealthy friend who used to send her liveried chauffeur to bring Miss Godfrey to lunch once a month, and sometimes another patient of Miss Godfrey's choice was included in the invitation.

A final category, special resources, picked up certain exceptional assets, which varied according to setting. As Miss Dietrich demonstrated, a private duty nurse was a prime resource at Countryside, but at Mountainside, private duty nurses were forbidden. In both facilities, a significant medical connection could be traded on—for example, being a retired physician, having a close relative who was a practicing physician, or having been a registered nurse. Of the four residents who were able to move from patient to boarder status, one was herself a retired physician, one had a brother in practice, and the third had two sons who were local physicians. (The fourth patient who managed to reverse roles had no medical connection at all, but had a former son-in-law who was an exceedingly active advocate instead.) At Mountainside, it was helpful to be a member of the sponsoring sect, to own an automobile, or to be the client of the Santa Claus Society, the pseudonym of a society that had as its mission maintaining the lifestyle of individuals with cultivated tastes whose last years were straitened because they had lived lives of service. This society had been organized to brighten the old age of elderly missionaries and selfless clergy.

Devised at the beginning of the study, the social resource inventory eroded somewhat as the study progressed but it was particular to Mountainside and Countryside and provided a rough guide to the assets of their residents.

Rules That Block Their Use

Mary Rogers (1974) has pointed out that when one crosses systems boundaries, one's role or the rules may change and suddenly one's sources of power shrink or become inaccessible. She describes infra-resources as the circumstances, conditions, or attributes that must be present before one can deploy one's resources. For example, at home a physician can prescribe but in another country, he or she would have neither the license nor the language but would have to wait for an indigenous doctor to act. The knowledge of the indications would remain but the ability to employ that knowledge would be compromised.

Perhaps no systems boundary marks a more abrupt change than the threshold of patienthood. Customary resources turn to lead because the infra-resources necessary for their deployment have vanished. New ground rules are in place. No resident illustrated this better than Mr. Sutton, who arrived at Mountainside's nursing unit perhaps not fully aware that he was destined to remain.

> A stroke two years earlier had left Mr. Sutton, then seventy-one, mentally alert, clear of speech, but paralyzed on his left side and incontinent. The latter was a source of distress to this handsome and immaculate man.
>
> After extensive rehabilitation, he had gone home, but successive hospitalizations for surgical repairs had undermined his initial gains. On several occasions he had been sent to a convalescent center while his wife took brief vacations to recuperate from the burden of

his care. These stays had been time limited and always
he had been able to see that he was taken back home.

Mr. Sutton had been and continued to be a very
controlling person. His life had centered around his
business, and it appeared that family life had centered
around not upsetting him and precipitating another
episode of chest pain. Now he switched to other methods of control. Ordinarily Mr. Sutton was an alert and
intelligent conversationalist, for example, but when
his daughters appeared he magically became a tearful
old man.

On the nursing unit, he skillfully provoked staff
members and then left them guilt stricken at having
been angry with a helpless patient. When a busy nurse
was tending his more helpless roommate, Mr. Sutton's
need for care escalated abruptly, as he implored her
help with tasks he normally performed for himself:
"Please part my hair."

When he was truly angered, he demanded to leave.
One night he stormed to the telephone to call a taxi,
to tell the police he was being held against his will,
to confront his family at the doorstep. But the phone
was a pay phone: He had a fortune in the bank, but
he didn't have a dime in his pocket because patients
were not allowed to keep money.

A nurse wheeled him off to bed.

Even a bedside telephone did not guarantee access to the outside
world.

Miss Godfrey's connections procured her many benefits in addition to the chauffeured luncheons. She had
a widely scattered circle of interested others. She fared
very well during most of her eight years in the home,
but toward the end of her life, she was intermittently
confused, depressed, and lonely. She missed her old
companions. On one occasion, her bed rail was up
and her cherished pink princess telephone was placed

just beyond her reach. She had been telephoning friends about the things that were bothering her and they, in turn, had called the administrator to complain on her behalf. The staff finally aborted this by removing the phone.

There were certain rules that particularly constrained patients.

1. Patients could not keep cash—and, in addition, the homes usually pressed for someone else to manage their finances. The homes' position was understandable. Many of the patients were very old and very frail. When they were ill, they often became less alert, which made it hard for the staff to collect their bills. If money was lost or mislaid, the aides might be accused of taking it. The other reality was that money could be used for purchases the home did not approve of or for tipping the staff. Perennially hopeful, one woman kept sending for mail-order hearing aids until staff resorted to intercepting her orders.

At Countryside, some aides contracted independently to do personal laundry, which entailed payment from the patient's account or by a family member. At Mountainside, any cash transaction between patient and staff member was frowned upon, first because the home's sponsors believed no one should be favored above others in the pursuit of care, but also because it gave patients reward power that might compete with management's controls.

This no-cash rule blocked many operations an adult might ordinarily engage in. A terminally ill patient, for example, wanted ice cream. The nurses were concerned about her poor appetite and refused on the official grounds that the home could not provide ice cream for one without providing ice cream for all. She could not send out for it because she had no cash.

2. Patients could leave the home only with their physician's approval and in the company of a "responsible" person. For practical purposes, this entailed a triple endorsement: approval by physician, nursing staff, and the family member, who had to sign a slip accepting full responsibility.

3. Patients could not wander out of sight on the grounds or go to the boarding unit. One resident who had known the home well as a visitor was surprised to learn that as a patient he could not visit

its library. Even the architecture conspired against it: Steps led down to the nursing unit, making it easy for boarders to visit there but hard for patients to leave.

4. Patients could not keep sharp objects (sewing scissors) or familiar medications. (This was the Balm Bengay generation.) Exceptions to the scissors rule were made for alert patients who sewed but concern was expressed about their roommates. Patients lacked secure drawers for possessions like these. Not rules but contingencies of space further limited patients' access to their belongings and what they could keep.

Mountainside boarders also lost certain freedoms, but most staff-imposed norms related to safety (restricted smoking areas) or household arrangements (posting notice if they planned to miss a meal) and therefore were broadly acceptable to the group. Residents were asked to sign out when they left the grounds, but there were no restrictions on their coming and going.

Peer norms were stated less forthrightly but were equally binding: There was a dress code, a taboo against sitting in the front row for anything, and a distinct pecking order. Shared generational values felt "right" and were scarcely noticed, except in their abeyance. The banning of liquor, for example, seemed absolutely correct to most members of this well-churched cohort.

Countryside boarders encountered two kinds of constraints. None had cars and the rural situation meant that they could not leave the home unless someone came for them. In addition, the owners were concerned about falls and required that no one bathe without the supervision of an aide. The fragmentation of the peer group reduced the clarity of their norms and led to the idiosyncratic imposition of sanctions.

Each of these rules or conditions in some measure limited residents' bargaining ability by making them more dependent on others, by limiting their access to other resources they might have employed, or by shrinking their range of opportunities and contacts. One set of contacts, the peer group, was itself a source of constraints but also of potential power.

Peer Alliances as a Source of Power

In both homes, the transfer of boarders to the nursing units could be expedited or delayed by the reaction of the peer group. This was reflected in the experience of three residents—one exiled to the nursing unit because the boarders demanded it, another misplaced but slow to go because of a countervailing need for beds, and a third protected from transfer by her symbolic meaning to her fellow boarders.

Within three months of Gretchen Elder's joining her peers in the boarding unit at Countryside, the group had coalesced against her. Mrs. Elder was indisputably alert and capable of self-care, but her morale score was among the lowest (4) and her clearly articulated complaints were more than the group could bear. Led by the most abrasive person on the unit, Mamie Slocum, they requested her removal.

Mrs. Elder was thoroughly aware of the other residents' feelings. The director of nursing spelled out the complaints many times. She understood which behavior they found offensive but appeared helpless to change it.

She was transferred to the nursing unit as Mrs. Flowers's roommate. Mrs. Flowers promptly protested. "She is much in disfavor," Mrs. Flowers declared. A small single room was found for her and partial peace restored. She constantly complained of a hot, itchy skin. She once said she wasn't lonely because she had so much to annoy her and detailed a list of physical symptoms. She frequently exclaimed, "I wish I had John's courage!" (Her son, John, had committed suicide.) She punched at her scalp with tweezers. Her eating habits, marked by bursts of greedy shoveling, led to further complaints. One day I found her at lunchtime seated at a card table near the veranda. She had been banished from the dining room because of the protests of her fellow patients.

This behavior was difficult to disrupt, but it could be done. It sometimes was possible to take her hands, remove the tweezers, and engage her in conversation. I often stopped to chat with her because she was a keen

observer and a ready source of information, but some
days all the content was drowned in lamentations.

Once Mrs. Elder's mentally ill daughter came to
visit her. On this occasion, the older woman was remarkably collected: She listened quietly throughout
the afternoon. When I offered the younger woman a
ride, Mrs. Elder promptly accepted and persuaded her
to go. When other family members came, Mrs. Elder
regaled them with moans and complaints, but when
this disturbed daughter arrived, she put on her own
robe of sanity and was again a mother.

Mrs. Elder still had status of a sort in the community because she
had belonged to the altar guild of the proper church in a nearby
suburb, but her social resource score (23) lay in the lower middle
range. The woman who routed her, Mamie Slocum, was a policeman's widow. Like Gretchen Elder, she had a low morale score (6),
but her resource score (31) was at the top of the middle range. She
was an undisputed leader in the boarding unit but not beloved; her
sharp tongue and cutting voice made her feared. She organized campaigns of silence against newcomers she disliked. She nicknamed
one unfortunate woman "the Creep."

"The Creep" was a timorous grey wraith, with a resource score of 18 (low) and a morale score of 4 (very
low). She asserted herself only when she saw another
resident with a cane that looked like her own, leading
her to believe the other woman had stolen it.

For the most part, she was aware only of her unhappiness. Once she was sitting, hat and coat on, suitcase beside her. Her sisters had told her they would be
picking her up on the weekend for a visit, and she had
been packed and ready ever since, although the weekend was four days away. Her confusion was complete:
One day she appeared with a bathrobe over her dress
and sweater and mismatching shoes.

So much senility was hard for the Countryside
boarders to bear and Mrs. Slocum's leadership was

hardly needed to organize a campaign against her. Nevertheless, her transfer was long delayed. Twenty-eight months after her arrival, she went to the nursing unit, and two months later she died. By that time, Mrs. Slocum herself was no longer at Countryside.

The grey wraith's slow transfer illustrates the interplay of norms with other considerations. By the official criteria for patienthood—a failure of self-care and the need for supervision—she required transfer more than Gretchen Elder. At the other boarders' demand, a place was set for her at a separate table. Her exile to the periphery may have served a function for the group by reminding them that there were behaviors they would not tolerate and, because she was quieter than Mrs. Elder, she was easier to ostracize. From a management point of view, however, when transfer was seriously considered, beds were in short supply.

In contrast to these cases, a Mountainside resident with a stigmatizing disability survived in the boarding unit because she had the support of her peers. She was mentally quite clear but few dysphasic persons receive a hearing attentive enough to establish this, at least not in settings where expectations are oriented to deficits.

Helen Windsor had a potent social asset in addition to her own indomitable will—symbolic significance for her fellow boarders and therefore their undivided support.

She entered the boarding home at sixty-two, following an abortive attempt to live at home after the stroke that had left her with a crab-like gait and scrambled speech. She was by far the youngest resident at Mountainside. Her stroke gave her special meaning for the group: She had had the affliction the residents feared most and she had retained her independence.

They struggled through her scrambled speech, they admired her courage, and they loved her laughter. When something struck her as funny, her mirth would ripple out softly, pick up, and then gush forth like a

torrent. Everyone else would laugh with her. She
brought them joy.

Over time, her physical condition worsened and her
once irrepressible spirits flagged. The boarders
watched her anxiously. A few months before her
death, she went to the hospital and all were intent on
her recovery, which at first seemed striking. They
proudly commented that her speech seemed better. In
succeeding weeks, however, she grew weaker. She had
difficulty dressing herself and getting out of her chair,
and she became uncharacteristically weepy. One evening at supper she saw the platter of tomatoes pass—
they were not on her diet—and tears ran down her
cheeks. She spent increasing time on her bed.

At last a senior boarder spoke to the administrator,
expressing the concern the whole group felt. It was
time for her to transfer, he said. Helen Windsor ac-
ceded to a temporary transfer to the nursing unit, then
signaled her acceptance by making it permanent.
Then, when she was ready, she died.

A few hours before her death, the administrator lingered by her bedside with a meeting calling but reluctant to go. "It's all right," Mrs. Windsor said and
dismissed her with a smile.

Until her need for nursing care was unmistakable to every
boarder, the transfer did not take place. Such a moratorium would
never have occurred for a boarder the peer group viewed as deviant.

The Limits of Negotiation, the Limits of Power

There are limits to negotiation and limits to power and a moving
balance between them. Outcomes are affected not only by what each
party brings to the exchange but by emergent properties arising
from previous transactions, impinging interests, unforeseeable options, evolving values, and the greater systems beyond.

In any setting, some norms are more negotiable than others:

In the introduction to this section, Mr. Schiller demonstrated that it was possible to negotiate the prompt removal of a breakfast tray. He simply displayed the health-threatening agitation that might ensue if his tray lingered too long, much as an ancient Japanese might have run his fingers along his sword to indicate that he would commit hara-kiri on the other person's doorstep if that individual did not do his bidding.

Mr. Schiller was not able to negotiate his way out of a bath, however, with either an adamant refusal or a rising pulse. Not taking a bath was simply not negotiable at Mountainside. The administrator equated cleanliness with godliness and good order, and her staff was prepared to escalate the pressures. One episode of bath resistance was resolved by sending for Mr. Schiller's son, who believed remaining in the home was in his father's best interests. The son informed the father there was no choice. The nurses handled another episode without outside assistance. If he would not shower, they would not help him dress. Since no one was admitted to the dining room who was not in street clothes, Mr. Schiller wheeled himself down to the dining room three times in his bathrobe and three times was turned back. He capitulated.

An encompassing system often sets limits for negotiation that are experienced as a local restriction, that is, as the "bad" agent rather than as the depriving system. In these situations, macrosystem constraints gather force when they reverberate with local predilections.

Normally sensitive to the feelings of her residents, Barbara Archer marched them through the monthly fire drills with the single-mindedness of a drill sergeant. Ruffled dignities and protests were disregarded as even the dying were propelled into place. She was moved by two imperatives: safety and the law. The state required fire drills and she took its regulations seriously. Other homes in the area were subject to the same requirements but I never witnessed elsewhere a fire drill of such intensity. At Mountainside the law reverberated with the administrator's preoccupation with safety.

The value of old alliances changes with the emergence of new needs and shifting relationships. Sources of prestige fade when no one remains who remembers. This is particularly true in homes for the aged, where time and turnover seem to accelerate as residents grow older.

> With a spray of white hair and flashing dark eyes, Ramona Everly was a striking figure at the study's start. She was clear of speech and mind. Like Sarah Penfield, she enjoyed prestige as one of the women who had sewn curtains and stitched cushions for Mountainside at its beginning. Because of her membership in the sponsoring body, she had many associations with members of the board and conversed with them when they came to supper before their monthly meeting. She and the administrator had known each other long before she entered the home. All of this strengthened her position in the home but ultimately provided the means of her undoing.
>
> Sarah Penfield, too, was a redoubtable figure, incisive of mind, well informed about the traditions of the sect, and much respected. The two women led the sewing group at which layettes were stitched and issues threshed out.
>
> Sarah Penfield had a keen eye and a sharper ear. She told the administrator that she had heard Ramona Everly criticize the management of the home to a board member. One remark cut Barbara Archer to the quick: When the board member commented on the splendid chocolates that crowned the repast, Ramona Everly confided that the administrator had saved them in the freezer from Christmas. Relations between the administrator and the resident chilled sharply after that. In Sarah Penfield's opinion, she had been disloyal to the home and she refused to share a table with her one day more. Barbara Archer saw that Ramona

Everly was never again table hostess and seating was rearranged to curtail these opportunities for chatting with the board. When Ramona Everly ceased to be table hostess, Sarah Penfield took her place.

Barbara Archer and Ramona Everly saw each other daily for another fifteen years, but there was always an edge of implicit criticism and mistrust.

Changing relationships fed into Ramona Everly's fall. Her rivalry with Sarah Penfield grew more intense as both women experienced a narrowing field of action. That year had been a particularly threatening one for them both. Ramona Everly's surviving daughter and her husband bought a property in another state and were talking about plans for his retirement. Sarah and John Penfield, then in their late eighties, were each deeply concerned about the other's health. She had experienced leg pain during much of the spring. When she had a bad fall, he declared, "My whole life was shattered." A diabetic, he was hospitalized with blood clots. He was the preeminent male at Mountainside and now his health was failing.

These changes affected Barbara Archer also. John Penfield had been a great source of strength during the early years at the home. As driving became more problematic, she often accompanied them when they went on trips. (These journeys were not lost on Ramona Everly, who commented that Barbara Archer was "overdoing it," going to too many conferences.) As the couple needed her more, her filial concern for John Penfield eclipsed her friendship with his wife's rival.

At the same time, the board itself began to include fewer members who remembered Ramona Everly as the active force she had been, planting bulbs, sewing for the annual fair, and speaking to concerns. No board member seems to have noticed that she was not quite so ever present as before.

Strauss (1978) has pointed out that the social order itself, the pattern of ranks and relationships, is always in process. Shifting more slowly than the flow of surface events, these provide part of the structural context of negotiations, as does also the larger climate. The larger climate in the 1970s was starting to suggest more

resident participation in decision making just as the aging of residential populations was beginning to militate against it. At association meetings, Barbara Archer was hearing her peers talk about
residents' councils. Most thought they were a bad idea, but in time
these would be a requirement and Mountainside would have one,
just as it currently held fire drills, although perhaps with less fervor.
Each home had its decision-making structure.

A final constraint on negotiation is to foreclose it by not opening
up the process at all. Exclusion is accomplished by definition of the
excluded parties and to stick, the definitions must be congruent
with the ethos of the setting. At Mountainside and Countryside
there were different definitions of patients and boarders, staff and
owners, congruent with the beliefs and values of managers and
boards. As Strauss would point out, these, too, slowly change
through the years.

In both homes, the needs of residents were taken into account but
the input of patients and, at Countryside, also of boarders was
hardly sought on matters affecting them as a body. This was partly
because it was assumed that patients, if not incompetent, at least
had few energies and little interest to invest in anything except life
maintenance. Countryside's proprietors viewed all residents, including boarders, as consumers: You consider the preferences of
consumers but you do not invite them to tell you how to run your
business. That remains a matter for the proprietors. Physicians—
and Countryside had mainly physician-owners—weigh their patients' concern with avoiding pain but they do not ask them to
titrate the dosage.

Neither home's management discussed with residents or their
families a matter most crucial to them all, rate increases, except as
an accomplished fact. It is safe to assume that Countryside's
physician-owners thought they were raising rates as an impersonal
marketplace response to the increasing cost of doing business. At
Mountainside, the struggle against raising rates was so tortured and
followed so much soul searching that the administrator and board
may have concluded that the issue was not worth discussing since
they had already examined every option.

In other matters, Mountainside's decision-making process was
generally more inclusive than Countryside's. In the boarding unit,

the reaction of the peer group was taken into account and their autonomy was substantial. Any act inimical to that autonomy was likely to be preceded by careful exploration with the group as a whole or at least with its weightier members. John Penfield was a useful spokesman. He generally knew the feelings of his fellow residents but, as a former president of the board, was able to place them within an administrative perspective.

In both homes, thought was given to patients' preferences for a late or early bedtime and to how they might feel about the assignment of a particular roommate.

> Although not consulted in advance, Mrs. Flowers was able to get rid of a succession of roommates she considered unsuitable. She simply established hegemony over the favored parts of the room. An erstwhile roommate complained that her African violets died because Mrs. Flowers kept the sunny windows for her own plants. She employed her TV as an offensive weapon. These maneuvers, coupled with her complaints about the intruder, ensured that any new roommate's exodus was only a matter of time. Staff members grumbled that she wanted a single room for the price of a double one, but beyond dragging their feet, there was not a great deal they could do since the new occupant usually wanted the change, too.

Staff encountered other limits to its omnipotence. At both homes, the ultimate sanction was transfer from the facility, but even this did not always work. Reportedly Mamie Slocum's family had been asked to remove her and declined. What was required to induce one of her daughters to take her home was a general rate raise that sharply increased the cost of keeping their mother out of their houses.

In the same vein, much circumspection attended efforts to contain the behavior of Agnes Chase, a member of Mountainside's sponsoring sect. Many of the causes she espoused with sufficient warmth to chill a supper conversation were precisely those supported by the church's more liberal members. Efforts to rein her in would have brought a committee to the administrator's door.

Both residents and staff found ceilings to their power. Within these limits they negotiated and renegotiated a daily balance.

CHAPTER FIVE

Champions Beyond the Walls:
Spouses, Relatives, and Friends

―――――――――――――

Champions beyond the walls is a particularly valuable resource. They are personally immune from reprisals although limited in what they can do for their resident because he or she remains when they go home. The most energetic of all these patient advocates are husbands and wives. No one demonstrates their effectiveness—and trials—better than Dr. Maria Magyar.

> From his entry into Mountainside's nursing unit, Dr. Ernest Magyar was an object of interest: He was young, handsome, and Hungarian—and tragically ill. That is to say, he was sixty-three and wheelchair-bound with multiple sclerosis.
>
> From his entry also, Dr. Maria Magyar elicited the hostility of the staff. She was an attentive wife. Her visits were as frequent as her employment permitted. While Dr. Ernest Magyar maintained a dignified reserve, Dr. Maria Magyar punctuated each of her visits by issuing a few complaints about his care to the staff.
>
> The result was extraordinary: Only a registered nurse could bring him a bedpan and that bedpan had to be immaculate. The tiniest deviation from perfect care was promptly noted by Dr. Maria Magyar on her very next visit.

The polarization of sentiments about the couple was striking. Under ordinary circumstances, Dr. Ernest Magyar himself would have been considered demanding, but as it was, he elicited only sympathy for being married to such a fearsome woman. Dr. Maria Magyar drew criticism as a magnet draws filings—her very approach caused a shudder. Staff members gave a sigh of relief when she went on a short vacation to her native Hungary. Staff members failed to see that her complaints, delivered like salvos, always followed a long conference alone with her husband.

What the Magyars illustrate is that it was useful to have someone outside to fight for you, that most residents had such a partisan—a relative, a friend, or a trustee—and that staff members preferred that it not be a spouse.

The Outside Other as a Social Resource

In dealing with troublesome relatives, staff members have two weapons: The patient's comfort lies in their hands and can be withheld, and they can threaten to return the patient to the complainant's care. These remedies are so extreme, however, that they are hardly helpful in day-to-day combat.

The outside other negotiates from a position of power: He or she generally controls the checkbook and, in addition, has access to the wider world and thus can affect the facility's reputation and perhaps even its license. Part of the impotence of patients, but not of boarders, is that virtually all their lines of communication exist with the sufferance of the establishment. As Dr. Magyar's case shows, a sufficiently resolute outside other can bring pressure to bear on the staff.

Dr. Magyar was exceptionally fortunate. He had the undeviating support and sympathy of a wife who appeared indifferent to, and even unaware of, the feelings of the staff. Moreover, staff members could not utilize Dr. Magyar's total physical dependence to capitalize on his hostage-like condition. Dr. Ernest Magyar was keen of mind and, if pressed, he could be cutting of tongue. Not only was

Dr. Maria Magyar undeterred by the disapprobation of nursing personnel, but reprisals directed at her husband would have evoked measures of counterdeterrence difficult to deal with. She was a professional herself and perfectly aware of her husband's rights.

In other cases, the threat of returning the patient to the complainer was more potent. Three factors entered the equation: the amount of personal care the resident required, the life situation of the caregiver, and the strength of the bond between them.

All relationships had their limitations, some more than others. A controlled study of families' use of respite services found that adult children tended to place the parent at about the point at which spouses were beginning to feel the burden of care—that is, when the frail person began to require personal, as opposed to instrumental, intervention. Children were willing to shop, houseclean, and do errands; they were less willing to bathe, toilet, and dress another person (Montgomery, 1988).

It will be recalled that Mrs. Flowers had a defender nearly as single-minded as Dr. Maria Magyar, but for mother and daughter, the threat of expulsion remained the night staff's trump card even though the administrator was unlikely to let them play it. Mrs. Flowers required a good deal of physical care and she could be demanding. Her daughter was eager to protect her own marriage and shared with her husband the care of his mother in their home. When she still lived in the community, Mrs. Flowers had been cared for through the joint efforts of her daughter and paid help. The daughter was quick to come to her mother's aid, but because the older woman lived in her own home, she had experienced frightening moments when the current housekeeper had failed to appear or when she had awakened alone at night. Mrs. Flowers was as physically helpless as Dr. Magyar, but she was as timid as he was acerbic. As a very vocal presence in the community that sent Countryside its most affluent patients, the daughter enjoyed leverage with administration. At the same time, all parties knew how unprepared the daughter was to cope with Mrs. Flowers at home and that it was unlikely she could find another facility for her mother as close to her taste. Thus when the night staff sedated Mrs. Flowers so heavily that it took her several days to recover, her daughter complained with considerable restraint. For a long time, Dr. Maria Magyar took her husband home on weekends, so she knew she could cope with him although she would have to get someone in when she went to work. This made her more immune to "redmail"—the threat of the patient's return. By the time his need for professional care exceeded her capacity, she had trained staff to meet her expectations.

The control methods employed by the patient were often a deterrent to taking him home. Mr. Sutton, for example, appeared bent on getting the home to expel him or on otherwise prevailing on his wife and daughters to take him home. His attentive family had made efforts to keep him at home and seemed unlikely to try it again: Mr. Sutton was precise about his demands and experienced chest pains whenever these were not met, so he remained a Mountainside patient.

Mrs. Flowers employed guilt. Her daughter's services were extraordinary—she brought plates of the raw oysters the older woman enjoyed; she took her and a chosen companion to lunch, manipulating two wheelchairs in the process; she sewed dresses for her; she arranged bridge games. Mrs. Flowers confided, "She does everything for me!" but when I tried to get her to say this to the younger woman, she could not. Instead, she inflamed her anger and subsequent guilt by regaling the daughter with her praises of the son, who occasionally paid a call on his way to the shore. She appreciated her daughter but she could not afford to relinquish some of her control by expressing satisfaction.

The issues then are how much the home wants the patient, how much the family needs the home, and how keen is the resident's sense of just how far the family member is likely to go. Affecting these is the method the resident uses to influence the outside other. These set the boundaries of negotiation.

Everyone Has Someone

More than four-fifths of the residents at Mountainside and Countryside had a spouse, adult child, or other kinsperson as the significant other who could be expected to support their interests, but the mere existence of such persons neither ensured their active engagement nor precluded other unexpected champions. Nevertheless, it is instructive to look at the other 17 percent, the twenty persons who did not have an outside other bound to them by marital or close blood ties. These lacked a living spouse, daughter or son, grandchild, niece, nephew, brother, sister, daughter-in-law, or son-in-law.

Only one was as bereft as that inventory suggests:

> Margaret Petersen's brief obituary said she was a "lifelong resident" of the area and that she had "no known survivors." The absence of any visitors supported the latter but her guttural accent raised doubts about the former. She herself said she was born in Paris and spoke French, Spanish, German, some Italian, and a little Portuguese. She had large blue eyes, the remnants of a fair skin, and a cancerous lesion on her forehead. She possessed a certain coquettishness that lent credence to the rumor that she was an old German actress. When I asked this eighty-year-old woman how old she was, she replied with a question, "How old do you think?" "Sixty," I lied. "Not *that* old!" she exclaimed, "Fifty-five." She had been married but how she got to the home, whether there had ever been children, or whether there were kinspeople someplace was quite unknown. Her social resource score was 12, the lowest it was possible to score.

All the others had someone—a cousin, an in-law, a trustee, or a friend. The cousins were often geographically, as well as consanguinally, remote and therefore not very active on the resident's behalf. Trustees and in-laws generally were more attentive to material needs than expressive ones. Friendship, indeed, often proved a stronger bond than kinship.

> Marion Bell grew up in a family of three marked by mutual support. At an early age, she allied with her mother to shield her father, an educator who had had a rather serious emotional breakdown. He was never as successful a provider after that but father and mother sacrificed in every way to forward her profes-

sional education. Later she, in turn, held a second job
to keep her mother at home with a nurse and, when
no other alternative was possible in wartime, to pay
for her nursing home care. She never married.

In retirement, she brought the skills of her profession to the service of her church. When she could no
longer get to the museums, the concert halls, and the
theaters, she left the city she loved and came to Mountainside. She had a few very good friends and the move
to Mountainside took her away from them. One friend
was a concert pianist, who used to journey to visit her
and always played for the residents when she came.

In late life, Marion Bell had the fragile beauty of
dried rose petals. Because of her limited means, she
clung to her room in the boarding home, but, at
eighty-two, she suffered fractures in a fall and there
seemed no alternative to a move to the nursing unit.
Her friend came, again played for the residents, and
spent much time at her side. After conferring with the
patient and the administrator, she agreed to manage
her finances for her. Marion Bell lived almost two
years longer. When her funds were exhausted, nothing
was said but the checks continued to come.

For some of these residents, a remote kinsperson was named in
the record, but a present friend was more active. One Mountainside
boarder listed her second cousin as the person to be informed when
she died but a male friend as the person most likely to know what
she would want.

Two friends of many years ended their days at Countryside together while a third friend, still in the community, stood by them.

They met more than forty years earlier when Dorothy Carroll, a teacher, placed her mother in the nursing home run by Rosemary Reynolds, a nurse. The
two women lent one another support during the dark-
est days of the Depression. The nurse accepted pay-

ment in the script that the county issued to its school teachers when funds ran out.

While still in her sixties, Miss Reynolds had a crippling stroke and was boarded with a family that sent her to a nursing home "like the dog to the vet's," as she ruefully phrased it, whenever the members went on a vacation. Eventually she came as a boarder to Countryside, where her friend, Dorothy Carroll, the teacher, had since become a patient.

Both women had as an attentive visitor a third friend, like Dorothy Carroll, a teacher. Dorothy Carroll died, and Rosemary Reynolds had more strokes, became a patient, and her life ebbed away with painful slowness. A month before her death, she was curled up in bed, gaunt, unresponsive to voice or touch. She was well tended by staff, but there was more than that— the nice gown, the cards taped nearby, the small potted plant. The surviving friend continued to come, as she had always done, to make sure she got good care.

There were other visitors whose sense of obligation was not so much to the resident as to someone who had died and whose duties they were assuming. Unless there was a direct personal bond, these surrogates tended to be dependable, to make good arrangements, but not to spend a great deal of time with the resident. This is consistent with Colleen Johnson and Donald Catalano's (1981) observation that the nephews and nieces of the childless elderly, acting out of a sense of obligation to a deceased parent, were often "managers" who served as intermediaries between patient and staff rather than direct caregivers themselves. One such surrogate was the widow of an aging spinster's nephew. She worked full time and lived nearly twenty miles away but stepped in when she was needed. Another was the daughter of the resident's best friend. When forgetfulness became an obstacle to the older woman's living alone in the city, the friend's daughter moved her to Countryside, where she could more easily watch over her.

Occasionally the benefactor was a person whose role was almost unknown.

When she was eighty-nine, Rebecca English's sole
remaining kinsperson was her brother's widow, who
did what was needed but did not come. Miss English
made up for this by referring to her ninety-three-year-
old roommate as "my daughter Flossie." She appeared
to derive comfort from her presence. The older woman
was cognizant of this and signaled me not to disabuse
her.

Miss English had a morale score of 3. When she
came to the item, "I have a lot to be sad about," she
quickly concurred. "My father and mother are gone
and I only have my sister and my sister's daughter.
That's all I have." The nursing staff reported that her
sister also had been single and had been dead for some
years, but that she called everyone, "My sister Florence." (I encountered only "my daughter Flossie.")

She was sad, restless, and sometimes seemed to be
in pain but was quieted by the presence of her roommate. Once when she was sick and confused, she
called, "Eliza, Eliza," presumably the name of an old
friend, and tapped on the metal bedside table. I called
her attention to the fact that the other woman was
sleeping and abruptly she was still.

The older woman occasionally attempted to correct
her, saying, "I'm Essie," but Rebecca English appeared not to hear and the roommate never persisted.
Fortunately, Miss English died first.

While Miss English's fantasied outside other was another patient
and therefore little help to her in social exchange, the roommate did
have one dependable visitor, her nephew's wife, whose visits provided a tangential surveillance for Miss English as well by bringing
an outsider into her room at regular intervals.

Three of the twenty had trustees, usually attorneys or bank of-
ficers, who were conscientious in their provision but relied upon the
home to let them know when the resident had a special need. The
trustees were like the distant cousins, not often present, but since

they were practicing their profession, they were more systematic in their service.

Several residents had unusual sources of outside support.

> One was Marcy Mae White, the English kindergarten teacher, whose former pupils rallied like nieces. She had taught their children, themselves, and possibly their parents. One was the primary outside other, aided by the rest. In the exchange, Miss White gave her personal interest and her alert appreciation of all that they did—she was the wonderful elderly aunt no one ever had.
>
> In addition to the honorary nieces, Miss White had a social worker from the Santa Claus Society. She received instrumental assistance from the society and expressive support from her "girls."

In contrast to the friendly Miss White, there was Miss Northern, who seemed indifferent to the companionship of those who came to her aid and sought only security and care from them.

> Miss Northern fastened on her former rector and demanded his help, so that through his efforts, she was able to leave Countryside for the church home of her choice. That facility was two counties away and once the clergyman had transferred her to its care, his duty was done. She lived there twelve years longer and died in her ninety-ninth year, undemanding as long as she was physically comfortable. It was reported that she sat near the door watching people come and go and awaiting a greeting from the administrator as he passed through. To the end, she was quick to distinguish potentially helpful authority figures, such as the clergyman, from mere peers.

The largest group of residents, 41 percent, had adult children, and in addition 30 percent had some other kinspeople—nieces, nephews, daughters-in-law or sons-in-law, brothers, or sisters. Consistent with the literature, there was a female descent of service: daughters, daughters-in-law, nieces, and sisters before sons, sons-in-law, nephews, and brothers (Brody, 1985; Kingson, Hirshorn, and Cornman, 1986; Montgomery, 1988; Stone, Cafferata, and Sangl, 1987) although there were notable exceptions.

> Mrs. Schultz's successive sons-in-law were the persons concerned about her care. Her granddaughter lived nearby but was busy with young children. Her daughter had died but the two men kept in close touch. The daughter's first husband, the father of her child, often met his successor when both men came to call. The second son-in-law paid a brief visit every day on his way home from work.

The difficulty with friends was age and distance. A couple from her hometown visited one Mountainside resident every three weeks but eventually the visits ceased. The friends of elderly residents were themselves old and too often there came a time when they stopped driving, so for those who had lived there long enough, the home itself became the significant other.

The Difficult Minority: The Still-Married

The most difficult significant others from the viewpoint of staff and the most loyal from the perspective of residents were husbands and wives. A disproportionate number of complaints were made about this small minority. Whenever possible, staff members endeavored to deal with the adult children or their surrogates (Schmidt, 1987). Of these there were plenty: More than half of the residents had adult children and well over three-quarters (77.6 percent) had either adult children or nieces, nephews, or grandchildren. The residents with husbands or wives were less numerous.

The still-married were deviant to the system in a number of ways: They were the fewest (12 percent), the youngest (mean entry age, slightly less than seventy-eight) and often the first to die (mean death age, eighty-five). Since spouses were the slowest to place, if they entered early, it signified that they were the sickest or the most confused. As couples, they generated the largest number of complaints from staff.

Dr. Ernest Magyar illustrates this well. He was half-way through his sixty-third year at the point of entry and already he had been in four previous facilities. He died shortly before his seventy-second birthday. His wife was assertive on his behalf and staff members would have preferred not to deal with her at all. After her retirement, she would have liked to rent one of the small apartments on the grounds: None was ever found available. In her seventies, she was commuting by bus to spend as many hours as possible by his side.

Actually Dr. Maria Magyar was well aware of staff's response. In a memoir written after his death, she said, "My spending generous amounts of time in the nursing home did not seem to delight the staff. I was already an exception in contrast to other visitors rushing in and out. [Ernest] complained very little to the staff and rather chose me to hear him. I invariably fell into the trap and did the complaining. They found me 'too demanding' and 'overbearing.' My contention was that I knew my husband's needs better because I was his wife and also a clinical psychologist. They were not impressed. Maybe the administrator of the nursing home summed up our differences most succinctly. 'Your husband does not get the care that you want him to have but he gets good care.'"

The administrator was correct in both respects: Ernest Magyar's wife would have liked him to have a very different kind of care and, because Mountainside was subject to organizational, economic, and legal constraints, its essentially caring staff could not provide it. These constraints structured the home's relations with all its residents, but the level of staff-spouse tension varied according to the pattern of entry.

Patterns of Entry and Response

Because the still-married residents were so few in what was largely a company of widows, the discussion will include other couples as well even though they entered the home later and were not part of the original cohort.

Although typical in so many ways, the Magyars represented just one of four patterns of entry, each of which elicited a somewhat different response from the staff. To understand this, it is necessary to consider task complementarity and the effect of different levels of accountability and control.

Litwak (1985) has described *task complementarity* between formal and informal systems: the formal system is best at doing those things that can be standardized and routinized, at performing repetitive tasks, while the informal system excels at the more individualized kinds of service.

Thus family and friends are better at shopping for the patient, reading to him, and providing small treats—all of the services that individualize the resident and affirm his or her identity as a person. The family can adapt routines to the patient's preferences. Over the long haul, however, its members become exhausted: The primary caregiver of a seriously disabled person in the community works three shifts; nursing home personnel work just one.

In contrast, the staff can provide quantities of care over long periods of time, but to do so efficiently, it must routinize the tasks, as much as possible treating one patient like another and reducing patient choice. Meals must be served at hours that fit the work day of kitchen staff and synchronize with nursing; baths must be scheduled by the day of the week to achieve a predictable work flow for nursing assistants.

At home, the primary caregiver, usually the spouse, did many of the same things that staff does in the nursing home but did them in a more patient-centered way. It will be recalled that adult children were more likely to perform the instrumental activities of daily living, such as balancing the checkbook and shopping, while spouses were willing to continue when the patient needed help with personal care, such as bathing and dressing (Montgomery, 1988). Therefore, more than the adult children, spouses were likely to feel, as Dr. Maria Magyar did, that they knew how that care should be given.

The stress occasioned by their complaints may be unevenly experienced. Much of the maintenance care in nursing homes is provided by paraprofessional staff members who have more experience but often less education than the family caregivers they displace. They feel competent to act but less able to articulate why they are

doing what they do. They are more threatened by a barrage of questions and suggestions than the nurses, who have their professional
education to attest to their expertise.

The very families that are complaining about the depersonaliz-
ing nature of the care would suffer greatly if costs were allowed to
rise. The facility is caught between letting prices rise and being
pilloried as unfeeling. Whether proprietary or nonprofit, the home
must try to keep costs down because the burden is borne chiefly by
individuals and taxpayers. For this reason, staff members are compelled to do in an institution-centered way what the spouse has
done at home in a patient-centered way. Because neither fully grasps
the difference, friction is inevitable.

Staff members believe that if families knew how to take care of
the patient, they would not have to turn to them for help. Having
delivered the patient for professional care, however, they should not
interfere. Family members view staff as insensitive, rigid, and hard
to teach. Each is critical of the other.

> During his first years at Mountainside, Dr. Maria
> Magyar took her husband home each weekend. In the
> summer, this meant a weekend at the lake that Dr.
> Ernest Magyar loved.
>
> The nurses were quick to point out that Dr. Maria
> Magyar idly watched while her husband struggled to
> transfer himself from wheelchair to car. They reported
> that he returned exhausted, with bruises and abrasions
> from falls. After these holidays, Dr. Ernest Magyar dis-
> played the fatigue of an apartment-bound pet who has
> spent a happy weekend in the country chasing rabbits
> and squirrels.

Dr. Maria's memoir makes plain that she was perfectly aware of
his struggles with the wheelchair but equally alert to his need to do
for himself (personal communication, October 14, 1984). She sometimes reproached staff for its failure to stimulate him to be more
independent. What she may have failed to recognize was the difference between her husband's eagerness to show her what he could

still do and his willingness to accept staff's help in coping with the same logistics.

Because Mountainside and Countryside had both boarding and nursing units, they illustrate clearly how the level of care and control influences the staff's response. Humanistic concern did not stop at the infirmary door, but staff accountability and labor intensity increased sharply.

In Goffman's (1961) total institutions, a relatively small staff was able to manage a large number of residents through uniformity and centralized control. Litwak's (1985) nursing home provides a high level of care by standardizing and routinizing to the greatest degree possible. Although the staff-patient ratio may appear high, it is low in relation to the amount of service that must be provided. Personnel is the major item of cost.

When the then-director of nursing at Mountainside was urged to be more flexible in her dealings with Margaret Wesley, she replied that she had to apply the same rules to all. She was correct, not in her assumption that bending the rules would lead to anarchy but in her conviction that anything less than perfect uniformity would make management more difficult.

The Magyars' insistence that only a registered nurse could fetch Dr. Ernest Magyar's bedpan entailed endless explanation and adaptation in a setting where shifts changed at eight-hour intervals, where the composition of each shift varied by the day of the week, and where most patients' bedpans were brought by aides.

The nursing home differs from other total institutions in the level of accountability to which it is held. Because its population is perceived as harmless and helpless, the issue is safety. In no other setting except schools and hospitals, and perhaps not even there, are staff members held to such a high standard for their residents' safety. This acts as a formidable obstacle to autonomy and also to informal helping. When one patient wishes to assist another or when a family member spontaneously reaches out to aid a patient, staff members intervene lest the patient be hurt in the process and they be held to account. Spouses upset this order when they wish to do for the patient themselves or when they protest at what appear to them to be needless restraints. In the boarding units of our two homes, these tensions existed in a much smaller measure: Boarders were considered less helpless and staff held less accountable.

The still-married residents admitted to Mountainside and Countryside followed four patterns of entry:

1. A well-functioning couple entered the boarding unit together. For these pairs, entry was often part of a late-life plan. They came because their neighborhoods changed, help was harder to get, or some illness had given them a premonition of future need, and they did not wish to become dependent on their children if health should fail.

These couples were welcomed, first, because they introduced another man into a setting peopled largely by women and, second, because of the functions they could perform, often as a team. Such a pair were the Penfields. As members of the sponsoring sect, John and Sarah Penfield had taken leadership roles in the founding of Mountainside. They agreed that when they were eighty, they would enter the home as residents. Both enjoyed good health and clear minds, and he continued to drive. They occupied positions of peer leadership, based upon their current, ongoing contributions to the life of the group and their role in its history.

A second couple, the Reardons, moved to Mountainside after a "bad" winter, marked by snow shoveling, trouble getting help, and bouts of influenza.

> The Reardons had been "beautiful people" in the 1920s, handsome, well educated, and moderately affluent. Their two adopted sons lived several states away. Their transfer to the home constituted something of a retreat. At the point of entry, they were in their early seventies, considerably younger than the Penfields, then in their late eighties.
>
> More inclined to reading and writing than needlework, Prudence Reardon did not compete in any way with Sarah Penfield's leadership of the sewing group, but as a resident valued for her sound judgment she soon became a table hostess. As they possessed two of the keener and more critical minds, she and Sarah Penfield became good friends.

It took Ron Reardon a little longer to find his niche. When he undertook John Penfield's task of making the nightly inspection and locking up the boarding unit in the older man's absence, the latter was quick to point out the deficiencies of his performance. Eventually, he found a job that competed with no one: He made the necessary phone calls to arrange for a minister, priest, or rabbi to lead the Sunday evening service. The two men never got along as well as their wives.

In time, one spouse would become ill and be transferred to the nursing unit, but their relationship with staff there had already been established. Short illnesses or ambulatory care had led them to accept the nurses as the guardians of health, and the nurses did not have to compete with a recent pattern of spousal care. At the same time, their boarder status had accustomed the nurses to treating them as possessed of some competence.

These couples often had a backlog of social credit. Staff members might regard the healthy partner as excessively demanding on the other's behalf, but they could recognize this as a manifestation of understandable anxiety.

2. An impaired couple entered the nursing unit because both needed care. These patients did not fit the nursing unit's policy of assigning same-sex roommates. (For facilities that accepted Medicaid, a second complication could arise if the spouses were approved for different levels of care [Locker, 1976]: One might be perceived as needing only intermediate care and the other, the full resources of a skilled nursing facility.)

When Mr. Manon suffered his first heart attack, he was forced to place his mentally frail wife at Countryside. He continued as an attentive visitor until he, too, was admitted after a stroke that spoiled his speech and left him with other deficits. Seven months after his admission to the nursing unit, the facility had an urgent need for another "male bed" and Mr. Manon was

moved into his wife's room, but only after the director
of nursing had "cleared it with the children."

Staff members appeared to take comfort from their
view that he was too confused to know she was there,
but the director of nursing noticed a behavioral
change: He no longer called out as he had been doing
whenever he was lonely and bored.

3. One member needed nursing care and the other came along.
Among persons in the study cohort, this took two forms, each elic-
iting a different staff response. One, illustrated by the Wesleys, involved a well spouse who entered the nursing unit to be with a
chronically ill partner. From the moment the director of nursing
slipped an identification bracelet around Margaret Wesley's wrist,
staff members worked endlessly to train her to be a patient, not from
malice but because they did not know how to deal with a well
person in a setting designed for the impaired.

In the second instance, the well member entered the boarding
unit to be close to a spouse who needed nursing care. After her own
retirement, Dr. Maria Magyar sought such an arrangement but was
never able to effect it. Two men were more successful; in the end,
however, both spent less time rather than more with their wives.
One of these was Mr. Kenworthy, whose wife had had a stroke.

Mr. Kenworthy placed his wife in the nursing unit
and entered the boarding home himself. After breakfast each morning, he walked over to the nursing unit
to spend the day at her side. Because he had been taking care of her, he felt quite clear about what was
needed and made a number of suggestions to the staff.
Very quickly staff members decided that it was bad for
Mr. Kenworthy to spend so much time in the nursing
unit. The nurses spoke to the physician and he told
Mr. Kenworthy that he was interfering with his wife's
adjustment. Reluctantly he gave up his role as
guardian.

A year later, staff members had a different complaint: Mr. Kenworthy was visiting his wife only

briefly and spending much too much time with an
agreeable companion in the boarding unit. They were
sure his wife sensed the reason for his neglect and was
upset by it.

4. One member came for care while the other remained in the
community. This was the most common pattern and it, too, led to
conflict. The Magyars illustrate this case in every respect but one:
Because Dr. Ernest Magyar's daughter by an earlier marriage was
largely unavailable, staff members could not make their usual effort
to bypass the wife and deal with the adult child.

From the viewpoint of staff members, the spouses had established
their incapacity by placing the patient. This was especially true in
the case of wives, who already belonged to a stigmatized category
as older women.

The adult children were closer in age to staff members and tended
to define their own duties as staff did. They saw themselves as shopping for the older person, paying bills, and visiting, but they were
willing to leave personal care to the professionals. Since most of
them had not nursed the patient at home, they were more likely to
bow to professional authority and they were less likely to see their
primary roles as those of advocates, educators, and caregivers. In
short, they fit staff's notion of appropriate task complementarity.

The effort to transfer responsibility from the spouse to the children was demonstrated most plainly in the home's interaction with
the Wesleys.

> As she had always done, Margaret Wesley managed
> the couple's checkbook and paid their bills. Month
> after month, the bookkeeper pointedly mailed the fa-
> cility's bill to her son and month after month, he re-
> turned it to his mother for payment.

At the heart of the struggle were conflicting role definitions.
Society prescribes that spouses be the primary protectors of one
another, but nursing assigns to the nurse the duty of safeguarding
her patient. Actually these roles are less competitive than their
crossed assignments suggest because their main domains are differ-

ent: The nurse's is health care and the spouse's is the expressive and social life of the partner. This distinction is sometimes drowned in strong emotion when fear, anger, guilt, and sorrow are aroused by the threatened relationship. Displaced from a central role, spouses may attempt to assert their competence and loyalty by finding fault with the professionals who seem to be taking over.

For their part, staff members may be reluctant to engage in the simple acts of role maintenance that might reduce tension, lest any encouragement provide an opportunity for the self-appointed patient advocate to stir things up some more. In addition, the realities of a litigious society dictate that staff members take over most of the instrumental tasks, such as helping the patient transfer from bed to chair and administering medication. However, they could acknowledge the spousal role by consulting the patient's lifelong partner about some of the patient's preferences and by sharing some part of the patient's care. There are a number of symbolic acts of nurture the spouse could perform, such as feeding the patient dessert, taking the patient on wheelchair walks, writing letters, and grooming (Schmidt, 1987). For example, Margaret Wesley read the financial section to John Wesley every day and at the end, Dr. Maria Magyar often fed her husband.

For most of Ernest Magyar's long stay, the warfare between staff and spouse continued unremitting.

> When work or weather made it impossible for Dr. Maria Magyar to come to Mountainside, she telephoned. The conversation always began, "Hello, this is Dr. Magyar; how is my husband?"
>
> The staff never failed to respond, "Yes, *Mrs.* Magyar . . . "
>
> Dr. Magyar had her revenge, however. Conversations with her husband were always perfectly private: No one on the staff spoke Hungarian.

For both partners of the well-functioning couples who entered together, there was a substantial benefit. Their entry was eased and their status enhanced because they came as a couple. When statuses changed, they were among people who knew and understood them.

In the case of the Penfields and the Reardons, when the men became
patients, the wives were supported in their spousal roles, as staff
members recognized the anxiety that lay behind their queries. When
the husbands died first, and the women were widowed, all the peer
group shared their loss, for most of the others were widows or widowers, too.

When two impaired persons entered the home, however, staff
members had difficulty thinking of them as still a couple. It was as
if each had come into a new state of being and former relationships
were no longer relevant. When Mr. Manon's wife died, his loss went
unacknowledged. This appeared to be due to his dysphasia as well
as to staff's inability to see that there might be a lingering tie between two damaged persons.

> Mr. Manon had been a supportive spouse until he
> became a patient himself, then his situation changed
> abruptly and he could help neither his wife nor him-
> self. Dysphasia carries an overriding stigma: It is as-
> sumed that a person who cannot speak coherently
> cannot think or feel either. Only Countryside's direc-
> tor of nursing, Winnie Mason, remembered him when
> he was witty and well, but even she perceived him now
> as utterly uncomprehending.

This is not a necessary conclusion to a common life. In a public
facility, an older physician delayed the transfer of a sick old man
so that he could spend his days sitting by the bedside of his dying
wife. The difference may have lain less in the sensitivity of the
physician than in the fact that the sick old man was clearly alert.

Had either of the Manons been mentally alert, their bond might
have been acknowledged, but staff members assumed that Mr.
Manon was unaware that his wife had died although she was in the
bed next to his. They did not discuss her death with him. I did. He
acknowledged her death but, as I was unsure because his speech was
so limited, I asked another question, "Do you think she knew you
were here?" He replied with one word, "Just." It is therefore quite
possible that the two old people found comfort in one another's
presence—or, at least, that he might have. She was nearly coma-

tose—a prettyish mummy lying immobile—before they moved him in with her and any possibility of awareness of each other was clearly beyond staff's thinking.

In the two remaining entry patterns, the benefit to the patient of the nearness of the spouse was sometimes balanced by the cost to the spouse. After his wife died, for example, Mr. Kenworthy and his pleasant companion in the boarding unit drew apart. When he entered the library to wait for breakfast, she eyed him anxiously, but he quickly disappeared behind his newspaper and she returned to hers. Perhaps both of them were responding to subtle pressures from the group. After a few months, he moved to another home.

The husbands who remained in the community were remarkably attentive to their wives and generally they received more respectful attention from staff.

> The ancient Commodore tottered in each afternoon and kissed his wife's upturned cheek. Then he clasped her hands across the tray of her gerichair and the two nodded together through the afternoon while his young driver read novels and drank coffee. When the driver went away, the visits became infrequent. The Commodore himself was having health problems and the practical nurse who stayed with him now was unable to drive.
>
> Another attentive visitor was Mr. DeYonge, a retired stockbroker, who perceived his wife only as she had been. He provided private duty nurses and came each day and read the *New York Times* to her.
>
> Mr. DeYonge insisted that his wife be properly dressed, wear her jewelry, and have her legs shaved—an arduous task that required five aides. When one of the private duty nurses billed Mr. DeYonge for a tetanus shot and broken glasses after Mrs. DeYonge bit and hit her, Mr. DeYonge only expressed the view that his wife must have been terribly upset by the incident.
>
> For her part, Mrs. DeYonge was a sad, demented lady. When I administered the morale scale, she said

to me, "I've never been so much alone in my life. Horrible. It's as if I were dead."

On the anniversary of her death, Mr. DeYonge sent flowers to "the girls at the nursing home." His wife had been at Countryside five years, and except when he was ill, he had never missed a day.

A third visitor was Mr. Skinner, a textile yarn salesman who continued on the road to pay for his wife's care. They had been married fifty-eight years; he had known her since she was nine and he was eleven.

Unlike the broker, he was keenly aware of changes in her condition and two months before her death, he commented that she seemed to be slipping away. I saw her first in the wheelchair and later always in bed. She made soft crooning noises.

After her death, he thought he would keep on working, but seeing his neighbors in the retirement community failing around him, in the end, he decided he would move to where medical care was more available. He also wanted to be nearer their daughter. He was thinking of his own old age: He was then eighty-three.

As high as the cost was to a man, life seemed even harder for the patients' wives.

Mrs. Mangeni came daily for more than nine years while her savings went for her husband's care. No one thought the tough old man, so mangled by his stroke, could live so long. A factory worker, Mr. Mangeni had bought a bit of land, owned his home, and was enjoying a modest sufficiency when he had a crippling stroke. There was sadness at the sale of the land. During her husband's last summer at the home, Mrs. Mangeni confided that many girls had telephoned her son when he was young and she had been sorry that he had not married. Now that he was the primary support for his father, she realized it had been for the best. For a long time, the home accepted partial payment but, in the end, Mr. Mangeni had to move to a Medicaid facility, where he died three months later when he was almost ninety-seven.

Ironically, after Margaret Wesley had worked out a pattern of life for herself within the narrow confines of the nursing unit and after she had accepted its restrictions as the price of remaining with her husband, she was diagnosed as having cancer. She died a year and eight months after nursing home admission, and her husband, whose health had occasioned their entry, lived more than eight years longer.

Her husband's third year at Mountainside was especially hard for Dr. Maria Magyar: Her mother died in Hungary and because he was very ill and hospitalized at the time, she could not go; she passed her sixty-fifth birthday and was forced to retire, unwillingly because money was a worry. My notes at this time record that when I saw her walk past the window, "she looked old, deeply troubled."

After that, life seesawed up and down for her. With the progression of his disease, her husband experienced less pain and more serenity. Her fear for her own old age was eased when she became a client of the Santa Claus Society. Her husband joined her Protestant faith. Her car, twice vandalized, was stolen; after that, she came by bus. So ingrained was the habit that she continued to call the home for a while after he died. She sent me the manuscript of her memoir and we corresponded about it. Then there was silence. Five years after his death, I received a letter from her friend. Dr. Maria Magyar had died of cancer a month after she herself entered a nursing home. She had asked the friend to let me know.

She had served her husband well: He had had wonderful care all those years, but she had to fight the battle to obtain it.

The institutionalized elderly are often presented as stored away in medically certified warehouses and forgotten by their families. Few residents in this study could be described as abandoned: Even the comatose and the childless had someone who inquired, who came, and who cared. The support of these concerned others was often breathtaking, like that of the granddaughter who spent her savings for her own old age to keep her grandmother in the home of her choice, and of the niece who made hot, dusty two-hour train trips each Saturday to spend time with a childless aunt. The family has not forgotten, and when there is no family, others often take its place.

CHAPTER SIX

How Residents are Controlled: Penalties and Privileges

———————◆———————

No system can function without controls. The mistake lies in assuming that they all flow neatly from a single source. The organizational charts have contributed to the fallacy by showing only the lines of formal control and ignoring the informal processes that sometimes support and sometimes challenge them.

Technically, controls at the two homes emanated at Countryside from the owners and at Mountainside from the board members and the religious organization they represented. But if residents of the two homes had been asked where the power resided, they would have indicated the administrators and the directors of nursing. Actually the controls were more diffuse than that; their effectiveness varied depending on site, staffing, resources, the focus of state regulations, and current consensus. Thus, for example, although Mountainside's administrator and professional nurses addressed the elderly patients by title, a wave swept through the home of nursing assistants calling them by their first names, which upper-level staff seemed powerless to check. As the innovator of the movement asserted, "This is their home. Using their first names makes them feel more comfortable." She was then asked if it would make patients feel more comfortable if they called the director of nursing by her first name. Her reply is lost to history.

What seems beyond dispute is that the rebellion would have been short-lived if their addressing patients respectfully by title had been a concern of the licensing agency—management would have seen to that. In the meantime, the nursing assistants' counterpolicy may have been reinforced doubly—by the mild disapproval of professional staff and by peer sanctioning of their own members who did not follow suit.

The relationship between staff and peer norms and their sanctions differed in the nursing and boarding units. Because regulatory authorities held the homes to account for the care of their patients, the staff exercised strong surveillance and control in the nursing units. The patient peer group was too fragmented to enforce its own values or even to agree as a body on what they were. Lacking a coherent group voice, patients and their families were forced to bargain on an individual basis, and, in major disputes, to rely on staff. In the boarding units, both administrators were concerned about resident safety but otherwise the residents themselves defined much of what was acceptable and what was not. This was especially true at Mountainside, where the peer group was larger and more cohesive.

This chapter will begin by looking at resistance in the nursing units, where structural supports for staff dominance were strong and patient resources were weak. After describing staff and peer norms for boarders and patients and the sanctions that enforced them, it will relate how the system tried to heal itself when its extreme penalty, exile, had been imposed and will close by discussing conformity as a matter of choice.

The Nursing Units: Countermoves of the Weak

The level of institutionality is high in the nursing units and, because patients depend on their caregivers for essential services, it is customary to think of them all as the passive victims of staff. The error lies in the status generalization that assumes that mental incapacity invariably accompanies physical deficits and that the lack of acuity necessarily assures the absence of will.

Drawing on his field observations at St. Elizabeth's asylum, Goffman (1961) described four inmate responses to institutional totality. These can be seen in attenuated form in the nursing units:

1. *Situational withdrawal* ranges from the cocooning of alert

patients who remain in their rooms to the flight into psychosis of the mentally frail.

Two alert patients, Ernest Magyar and John Wesley, eschewed all scheduled activities except meals and the obligatory shower. They declined to be "batched" with other patients; they were able to define a narrow territory as their own and control it. So fiercely did they defend their rooms that staff members were diffident about coming in without knocking. Patients with more limited capacity withdrew by other means. For example, much of Mrs. Middleton's delusional content related to entertaining others. She terminated one interview with a brisk announcement, "Well, I must get home and bake a pie. The ladies are coming." With that, she propelled her wheelchair out of the room. Delusions generally conjured up days of strength and power. As in Richard Emerson's (1962) cost reduction operations, they redefined the situation, which did not solve the power imbalance but probably reduced the pain.

2. With *intransigence*, the individual opposes anything the institution has to offer or that a staff member proposes. It takes great determination to remain negative when all the obvious rewards are in staff's hands, but even a nurse's wrath may be rewarding to the patient who has extorted it. In an indifferent world, dislike entails recognition and thus provides a relationship, even if it is a bad one. Intransigence seems to sustain certain residents in the maelstrom of a dissolving or despairing life.

> Ramona Everly entered Mountainside at eighty. At eighty-nine, following a hospitalization, she returned to the nursing unit and refused to leave it. This was remarkable because earlier she had expressed her dread of becoming a patient and losing her solace—listening to classical music on her radio late at night.
>
> In the nursing unit, she steadily provoked the administrator and the director of nursing. Neither was a match for her because the power differential compelled them to be forbearing. For example, knowing the administrator prided herself on providing the residents with the little treats of life, she implied that

they had a Spartan existence with a single trenchant comment: "We are all Trappists here."

She refused to attend the sect's Sunday morning worship meeting but went instead to the formal service led each Sunday evening by visiting priests, rabbis, and pastors of other faiths. Since she officially belonged to the sponsoring sect, this was difficult for its members to ignore. Once near the end of her life, she spoke of her disappointment in the "great Presbyterian God." (The sponsoring sect was not Presbyterian.)

What seemed to lie behind this was a great anger at life that had taken four of her five daughters but would not let her go.

3. In *colonization,* the patient uses the nursing home's resources in ways that disconfirm its purpose, much as nineteenth-century colonizers collected native people's goods while nihilating their beliefs. These patients affront staff members by disregarding their views of their relative statuses, implying by their demands that they are not there to be supervised but served. Staff members respond by collecting evidence to establish that patients' failing to see things their way is evidence of their sickness, a procedure that is not difficult since no one sounds quite sane if monitored twenty-four hours a day.

> When the staff pressed Margaret Wesley into patient-hood, she capitulated with a vengeance. She spent long lazy mornings reading in bed. She asked nurses to fetch things that were near at hand. This is what they had been telling her to do, only now it seemed somehow different: She was not acting as if she were incompetent; she was treating them as if they were maids.

4. In *conversion,* patients accept staff's view of their own moral worth, which provides a goodness-of-fit between their respective

roles. If the colonizers irritate staff members by rejecting their values, the converts provide reassuring confirmation.

Many persons at Mountainside and Countryside did not need conversion: They had accepted the patient role before they came. These were chiefly alert individuals with well-established illnesses. Some had been processed by hospitals and other facilities earlier and they appreciated these homes for their good physical care.

> John Wesley was such a patient. He arrived after a long battle with Parkinson's disease and revealed his identification at the start when he complained that the breakfast was too big for "invalids like us."
>
> Ernest Magyar had been living with his multiple sclerosis too long to deny it and he, too, accepted the role, although on his own terms. Both men had exchanged their wives' nursing care for that of competent professionals.
>
> Another resident, Mora Kelly, also settled comfortably into the patient role: She had been trained for it. This ninety-four-year-old woman had been an early graduate of a famous hospital's school of nursing. As such, she received preferential treatment at Countryside, where the director of nursing herself provided much of her bedside care. Procedures were carefully explained to her nurse to nurse.

All three enjoyed favored status. Staff members accepted a certain demandingness on their part because each so clearly saw staff's role as they did and because each was alert.

Whether their conversion was a triumph of socialization or whether the siege itself had become unbearable, most residents in the nursing units yielded to the patient label in time. Even the confused were converted.

Tobin and Lieberman (1976) concluded that the change in self for which institutionalization is blamed begins with the rejection leading up to entering the home. This was true in the case of Elizabeth Jordan, who fitted the classical pattern of conversion.

> Within a three-month period this eighty-two-year-old woman lost her husband, her car, her home, and her freedom.
>
> After her husband's death, she became guilt-ridden and immobilized. She had promised to protect him from death-prolonging measures, but once he entered the hospital, she could only watch helplessly as protocol took its inexorable course. She blamed herself greatly. She was very dependent at this time and after an automobile accident, she gave up driving, which increased her need for services from initially willing friends. When she burned her leg with a heating pad, physician and friends expressed concern about her living alone and placement followed. One of the friends, a real estate dealer, sold her house.
>
> When she was interviewed four months later, she said she had thought they were talking about her entering the boarding unit. By this time, she was presenting herself as helpless, forgetful, indecisive, and plagued with urinary problems beyond her control, although there was no evidence of memory deficit. The urologist reportedly dismissed her urinary problems as due to age: He made no report to the home. As a complicating factor, she appeared to be using her urinary symptom, urgency, as an excuse whenever she was pressed to do something she did not wish to do. She declared that patienthood provided few opportunities for initiative and that with inactivity, she was becoming less able.
>
> She responded to her situation with a deadweight passivity: She would not select her own dress or turn on her radio—she waited for staff to serve her. In desperation, they sometimes delayed, but she outwaited them.

A year later, she was spending much of her time in a wheelchair. She said she had had a stroke although there was no record of it, no readily visible residuals, and her memory and word-finding skills continued intact. She was able to walk but tortured nursing assistants with her slowness.

Staff members responded with a mixture of irritation and concern. They knew she could do more, but they did for her because there was not time enough to wait for her to move.

She had been referred for psychological and psychiatric testing but neither psychiatrist nor psychologist sent a report to the home, provided consultation that might guide its staff, or offered treatment.

Mrs. Jordan illustrates the complexity of these situations: Neither she nor the staff could be mobilized enough to move her to a lower level of care—she did not have the will and they did not have the time. She suffered from Engel's (1968) "giving-up, given-up" syndrome: Physicians failed to treat her, friends institutionalized her, and staff members sensed that she could do more but did not believe she ever could do enough to leave their care. Alert enough to state that inactivity was eroding her capacity for independence, she nevertheless went out of her way to confirm a role she professed to resent. She sat waiting for someone to dress her. She employed her urinary symptom as a reason for staying close to the bathroom, but she talked nearly an hour in our interview without the slightest evidence of urgency. She was perfectly in control and so was staff, but an impasse existed between them.

Whose Rules?

Not everyone in a system is equally invested in all of its norms. The nature of particular norms tells who has a stake in their enforcement, the interests that lie behind them, and the solidarity and divisions likely to be found in the setting itself. The written and unwritten rules that governed life in the two homes fell into four broad categories:

1. *Maintenance norms* regulated behavior affecting the homes' main task, taking care of elderly people. Typical maintenance norms required boarders to be on time for lunch and patients to accept medication promptly when it was offered.

2. *Security norms* protected the safety, property, and territorial rights of residents and the property and equipment of the home. These related to such matters as fall prevention, leaving the grounds, bed rails for patients, and fire drills for everyone.

Because security norms elicited a high level of compliance, the safety aspect was often emphasized even when the norm served other ends as well. At Mountainside, smoking was confined to a small area near the nurses' station and boarders who wished to smoke were required to go out of doors or to the nursing unit. This was presented as a fire safety measure although making smoking inconvenient was strongly congruent with the religious beliefs of the sponsoring sect.

Security and maintenance norms were instrumental in character because they helped staff members with such tasks as housekeeping, nursing, protection, and resource management.

3. *Norms of external image management* were intended to enhance the system's status as a collectivity from the residents' perspective and as an institution from the viewpoint of management. Because each member drew some of his or her public identity from the shared reputation of the group, all had a stake in how the others presented themselves. One boarder described a reluctant bather as "not the kind of person we have here" and added, "She created a bad impression of us." These norms dealt with such matters as dress, deportment, and personal hygiene.

4. *Norms of internal tension management* limited behavior that might have an adverse effect on the emotional climate and interpersonal relations within the home. These governed topics of conversation and the more overt forms of competition. A social work intern was distressed because she could not get residents to express their differences more openly in the group she led. John Penfield explained that they lived too close to one another for that. There

were rivalries and disagreements at Mountainside, but boarders managed most conflict by avoidance and suppression.

Norms of external image management and internal tension management are expressive in character because they regulate the emotional and social climate of the home.

The relative investment of patients, boarders, and staff in the four classes of rules was tested by means of a norm sort: Residents and staff members were given four norms to rank in order of importance. The packets differed for the two homes' boarding units but were alike for their nursing units. These are given in Resource B. Some of the responses said a good deal about life in the homes.

At Countryside, nine of the twelve boarders gave first place to "Guests should not say things that hurt the feelings of other guests," and two others ranked it second. Mamie Slocum, the resident Robespierre, placed this norm last.

While weighing "Patients should respect the safeguards the nurses provide for their protection, such as bedrails and soft ties," one chronic offender explained that she went over the foot of the bed to get to the bathroom because the nurses and nursing assistants did not answer her bell. She added thoughtfully, "Put yourself in the place of someone running one of these places—first, you've got to make people safe."

One item proved to be an unexpected touchstone. It was "Patients should not act silly, making visitors think this is a place for crazy people." Patients responded so universally with a chuckle that failure to laugh was taken as a sign of noncomprehension. Even the dysphasic Mr. Manon, whom everyone assumed never understood, burst into laughter. Many staff members were upset by this item and hastened to explain, "They can't help it." Although staff accepted a certain amount of craziness, they appeared to be disturbed by the imputation of intent: If patients grasped the norm and still violated it, it meant they were more aware than staff members liked to think. Mountainside nurses argued that alert residents were not so much socially embarrassed by regressed patients as uncomfortable because they were a portent of what they, too, would become.

When first choices were scored, nodes of cohesion and of fragmentation came into view. As expected, 79 percent of staff members put instrumental norms first and 53 percent of residents favored expressive norms (phi .33, X^2 = 14.6, 1 df, $p > .001$). The residents' endorsement of expressive norms was diluted because the second largest group of resident first choices was the security norm, whereas staff's first choices were divided between two instrumental norms—safety and maintenance. The division is hardly surprising, because staff members were concerned about getting their work done and residents were more interested in the emotional climate within which they lived. The two groups showed substantial agreement about the importance of safety norms: 40 percent of staff and 27 percent of residents placed them first. Thirty-nine percent of residents made the internal tension management norm their first choice.

The external image management norm received shorter shrift from both groups than field observation had suggested. Only 6 percent of staff (and no nursing unit employee) ranked it first and only 14 percent of residents made it their first choice. Moreover, it was the last choice of 72 percent of staff members and of 45 percent of residents. This was highly inconsistent with the peer pressure observed and reported at Mountainside, where there was substantial concern about dress and decorum.

A cross-over effect between the nursing and boarding units reflected patterns of dominance. Patients' first choices were divided almost equally among categories, showing a general lack of consensus among them. Although they lived in physical proximity, they were isolated by social withdrawal. In contrast, nursing personnel showed substantial agreement. They strongly favored maintenance and security norms (45 and 42 percent).

Boarders agreed among themselves—56 percent placed internal tension management first—while boarding unit staff lacked a strong modal choice. The closest they came to one was 37 percent for the security norm.

In the nursing units, the nursing profession was dominant and employees worked in relatively close contact with one another. Even the laundress followed the nurses' modal pattern of security, maintenance, internal tension, and external image management norms in that order. The ranking reflects the professional nurses' strong sense of total responsibility for their patients' safety and care, and other staff members in the unit accepted their value system.

On the other hand, boarding unit employees (bookkeepers, tray girls, maids, and kitchen help) had less contact with one another: Their profile of first choices was scattered like that of the patients, who also lacked group cohesion. Boarders, like nursing personnel, showed strong agreement. Boarders voted solidly for internal tension management (56 percent) and only secondly for the security norms (19 percent) while boarding unit staff placed security and maintenance norms first by a relatively small margin. These employees gave external image management its highest percentage of first places (18 percent).

A resident's conceding the importance of a norm did not guarantee that he or she would obey it. Mountainside boarders who short-circuited the sign-out sign-in norm by doing both on their return nevertheless ranked it high, and patients who undid soft ties and climbed over bed rails endorsed the safety norm. John McDevitt, who put the bath safety rule ahead of internal tension management, was the Countryside boarder who objected most to having the aide supervise his shower.

This supports another observation: While staff members assumed that the system's deviants simply did not understand, the deviants themselves showed a striking awareness of how others felt about their behavior.

> When John McGreevy was asked about the spoken and unspoken rules in the setting, he hesitated and the question was rephrased, "What bugs them most?" There was a pause. His voice dropped. "Me," he replied.
>
> The way Mr. McGreevy "bugged" them was by arriving late at meals with his cane thump-thumping and bump-bumping through the Mountainside dining room when the boarders were having their silent grace. This was Mr. McGreevy's protest at having been placed by his children in this hotbed of Protestants. Once seated, he murmured a prayer of his own.
>
> I resolved that on the day I was visiting I would not allow him to earn the opprobrium of his neighbors, and so I cut short our interview, reminding him that

lunch would be served in just fifteen minutes. On that day, as on all others, however, Mr. McGreevy arrived late, paused outside the door and again made a noisy entrance during the silent grace. Half-way through his odyssey, heads bobbed up in irritation and prayers gave way to glares.

Staff Norms, Peer Norms. Who Enforces?
Who Obeys?

Deviance is identified by the reaction it arouses (Schur, 1980). Whether individuals are seen as advocates or agitators depends as much on where they are and who is doing the sanctioning as on the behavior itself. Whether the stigma sticks depends on the support they can muster and the climate of judgment. The observer has only to note the response.

At Mountainside and Countryside, there were two kinds of deviance: *deviant behavior*, which it was believed that offenders could stop, and *deviant essence*, which it was thought that they were powerless to change but for which they could make amends by accepting their stigmatized state and keeping a low profile. Both peers and staff members made efforts to sanction norm-violating behavior, but, in general, they tried to distance individuals adjudged to have deviant essences and punished them only for the presumption of intrusion.

A music-loving patient illustrated the difference when she instructed me to take measures against persons who were chattering during the music group: "If they are boarders, tell them to be quiet. If they are patients, take their wheelchairs and push them out!" Her assumption seemed to be that the boarders might respond to reprimand but that noisy patients had spoiled essences which no amount of censure could correct, and therefore the solution was removal.

Some persons were perceived to behave in ways they could mend and, at the same time, to possess essences that were both unalterable and flawed. Myrtle Weatherford was such a resident. She affronted her fellow boarders by violating expressive norms and offended the Mountainside administrator by disregarding those relating to safety.

By all reports, Mrs. Weatherford had been a "mom" who was quite prepared to accept a secondary role ("My husband didn't think women should drive") and comfortable with dependency. She elevated authority figures and then was angry with them when they did not meet her needs and hurt when they found fault. In her early eighties, she was a small, nicely rounded woman who suffered from dizzy spells and was irritated by efforts to control her behavior.

Her tablemates disapproved her loud voice and her discussion of taboo topics, such as her urinary accidents. Her table hostess, a former physical education teacher, was flatfooted in her reformatory efforts: "We don't do that," "That isn't done," and finally, "Ladies don't . . . "

The last was too much. Myrtle Weatherford bridled. "I consider myself a lady. I read the etiquette books!" Heads turned, since she spoke rather loudly.

Seeking to mute the impasse, a tablemate replied, "There are many definitions of a lady."

Mrs. Weatherford belligerently demanded, "What are they?"

The other boarder, a former efficiency expert, copied a list of definitions and put it in her box. Reportedly, after all that, Mrs. Weatherford said she didn't want to read it.

Her brushes with the administrator proved fatal. No norm elicited more steadfast enforcement from Barbara Archer than compliance with fire drills. When the alarm sounded, Mrs. Weatherford stepped quietly into a bathroom. When the administrator commanded her to join the others in the drill, she said she was too dizzy and, apparently to prove her point, wove so dangerously on the fire escape that the administrator was forced to pull her in.

The next time there was an empty bed, she was transferred to the nursing unit, contending all the while that she had not been told and did not belong there. Her physician supported the move because there had been difficulties monitoring her blood pressure and supervising her medication in the boarding unit. In the past, she had appeared to enjoy short stays in the infirmary but now she was angry at the change of status.

After two falls, she was told she must use a walker and, finally, that she must either use the walker or leave. One morning she informed the nursing staff that she was departing that day. When her daughter and her niece came to move her, they disclosed that she had applied to Sunnyvale nursing home some weeks earlier and had been awaiting a bed. She smiled triumphantly as she departed, quite ignoring the fact that she would be a patient there, too.

Myrtle Weatherford might have survived longer in the boarding unit if she had curbed her angry behavior. She was aware of the group's disapprobation but insensitive to its "feeling rules." From the viewpoint of her fellow boarders, her indignation was inappropriate to either her talents or her status. Her essence was not ideal but might have been tolerated if she had remained quietly in the background. As it was, her peers strongly endorsed the transfer. For the home, the transfer served the function that status deescalation always does: It told the group which behavior was taken seriously (in this case, that fire drills were sacrosanct).

The sad wraith whom Mamie Slocum christened "the Creep" also had a spoiled essence. There was no single behavior the Countryside boarders expected her to change: They just wanted her to stay away. The evidence of her internal exile was plain: Five places were set at one table in their lounge and at the other, just one.

For her part, Mamie Slocum was successfully intransigent.

When an inspector found her lying on her bed, smoking, she refused to put out the cigarette. Afterwards Ernest Miller reproached her, and she retorted that she was not afraid of the inspector.

"Yes," replied the unhappy administrator, "but I am."

Mrs. Slocum continued to smoke in bed. There were other enormities. She showered in the men's bathroom, for example, because she found it more convenient.

Even with all of this defiance, she was remarkably immune to reprisals. Threats to demand her removal were unavailing since there was nothing she wanted more than to leave. When the management asked her family to take her away, however, the family refused. There was no way Countryside staff could invoke its second-level penalty, demotion to patienthood. They had no excuse: She was mentally alert, articulate, and managed her self-care meticulously.

Her peers were no more successful than management. Mr. McDevitt, the dominant male, avoided her. Mrs. Gladwin took her meals downstairs. All the others detoured around her except Mrs. Florentine, a timid eighty-seven-year-old whose English had eroded with the years and who obeyed her commands. Mrs. Slocum complained about the elderly Italian woman but helped her make phone calls to her daughter-in-law.

Mrs. Slocum was immune to sanction because she wanted nothing the home had to offer. She was depressed and angry. Her resource score was high but her morale score was low (6). When she came to the item about loneliness, she penciled in, "Very," but there was no one at Countryside she wanted for a friend.

Her unhappiness was understandable. The end of a difficult marriage forced her to seek paid employment and provided her first taste of independence and success. This was cut short by cancer. After she had a stroke, her physician said she should not live alone, and her family placed her at Countryside near a granddaughter, who promptly moved away. She was bitter because her eldest daughter refused to give up her job to take care of her on the grounds that her wages were needed to send her own daughter through college.

"She puts her daughter ahead of me," she declared with a poorly suppressed sob.

In the end, her wishes were realized when a widowed daughter took an apartment for the two of them. What the home's requests and her own had failed to do, rising rates accomplished.

Countryside boarders had a fellowship to withdraw and approval to bestow, but Mrs. Slocum was as immune to their sanctions as to those of management: She had no desire to be universally loved and she fed on others' rage. Her tongue was too sharp to ignore. Sometimes she attempted to organize campaigns of silence against newcomers she disliked. When an inoffensive new boarder arrived, Winnie Mason addressed Mrs. Slocum forthrightly, "Lay your mouth off him!" The other men gathered around him to protect him, like a ring of covered wagons.

In the micropolitics of the home, residents sometimes made certain that sanctionable behavior came to the attention of staff. Peer power was exercised mainly through these informal channels: Since its existence was unacknowledged, there was no formal provision for its expression. During the period of the study, neither home had a regular residents' council and it is questionable whether one would have helped. (Even today's residents' councils appear to be more an activity than a forum because, as Devitt and Checkoway [1982] point out, they often take up nothing more controversial than the menus.)

In dealing with errant boarders, management's major sanction was demotion to patienthood. Becoming a patient in itself created a deviant essence and handicapped the resident in further negotiations, and the transformation was abrupt.

In discussing the ways being deviant with its accompanying stigmatization accomplishes containment, Schur (1980) says that first, it boxes persons into a category, such as "patient," that tends to obscure their total selves. It also provides seven particular kinds of containment, all evident in the nursing units.

1. *Social-psychological containment.* In the eyes of others and often their own, stigmatized persons acquire a master identity that overrides all others and sometimes lowers their self-esteem, contributing to a helplessness syndrome.

All patients bore on their wrists identification bracelets that implied they might not know who they were or, if they did, might attempt to conceal their discreditable identities and "pass" as "normals." The ensuing quarantine took on a physical dimension, which was illustrated when boarders and patients met together for a music group. The staff clustered patients in front, ostensibly so they could hear, while boarders seated themselves in back. A gray area was created in between when a boarder chose to sit beside a former neighbor or friend who had recently transferred from the boarding unit.

2. *Interpersonal containment.* The stigmatized become less attractive as partners. Conversation with them is hurried, and their contacts and opportunities to be with the more fortunate are limited.

While boarders went to the library, the city, and even on trips, patients could go out only when escorted by a "responsible person" who controlled the contact.

> When Miss Godfrey wanted to attend a garden party and proposed paying one of the aides to escort her, the administrator flatly forbade it. The members of her thinning circle who would be at the party were themselves elderly and dependent upon others to help them get there, and her nephews were far away. In the end she had only the consolation of knowing she had been invited, that she was not utterly forgotten by the world outside. Since even those who invited her did not facilitate her attendance, this may have been the modest intent behind the invitation.

3. *Economic containment.* Labels, such as ex-convict or former mental patient, interfere with access to jobs, loans, and other resources.

Patients were not allowed to keep money for two reasons: If it

were lost, they might have accused staff of stealing it or they might
have used it to tip the aides and get an undeserved advantage. Either
implied a discreditable essence: in the first instance, incompetence,
and in the second, a conniving nature.

Administrators would have pointed out that the patients still had
money—it was just being kept for them. Asking for petty cash,
however, laid them open to counterinquiries about what they intended to do with it. Whenever possible, therefore, Mountainside
endeavored to have a relative or a bank manage patients' funds, an
arrangement that made it unnecessary for the home to negotiate
with them by removing this resource from their control.

4. *Visual containment.* Deviantized individuals are encouraged
to keep evidence of their condition—and often themselves—out of
sight. Thus "normals" are preserved from outrage or pity.

Visitors to Countryside often protested because one entrance
brought them face to face with a circle of that home's most impaired. (This arrangement ensured the patients better care by keeping them close to the nurses' station.) More generally, nursing
homes present their architectural facades uncluttered by wheelchair-
bound reminders of human decrepitude, by keeping patients out of
their lobbies.

5. *Geographical containment.* Patients were barred freedom of
movement and access to certain areas that were open to boarders.
Boarders came to the infirmary as convalescents, as visitors, and
even as volunteers, but in each instance their boarder status was
clearly acknowledged and their stay in the nursing unit, time-
limited. For patients, the boundary began at the door. In each home,
there was a physical barrier that was not originally intended for
containment but that accomplished it nonetheless. At Countryside,
a flight of stairs separated boarders and patients and although some
boarders elected to eat in the main dining room that was also used
by patients, they neither shared tables with them nor lingered in the
lobby. At Mountainside, five or six steps made the nursing unit easy
to enter but hard to leave. The symbolism was obvious but
unintended.

6. *Pharmacological and electronic control.* Chemical "strait-
jackets" and electronic alarm systems can restrain as effectively as
institutional walls. Except for night staff's medication of Mrs.

Flowers, however, I did not observe the misuse of psychotropic medications for behavioral control. Nevertheless, this remained a possibility in the nursing units, one the boarders were not exposed to.

7. *Physical containment.* Despite deinstitutionalization, prisons, mental hospitals, and special schools still persist. Every total institution provides physical containment—and the nursing home is no exception.

Patients were kept within a demarcated area while boarders were free to come and go. Margaret Wesley, for example, reported that she had found a pleasant spot in the garden for reading and then, having foolishly mentioned it, was promptly told not to go there any more, that she could be seen from the boarding unit.

With so many controls for a group of frail persons dependent on their caregivers, it might be assumed that deviant behavior never occurred in the nursing units. Boarder norms were divided between those requiring action and those demanding restraint but most patient norms asked only passive compliance. To score the full 18 points on the norm-conformity instrument, a patient needed only to "go along."

Nevertheless, patients' mean norm-conformity scores were slightly lower than those of boarders: 15 as opposed to 16. Patients were less conforming to peer norms than to staff norms while boarders were equally responsive to both. The patient peer group was fatally weakened by its lack of cohesion. The occasional small alliances that existed offered some friendships, but even these were frail because all were in competition for the services of staff. With favors to bestow and comforts to withhold, staff members had the greater leverage.

> Ellen Landsford was a soft-spoken school teacher in her nineties. Her tiny frame was racked with arthritis. Whenever possible, the nurses let her take the last bath so that she could soak in the warm water that eased the pain. For them, her obvious pleasure was enough.
>
> She did not fare as well with the nursing assistants. When things disappeared, for example, she suspected them of stealing. She was both deaf and a little forgetful: Sometimes, perhaps, she had put an object away

and forgotten that she had done so, and occasionally, as with her scissors, it had been removed and she had not heard the explanation. (The scissors turned up in the administrator's office: They had been confiscated as a safety precaution.) The nursing assistants were aware of her suspicions—she did not hear their footsteps one day when she was telling me about the loss of her scissors. Of the nursing assistants who dressed her, she complained, "They push and pull me so!"

She was quite clear about her own misdemeanors: She often crawled over the foot of the bed to get to the bathroom and she sometimes refused to take her medication, "but not for that nice nurse who helps with my hearing aid!"

She summed up her existential predicament, "How can I complain when I am in this beautiful place with these pleasant people and good food? But I'm tied and that's not so pleasant. . . . I'm not free."

Since patients' bad behavior was attributed to a deviant essence, senility, and believed to be inaccessible to reason or remembrance, staff tried to control it with soft ties and bed rails, much as one blocks a baby or a puppy with a barrier. For the most part, the assumption that patients had deviant essences therefore appeared to protect them against "punishment" but it cost them their freedom.

The ultimate norm violation was the inability to pay one's bill, and the penalty was exile to a Medicaid facility. Moral opprobrium attached itself to the financial misfortune. Transfer implied that the transferees' families could not or would not come to their rescue, that they had been bad parents or their children were ungrateful. There also may have been the sense that they had lived too long or had been improvident. The view that most exiles and their families held about the homes was even simpler: They had taken all their money and now they were casting them out.

What is noteworthy, however, is that not all persons whose funds were depleted had to move. At Mountainside, no member of the sponsoring sect was ever forced to leave on that account. In addition, reduced rates were accepted for many months for some who had been there a long time. Some were rescued by a deus ex machina, such as the Santa Claus Society or persons like Marion Bell's friend, who never told when Miss Bell's own funds were exhausted but simply paid the bill.

When a Medicaid move did occur, there was generally an angry family, an unhappy old person, a distressed peer group, and an embarrassed staff. Each put a different face on the transfer.

Reconstructing the Reason for Exile

According to the "just world" hypothesis, people must believe that those who suffer brought the calamity upon themselves, otherwise, there would be nothing they could do to avert similar misfortune. The same assumption enables those who are distressed by the victim's fate to reduce their own discomfort (Jones and others, 1984). In both the proprietary and the sectarian homes, staff members evidenced disquiet when a resident was forced to leave, and a process of "repair" work attended the departure. In addition, the family and the patient, if he or she was aware, began to prepare a more palatable explanation.

Almost invariably, departures were from the nursing unit, since it was its cost that exhausted funds.

> Gladys McCulloch came to Mountaindside in her eighty-first year after her widowed son remarried. They had shared a double house so that she could take care of his children, now grown. She was a discreet, homey woman, not of the highest status, because her husband had been a cabinetmaker, but a skilled needlewoman, which provided a basis for companionship and pattern exchange with some of her neighbors in the boarding unit. Her son visited often and members of her church included her in their special events. The boarding unit was within her means.
>
> A year before her death, she confided that she had not opened her sewing machine because she had had pain in her chest. In the weeks that followed, she spent more time sitting in her room or resting, but she was

careful not to complain lest this suggest the need for
more care.

Five months before her death, she fell and went to
the nursing unit for several days, but she was not dis-
couraged because she was able to return quickly to the
boarding unit. This stay lasted only a short time; before the month was out, she was in the nursing unit
again, this time permanently. She was unsteady and
she also was nauseated. Staff members worried about
her many and quite uncharacteristic complaints.

Her son, who was divorced and in debt, came nightly and they
had feverish conversations by her bedside. She was alert but depressed and confided to friends that she was no longer happy at
Mountainside, a report they seem not to have challenged. She was
plainly dying and the hope was that her life might end before she
had to move. Forty-seven days before her death, she was transferred
to a large proprietary nursing home that did accept Medicaid
patients.

In this case, the resident saved face for her son by saying she
wanted to go. The same tissue served the home and her fellow
residents. For administration, the case had posed an ethical dilemma: Accepting less than full pay for one resident ultimately
increased the rates for all. For staff, counting her complaints was
less painful than seeing her distress. For her friends, believing that
she wanted to go provided a little balm, and for those who had
viewed her as "not quite our kind of people," her late disaffection
provided a welcome confirmation that perhaps she was not really
entitled to their consideration after all. The terribly ill woman provided a way out for them all.

Many exiles-to-be were not as much in command as Gladys
McCulloch. Often the confused were not told for fear that they
would understand, with the rationale that they would not remember
and they would be upset twice.

The saddest of these departures was that of Grace
Gladwin, a flamboyant figure until she ran down like
a wind-up doll. After less than three months in the

nursing unit, she was transferred to a Medicaid home. Her niece directed that she was not to be told, only that she was to be dressed and ready to go.

As a hospital administrator, Ernest Miller had known her when she was director of the visiting nurses, and he was saddened by her transfer. He saw her there in the lobby, dressed and made up by the nurses, and asked if he could give her a kiss. She smiled but asked, "Why?" Respecting the niece's fiat, he fumbled for an answer and said he was kissing her "Hello." When staff members discussed the case, their emphasis was on the niece's decision to remove her.

Conformity as Choice

The chapter began with the complexity of imposing controls, but controls were usually unnecessary because many residents elected to conform. Often these were the individuals who had the greatest choice.

There was a significant association between norm conformity and social resources (gamma .57, χ^2 = .00014; T 13.32, p = .000). No resident with a low resource score was a high conformer, but 35 percent of those with the highest resource scores and 34 percent of those with medium resource scores were high conformers.

When residents at the three resource levels are compared, the greatest difference appears in the percentages of low conformers at each level. Eighty-two percent of those with the lowest resource scores and 41 percent of those with the highest resource scores were among the lowest conformers. Those with resource scores in the middle range included fewer low conformers (39 percent) than either of the two extremes.

This suggests that those with the fewest resources also had the least to lose—even their best behavior was unlikely to win them good rewards. An old woman in a gerichair, for example, would have little to gain by being "good." No one would spend extra time with her simply because she was quiet and uncomplaining.

Those with the highest resources enjoyed relative immunity from sanctions and were less dependent on the home and their peers because they had other options. Those at the middle resource level had rewards to gain by conforming but fewer possibilities of leaving if life in the home turned sour.

Stated more positively, many of those who could leave but stayed were those who perceived the home as their very best option. Because they shared its values, these residents did not see its norms as constraints at all but simply as perfectly natural courses of action.

CHAPTER SEVEN

Changing Patterns of Support and Power as Residents Age

The cost of survivorship is finding yourself alone. This can be hard to bear when other supports are slipping away. The men and women at Mountainside and Countryside drew on inner strengths and outside allies in their negotiations with the environment, but as elderly survivors, they brought ebbing energies and altered networks to their final years.

Changes in their peopled world often combined with a biological winding down to create different patterns of relationship. Kahn (1979) and Antonucci (1985), who both credit David Plath for the first use of the term, describe *convoys of support*. The convoy accompanies the person through life but there are shifts in its character and composition. Antonucci mentions loss and replacement but the convoys of the very old may not be so much depleted as different, with health personnel as the instrumental others and one or two key visitors. The diminished group may be all the individual can tolerate.

> Although she got along civilly with her neighbors in the nursing unit, Clarissa Bennett, eighty-six, commented that only two individuals mattered to her: her son and her younger brother. Both were faithful visitors. One day I found her quietly crying. Her son had

told her he might have to move away because of his
wife's arthritis.

This chapter will illustrate the shifting balances between personal strengths and the help of others and between sources of support inside and outside the home. Then it will examine the changes
in the network of families and friends that lead to increasing re-
liance on caregivers and fellow residents. Finally, it will consider
the effect of these changes on peer leaders as they age.

The Shifting Balance

When sensory acuity fails and mobility diminishes, individuals
experience a shrinking environment, especially when they also lose
America's symbol of adulthood, the keys to the car. Agnes Chase
illustrates this drawing-in in the final years of life.

> Agnes Chase's rickety old car was at once an emblem
> of freedom and a social asset. At the study's start, she
> was driving several old friends to their summer place
> for a shared vacation in the country. The car played
> an equally important role in her daily life at Moun-
> tainside, where she transported fellow boarders to
> meetings and performed errands for those less able to
> get about. With her car, she drove to peace demonstra-
> tions, engaged in prison visiting, and supported the
> League of Women Voters.
>
> At eighty-one, she enjoyed a high resource score
> (38) and high morale score (18). Her manner was di-
> rect and forceful, but her good will was apparent. In
> the home, she was a table hostess and also went each
> morning to the nursing unit to help feed patients.
>
> Even then, she was an impetuous driver, often more
> preoccupied with the cause she was espousing than
> the traffic. When evidence accrued that eye and atten-
> tion were no longer so sharp, Barbara Archer asked
> her not to take passengers. At eight-six, when await-
> ing cataract surgery, she gave up driving altogether,

but with great reluctance. Meetings had to be on the bus lines now or within walking distance. The old physical education teacher's athleticism served her well for a long time, but in the end failing memory shortened her range.

Boarders who arrived when her powers were declining did not perceive her redeeming warmth and honesty. She had always been attentive to the needs of others but somewhat insensitive to their feelings. Now she was missing cues and her increasing irritability made matters worse. When a tablemate who was forgetful lost his thread, the other boarders quietly came to his aid, but they did not do the same for her.

Her morale declined sharply when she was eighty-nine. She had just had her second cataract operation. A few days before the surgery, she had traveled to a major peace demonstration, but when she recuperated, her physician asked her to curtail her activity. She was no longer a table hostess, and she was noting a decline in hearing. She spoke about awakening at 5 A.M. and worrying about money. Sadness began to show beneath the optimistic replies to the Philadelphia Geriatric Center Morale Scale, as she talked about the death of her parents and the lack of family and friends.

After her ninetieth birthday, she commented that she hoped to die soon. ("I wouldn't want to be an invalid. It would drive me crazy.") As her confusion increased, she worried about poverty more, forgetting she had the protection of the Santa Claus Society.

Three days after her ninety-second birthday, she had a stroke and became a patient. On the whole, she was remarkably cheerful, and with her short curled hair and her small trim figure, she looked handsome and vigorous even in her wheelchair.

What was striking at this time was how obliterated her memory could be while her personality remained so unchanged. When I took her for a wheelchair walk in the garden, she greeted each familiar spot as new and interesting but expressed passing concern about how she would ever get back to where she lived.

On another occasion, she and three other patients were awaiting the reader, who never appeared. She was telling one of them how to operate his wheelchair. She maintained he wanted to leave the room, although he said he did not. To break the impasse, I suggested he wanted her company, and he assented. She smiled, but a few minutes later she was telling him again how he might turn his wheelchair so he could leave. This penchant for helpful advice giving was not uncharacteristic of her earlier days.

Jean Blackwell was a boarder with whom she had both collaborated and quarreled over the years. They shared common social concerns that brought them together, but they held clearly articulated opinions that often set them apart. Jean Blackwell was very attentive to her now and visited her twice a day. The director of nursing credited her for Agnes Chase's current contentment. She kept her more alert.

When I saw her for the last time, nine months before her death, she seemed to have had more little strokes. She was rather like an old warship, its battles fought, riding at anchor and waiting for a more decisive ending. She was dozing her days away.

Agnes Chase had performed acts of kindness for many persons. She lost personal contact with most of them in her final years, but when she died, the memorial service was packed with friends. They had not forgotten her after all.

Agnes Chase had come to Mountainside because the only relatives she had were cousins in England. Much of her life was richly peopled, but she did not wish to be a burden to her friends. As she experienced the biological deficits of aging, she lamented her lack of family; she had gained another resource, however: the institution. Nursing personnel were grateful to her for not being as difficult as they had anticipated. During her final years in the boarding unit, she had often been frustrated by those whose concern for her safety interfered with her projects, but in the protected setting of the nursing unit, the same people were seen as facilitating rather than balking. The nurses gave her good care and she accepted it gratefully—they had become her family.

The Changing Character of the Convoy

The most enduring support system is the family. The family differs from friends in having both horizontal and vertical reserves: When a vacancy occurs, it can reach into its own reservoir of intra- and intergenerational replacements.

The difficulty is that the intragenerational replacements—siblings and spouses—are also old with mobility problems of their own and the intergenerational replacements, except adult children, tend to be less intensely involved. It is not surprising that the children often live near—this is a consideration in the older person's choice of a last community residence and the children's in the selection of a facility for their parents. The young old wish to be close enough to help their children with their families and the children want the old old nearby so they do not have to travel to them in emergencies. Nieces and nephews, who lack these agendas, frequently live farther away, as do cousins. Members of the middle echelon are pulled toward their own children in relationship-replicating patterns. Grandchildren are a special case. If the grandparent has participated in their care there may be a special bond, but grandchildren tend to be young and preoccupied with their own launching. They are emotionally bonded to grandparents but less constrained to live nearby.

The facility, like the family, possesses the relative immortality needed in a long-term care provider and it, too, can draw on a broader base. The institution's equivalent of the family's "other hands" (siblings, in-laws, and nieces or nephews) is shifts. What the family has that the institution lacks is the reinforcing effect of special emotional ties and social expectations. This is not to say that staff is uncaring or that there are no norms to admonish it, but only that its ties and regulations lack the compelling personal quality of those governing the family's service to its senior members. Needless to say, however, neither individual families nor institutions quite live up to these models.

Unlike family members who may have little choice, friends are voluntary members of the convoy, but because they tend to be age peers, they are subject to attrition.

From her in-depth interviews with the elderly, Kaufman (1986) concluded that for many, children and grandchildren were the closest friends. Families provided support and intimacy; friends provided companionship. Close friends were long-time friends of at least twenty years. Some of Kaufman's respondents were saddened at having outlived most of their friends and all declared that you do not make close friends when you are old. This is supported by a larger study that found that older persons tend to have thinner networks, that they have known their members longer, and that 82 percent of them are family (Troll, 1986). When residents entered the home, for example, their networks had already thinned and sometimes entry itself combined with their reduced mobility to separate them from the kind of neighborly contacts that keep acquaintance-ship warm.

We saw in Chapter Five that spouses were patients' most active advocates but that most residents had outlived their husbands or wives. A few residents still had sisters or brothers but more had survived them. For the largest group (41 percent), an adult child was the significant other. For a second group (18 percent), it was nieces and nephews. Grandchildren were less likely to be listed as primary unless their parents were dead, but they were visible and active.

Sometimes residents had nursed a spouse or friend at home and thus prevented that person's placement. After his or her death, they had a heightened sense of their own mortality and began to plan for themselves. ("My minister said to me, 'You've taken care of your friend. Now what are you going to do for yourself?'")

Often when an individual entered the home immediately after the death of a household member, it was apparent that he or she had been dependent on the decedent for care. The "backup" kinsperson, often a nephew or niece, was less likely to take the older person into his or her own home (Johnson and Catalano, 1981). Even adult children might be unable to provide personal care (Montgomery,

1988) or reluctant to commit their spouses to a burden they themselves otherwise might have been willing to assume. In these cases, the character of advocacy differed. Often the second-echelon significant other (noted in institutional records as the person to be contacted) was geographically removed and therefore responsive to institutional initiatives rather than proactive on the resident's behalf. A case will illustrate this pattern.

> Miss Godfrey entered Mountainside three days after the sudden death of the younger sister who had been caring for her. Miss Godfrey made it quite plain that in her opinion if her sister had not worked so hard on plans for her college class's sixtieth reunion, she might have survived longer to provide her with companionship and care. Nephews phoned and sent holiday gifts, but they lived in another state. She had not intended to end her life in "a home with a capital H."

Research findings suggest that relatives of confused residents visit as often but do not stay as long (Moss and Kurland, 1979). When verbal communication falters, companionship in the ordinary sense fails and the purpose of the visit becomes surveillance. This was illustrated by Georgiana Longino, who bore a diagnosis of Alzheimer's disease before that label became common. She had a large, close family.

> When I first met Georgiana Longino, she was seventy-four and had been at Countryside two years. Her response to the morale scale item "How much are you lonely—a lot or not much?" was "A great, great, great deal."
>
> Her four sisters took turns so that she had a visitor each day. She had been the bookkeeper in the family business and, as the unmarried sister, had taken care of their mother when she had shown the same signs. The family had been able to keep the mother at home, with two neighborhood women paid to care for her while Miss Longino was at work. By the time she

herself needed constant supervision, however, this
kind of help was difficult to get at an affordable price.

By the time she was seventy-eight, she was in bed
all day, unaware but beautifully kept in pretty gowns.
When she was eighty-two, a sister declared sadly that
she could only pray for her. By her eighty-third year,
she twitched and had seizures. The sisters came a little
less frequently now and visiting became chiefly the
youngest sister's duty. Miss Longino died at eighty-
four. For the last six years of her life, she was almost
totally unresponsive, but the family continued to keep
vigil.

For some, however, transfer to the homes brought a renaissance
because it got them good care and release from strain.

John Post came to Countryside at seventy-four,
shortly after the death of his alcoholic son, with whom
he had been living. His brother, who brought him,
warned staff members that they would have difficulty
getting him to eat, but this proved to be no problem—
he promptly gained weight. Mr. Post approached the
food at Countryside with an enthusiasm best explained by his former diet, which he described as a
liverwurst sandwich for lunch and baloney and beer
for supper. He had lost a lung ten years earlier; even
a trip to the bathroom left him exhausted, and he
husbanded every bit of breath. Nevertheless, he did
well, enjoyed the attentions of his grandchildren, and
died two years later, five days after catching a cold.

Whatever Mr. Post's personal grief over the loss of his son, he
plainly benefited by being removed from his care.

Sometimes an untimely death reverberated through the family
system, indirectly leading to the placement of a vulnerable member,
which can be expected when the caregiver must pick up the roles
the dying person left. In the illustration that follows, however, the
process was more subtle. The whole family was immobilized by

the sudden loss of its youngest member, and the eldest became the symptom bearer.

> Kate Brigg's agitation increased sharply when the freeway death of her granddaughter plunged her daughter and son-in-law into grieving. She had been living "independently" with daily help from the pair. Now she began phoning at night that men were hiding in the shadows. The daughter and son-in-law took her into their home and, when that did not work, they moved her to Countryside, where she remained a restless, unhappy patient.
>
> Her morale score was very low. She begged visitors to take her home, not to the small house where she had recently lived but to her long-ago home, now a parking lot. Of her children, she said, "There were so many of them. They could have taken turns staying with me. I never left them alone."
>
> A year later, she was hospitalized with a stroke. Her girlhood friend, herself eighty-nine, expressed distress when she learned they were giving her oxygen. "She has nothing to come back to," she said. She prayed for Kate Brigg's death.

When the adult children retire and move away, they often remove the last prop to an older person's independence—a daughter or daughter-in-law. This changes the kind of help the family can provide. What ensues may be a shift from instrumental to expressive support.

> At eighty-four, Marion Greenway had strong organizational ties to the area: She attended weekly prayer meeting at her church, belonged to the order of Eastern Star, and was active in the local chapter of the Daughters of the American Revolution.
>
> Her daughter-in-law had helped with transportation and shopping, but when her son retired to the sunbelt, he suggested that she move to Mountainside.

She complied, but the gastric ulcer that followed suggested ambivalence. She eventually transferred to the
nursing unit but continued to go out to meetings,
escorted by friends. From distant states, her sons' families sent letters, gifts, and phone calls. She kept a
book of their birthday tributes by her bed: This seemed
to be all she needed.

The children of the very old sometimes die before their parents.
Several Mountainside residents survived a child: Sometimes they
mourned the long-ago death of a special son or daughter deeply.
But again, when the death itself occurred very late, their response
seemed strangely muted. It was as if they had experienced so many
deaths that death had become a friend.

Staff members who had worried about how to tell
Ellen Rutledge that her daughter's body had been
found were unnerved by her stoicism. Mrs. Rutledge
was ninety at the time and had been living in the
home fifteen years.
   The same staff members wondered if Rene Schmitt
understood that his second son had been killed when
answering an alarm as a volunteer fireman. He did, as
his account made clear, but by that time he was realistically concerned about his own health and had little
energy to invest.

In her ninety-fifth year, Ramona Everly commented on the loss
of people. She had always had a great many people in her life, but
in the end she shut them away as if in a deliberate withdrawal from
the weariness of living.

Whe she entered Mountainside at eighty, her husband
and four of her five daughters had predeceased her, but
she carried on a large correspondence with her grandchildren and her former sons-in-law, even after the
latter remarried.
   Her relationships with staff and peers at Mountain-

side appeared to reflect her concerns about members of the family. At eighty-six, her dissatisfaction with the home and her rivalry with Sarah Penfield reached a crescendo just at a time when she thought her surviving daughter and son-in-law were going to move to New England. One of our interviews was marked by a series of complaints about the home and then, almost without a break, she reported that a favorite nephew and a favorite grandson were moving out of state. She added that she hoped Loretta, the daughter, would not die. The interview ended when Loretta, looking very healthy, came to take her out.

Even after her transfer to the nursing unit at eighty-nine, letters and family visits continued to flow. Snapshots were at hand. One of her correspondents was a much-admired writer who shared her belief in psychic phenomena. An unrelated person, Grace, became a faithful visitor, bringing her small gifts of fruit.

At ninety-six, she continued to correspond with the grandchildren but regulated their visits. Grace and her daughter were her most consistent outside contacts. Her letters from the writer on psychic phenomena ceased as he, too, apparently experienced the lassitude of aging. As her eyesight failed, her letters became more difficult to read.

At ninety-eight, she wanted to die. Old friends and enemies within the home were dying. Evan Brewster, whose mending she used to do, had died when she was ninety-six. It was reported that she spent the day in bed when she learned of Sarah Penfield's death.

At ninety-eight also, she wrote each grandchild and all the remaining members of the extended family that they were not to visit her. Her stated reason was that she did not wish visiting to become a duty and a burden to them, but her daughter Loretta reported that they were crushed—they felt shut out.

She was tired: She commented that even breathing was a burden. On her ninety-ninth birthday, she ate

ice cream and then did not eat again. She had no intention of celebrating her hundredth, and she died
eleven days later.

Dr. Ernest Magyar had a faithful older friend who came from
another town to visit him each Wednesday. The two men spoke
Hungarian together and throughout his nine-year stay, his friend's
visits remained one of his pleasures. A few weeks before his own
death, his friend collapsed on the streets and died instantly. This left
his wife as his unfailing visitor, who came daily.

Shifting Sources of Support: Turning Inward

Families sometimes have been advised not to visit their newly
placed members too often on the grounds that patients become integrated into the life of the nursing home more quickly if they are
not cosseted by their relatives. It is unclear whether this proposition
is advanced for the convenience of staff or the relief of relatives. In
any event, it has been challenged by Restinas and Garrity (1985),
who found no association between the frequency of visitors and the
number of friends patients made in the home.

While the study indicated that visitors did not interfere with
adjustment, it also showed that the longer patients remained in the
home, the fewer friends they had. The authors contended that it was
not the conditions of institutional living that led to isolation but
changes in the patients' ability to communicate. Restinas and Garrity were speaking of friendships among patients in a nursing
home, which at Mountainside and Countryside were relatively few.
Even in their study, 35 percent of the patients were scored as loners.

With the passage of time, however, residents turned more and
more to resources within the home. This was a function of thinning
networks, declining energies, and long residence in the setting. This
shift was illustrated by Agnes Chase, who combined all the compo-
nents—diminishing connections, increasing care needs, and long
residence—but could only come to terms with a shrinking environment when it was matched by failing energies.

Because Agnes Chase's network did not include an intergenerational core of obligation, Mountainside was her elected "family" from the start and remained so for almost twenty years. It proved to be the enduring one as time reduced other relationships.

Her English cousins faded from written contact. Her strong community ties lapsed as memory impairment reduced her range. Her old allies in the boarding unit were removed by death and transfer and those who took their place saw only a willful woman with a failing memory.

She had always been a service giver. This was a frustration during her final days in the boarding unit, when every effort on her part to help was greeted with alarm or went awry. Only when the stroke lowered her energy level was she able to accept care from others.

Before he came to Mountainside, John Wesley had jettisoned much of his social baggage. His need for relationship was narrowly focused: He brought his wife with him and that was enough. He had no thought that he might survive her.

John Wesley's Parkinson's disease had limited the energy he had to invest in interpersonal relationships; he avoided other patients. Three of his four children lived out of state. He relied almost solely on his wife. Freed from giving him physical care, she stayed by his side and read to him, but in his second year at the home, she died.

Into this void came an exceptional volunteer, a school nurse who also was widowed. She introduced herself with the words, "I know what it is like." Thereafter she read the Sunday papers to him, telephoned him, and visited weekly. He drank up every word she said. Once I was with him when the phone call came. He smiled with pleasure. "Yes, Darling," he said, "I have been waiting." She continued as his friendly visitor during the eight years that remained

till his death. When we were alone, he continued to
speak of his wife: The new relationship had not replaced the old one but it had wiped away some of the
pain.

Nevertheless, he drew increasingly on sources of
support within the home. A nursing assistant, whose
manner was at odds with his own quiet restraint, became a favorite. As powerful as a crane, she moved his
emaciated body gently and made him comfortable. He
brightened when she came in. The director of nursing
helped greatly by accepting his need to control: She
recognized the fear, bred of helplessness, that lay under it.

While John Wesley had entered the home deeply dependent on
one person and Agnes Chase had found her meaning in many contacts around causes, Evan Brewster was still grieving for the wife he
had seen as the guardian of his health. Despite the cancer that
would keep him moving between hospital and home during the
next eight years, his energy level was relatively high and he was
open to all the support he received from his peers in the boarding
unit. In time, the home would replace his wife as an anaclitic object,
a role it filled well for dependent personalities.

As the last, late child in a large family, Evan Brewster
regarded himself as fragile. He married a nurse and
felt secure because of her close attention to every detail
of his physical well-being, but her sudden death
brought an end to his sense of security.

Shortly afterward, he was hospitalized for surgery.
As he reported it, his wife's nephew, who had grown
up in their household, announced, "Uncle Evan, you
don't have to worry about a thing!" When the nephew
explained that he wanted Evan Brewster near him so
that he could watch out for him, the older man failed
to understand that what he had in mind was a large,
impersonal nursing home. As a former banker, Mr.
Brewster watched his nephew's management of his

funds with misgivings. With the help of his nephew's wife, he got himself transferred to Mountainside, in the town where he had grown up.

At Mountainside, he quickly transferred his dependence on his wife to one of the nurses who had trained at the same hospital a generation or two later. He said that before he went to the hospital, he talked to her, she explained everything to him and then he knew it would be all right. He took comfort also from the fact that his physician's father had been an intern when his wife was at the hospital. In each of these relationships, there was a symbolic laying on of hands by his dead Matilda. Despite frequent trips to the hospital, he did remarkably well, remaining in the boarding unit except during his intermittent bouts of illness.

As death comes closer, the very old have little energy to invest even in the undemanding others who make up the tertiary tier. They are grateful for their presence, perhaps, and, if they are fortunate, there may be an aging daughter or son to sit by their side, but in the end, the very end, they turn inward and the last of the shifting sources of support is the gently ebbing life flow that characterizes natural death.

Old Leaders Fade

In the meantime, there were changes in the peer leadership within the homes.

What happens when peer leaders age is of interest on two levels: first, in showing to what degree social credit sustains status after the individual's contributions to the life of the group have peaked, and second, in raising questions about whether the general aging of the resident population reduces the likelihood of competent successors. Based on their study of thirty-six retirement communities, Streib, Folts, and LaGreca (1985) have suggested that the number of residents willing and able to take an active role in self-government may decline. This section will deal with the first question and begin to look at the second.

At the study's start, there was strong peer leadership in Mountainside's boarding unit. This meant that the boarders had an informal social structure coherent and cohesive enough so that they could enforce norms and so that management would consult them or at least consider their probable reaction in making decisions that affected them as a body.

There was less peer leadership in the boarding unit at Countryside and almost none in the two homes' nursing units. Some patients possessed high status but the social structure was such that there was no one who could mobilize the group. The staff was too advantaged and the patients too disadvantaged in social exchange.

At the beginning of the study, residents were asked to name "five people who live here" and staff members to list the three residents they would miss most. Dealing more explicitly with leadership would have been desirable but was viewed as potentially destructive to natural patterns of relationship. As it is, it can be said with certainty only that the replies captured salience. In the boarding units, however, observation strongly suggested that they reflected nodes of peer power as well.

Later pollings would have supplied more objective evidence about shifts over time than the qualitative impressions that follow, but these would have entailed interviewing subsequent entrants as well as survivors because leaders could not be leaders of their own thinning cohort alone. Field notes show that the ground against which these figures moved was constantly changing.

The top scorers in the Mountainside boarding unit were Arletta Franklin, John Penfield, Agnes Chase, Ramona Everly, and Sarah Penfield, in that order. In the Countryside boarding unit, only John McDevitt scored appreciably higher than his peers. Of the three whose scores of 9 came closest to his 12, two were pleasant, passive, and forgetful women and the third an Italian woman who had lost most of her English. In opting for these, all but three Countryside residents were walking around their most feared member, Mamie Slocum.

In contrast to Mountainside boarders, the patients most often named by their peers seemed to be not so much leaders as exemplars—they were alert, carried some outside cachet, and were relatively visible. Two Mountainside patients had relatively high scores. One, recently transferred from the boarding unit, was mentioned by four peers and ten members of staff. Staff members appreciated her unfailing consideration for others at a time when her health was failing and she was forced to transfer. She reached out to other alert patients, easing the isolation of patienthood. The other, Miss Godfrey, had been socially prominent in the local community: On his rare visits to Mountainside, the home's donor always stopped to chat with her; another old friend sent her uniformed chauffeur to fetch her for lunch. She was named by five peers and eight members of staff. She had salience if not influence.

Two Countryside patients also had higher composite scores than their peers and a third, Jane Green, was mentioned by seven staff members but not by a single peer. In my field notes, I described her as the "doll lady" because she spent her days sitting in a gerichair and clutching a doll, grinning as she saw the startled expressions of visitors. Quite obviously, the qualities that won the interest of staff members in the nursing unit were not qualities that engaged her fellow residents.

Mrs. Flowers was mentioned by four peers and five members of staff. Several factors may have combined to give her prominence— her own personality and community connections, the frequent presence of her daughter who did things for other patients as well, and her part in my study. She was a willing cover for my investigations: I used to wander around the home pushing her wheelchair. The other patient—a brisk, equitable woman who had taught domestic science to most of the older nurses and aides—was named by four patients and four staff members.

What Mountainside's leaders in the boarding unit had in common were high social resource and morale scores and a record of helping others.

> Arletta Franklin was mentioned by ten fellow boarders and five staff members. She was a large woman, thoughtful, even tempered, and disposed to be pleased with people as she found them. She had never worn glasses and at ninety-two she relied on sunlight for

reading, writing, and sewing. The basis of her leadership is clearly revealed in the note written at the end of her social resource inventory: "shares and does for all, intermediary for the silent, clarifies, fixes mail, helps with sewing problems." She was a table hostess. Spontaneously the others grouped around her.

At ninety-five, she fractured a hip and suddenly aging caught up with her, which she met with good grace. I interviewed her in the nursing unit two days before her death at ninety-six. She was reported to have had a series of small strokes, each entailing a "lost day," but she spoke of them calmly. The administrator commented that she was helpful with confused and restless patients. Her resource score had slipped to the high end of medium; her morale score had dropped only a few points and remained relatively high. Her worries concerned her daughter and granddaughters and the troubles they had, but her leadership qualities remained intact.

John Penfield was the long-term instrumental leader in the home: He made announcements, locked up at night, helped the administrator with her marketing, and drove whenever transportation was needed. His tablemates tended to wait for his judgments and he was often the spokesman when something was disturbing the group. He carried special authority as a tradition bearer because he had played an important role in the home's founding and belonged to the sponsoring sect. Nine staff members and five boarders mentioned him.

The following year, when he was eighty-eight, small blackouts and advancing cataracts forced him to give up driving. His diabetes was slipping out of control. Like Agnes Chase, he responded with increased irritability. He was critical of the younger men who might have assumed some of his roles, and in this way he blocked successors. He had little patience with the women who seemed to challenge his wife—sometimes

this led to sharp exchanges at the table. His relationships with the administrator remained that of father
and daughter but increasingly she was forced to try to
check his verbal assaults. His social resource score remained in the highest quartile, dropping by only a
point from his eighty-ninth to his ninety-second year,
but his morale score declined abruptly the year before
his death. He spoke of the frustrations inflicted by a
ninety-year-old body and said he felt less useful. He
played a less dominant role: He continued to make the
home's announcements and his peers listened respectfully when he spoke, but other tasks had fallen away.
In spite of this, he remained alert and well informed
on affairs within the sponsoring sect.

At the study's start, Agnes Chase and Ramona Everly both had
salience scores of 13 while Sarah Penfield scored 10. All three belonged to the sponsoring sect—of Mountainside's peer leaders, only
Arletta Franklin did not. All were table hostesses at one time or
another; each made distinctive contributions. Agnes Chase threw
her enormous energy into errands, gardening, and helping clear
tables when the tray girls were slow. She was overwhelmingly endorsed by her peers (nine mentioned her), which was surprising in
view of the coolness with which her causes were greeted later by the
more conservative members of the group. What the first cohort saw
was her spontaneous warmth and caring, but this was less apparent
to those who knew her only when events were slipping past her and
her frustration level was rising.

Ramona Everly was favored by her peers (eight mentioned her as
opposed to five staff members) and Sarah Penfield by staff (three
peers listed her and seven staff members). Both women had needle
skills and both were active in the sewing group at the home, but
Sarah Penfield was the official leader. This group flourished as long
as the two rivals joined forces. (It fared less well when the leadership
fell into other hands, but perhaps the day for gentlewomen sewing
layettes for the poor had passed.) They had been a formidable pair
but there was always tension between them so that ultimately the
administrator separated them under the guise of a general reseating.

The reseating of residents always involved several selective transfers. The rationale was that moving helped everyone get acquainted with everyone else. Under the cover of a general reshuffle, feuding parties were separated and persons whose conduct was a concern were advanced to the administrator's table where she could keep an eye on them or else moved to the outer reaches where they were unlikely to bother anyone of consequence. Thus as Agnes Chase became more forgetful and more irritable, she was demoted from being hostess at another table to merely being seated there to a position under the administrator's eye. Each move could be viewed as a waystation to the nursing unit.

Countryside's John McDevitt was named by seven residents and five staff members. He spoke with the authority of his two professions, policeman and tavern keeper, and was the boarding unit's dominant male. He named the other assertive boarder, Mamie Slocum. The other two who listed her were among her victims—Gretchen Elder, whom she had managed to get exiled to the nursing unit, and Margaret Dunbar, whom she had tried to keep out of the boarding unit altogether. As the group's high lord executioner, she did not lead its popularity poll but she did exercise power. Both Mr. McDevitt and Mrs. Slocum had high resources but low morale.

The enduring peer leaders were relatively successful in delaying or staving off altogether transfer to the nursing units, settings hardly conducive to the exercise of influence. Each fulfilled a distinct function for the peer group and the home. All had high social resource scores. Their prestige dropped, however, with their acuity, their resources for service, and their energy level.

So little peer leadership was apparent at Countryside that it is difficult to speak of successors. At Mountainside, John Penfield had done so much so long that those who might have taken his place hung back until the time had passed. At the study's close, the youngest and most active residents, who might have taken over, traveled, took courses, and pursued out-of-home memberships and family concerns. The others tended to husband their strength.

In their treatment of autonomy in retirement communities, Streib and his associates (1985) pointed out that the very motivation that propels people to retirement communities mitigates against their taking an active role in self-government. Retirees come seeking a more relaxed lifestyle. If this is true of persons entering a retirement community, how much more so of those choosing a home for the aged. Resident involvement in decision making brings greater commitment to the facility's norms but it becomes difficult to mobilize as persons enter these homes older, frailer, and with less energy to invest.

CHAPTER EIGHT

Good Deaths and Unhappy Departures

The residential career can be assessed conclusively only at its completion. Many residents who had experienced troubled passages earlier appeared to reach calmer waters at the end. For others, who had fared well in the system, illness, costs, or exile often shaded the final perception of the experience. And finally, some moved through each phase with such grace that the whole career was distinguished for its unity. In viewing all three paths, the salient feature is not that life wound down but how the residents coped with the winding down and how they were supported in the process. This chapter takes a closer look at their careers with attention to endings, morale, and identity maintenance.

A retrospective view places the difficulties in a more balanced perspective. The troubled passages commonly occurred at transition points as individuals moved from community resident to boarder, from boarder to patient, and, most traumatic, from patient to involuntary exile. (The routes to these waystations are shown in Resource C.) In the context of the whole, the storms may have mattered less for some than the long seasons in between, and for others, the turmoil may have left the landscape and the self so changed there was no going back even in the mind to the place or person that had been. Neither process can be known if lives are examined only at their crisis points.

John McGreevy's daughter-in-law commented that each time a responsibility was removed, he resisted strongly but functioned better afterward. That he would accept the Mountainside-nursing unit was not readily apparent, therefore, during the two days he stormed up and down its corridor protesting his transfer. Mr. McGreevy demonstrates both the enduring effect of cohort-specific experiences and the fact that a residential career need not be unalloyed to be the best that can be realized under the circumstances. In addition, he illustrates Lieberman and Tobin's (1983) theses about terminal decline and the maintenance of an acceptable self.

In *The Experience of Old Age: Stress, Coping, and Survival,* Lieberman and Tobin (1983) made a number of points that were supported by their research:

1. The context of late life is the sense of personal finitude.
2. The task of the very old is the preservation of a consistent self in the face of sensed inner changes.
3. As death nears, this task requires greater effort, resulting in withdrawal, some shedding of emotional complexity, and the avoidance of reflection that might threaten the self-image.
4. The task becomes more difficult when external demands for adaptation overchallenge an impaired coping system.

Their first theme is identity maintenance. Here their work is at once a tribute to the coping capacity of the very old and an implicit plea for caregivers to support efforts at identity preservation.

Their second theme, distance from death as a variable, arises from the psychological shifts they observed before physical changes were readily apparent. They retested their subjects at intervals and later compared the scores of those who died with the scores of their matched controls. The ego disorganization and the relative drop in cognitive functioning they observed in those nearer death were most apparent when the environmental call for adaptation was high and the perception of personal control was low, as, for example, when there was forced relocation. They distinguished these changes from the transient instability that sometimes occurs with acute illness and described them as a more enduring response to the struggle to maintain a consistent and continuing identity in the presence of failing biological competence—that is, as the individual's last fight against entropy.

They emphasize that these phenomena are only partly related to chronological age. The psychological countdown occurs at different ages for different people, but, like death to which it is the prelude, it becomes more endemic in the upper reaches. Their findings apply to the natural deaths of the very old, such as those occurring at Mountainside and Countryside.

Lieberman and Tobin combine their two themes when they call for a new psychology of aging that will take into account identity maintenance as an overriding concern and nearness to death as more relevant than chronological age. From such a retrospective perspective, the meaning of many contradictory findings about normal aging becomes clearer.

John McGreevy fit their model in two respects. First, he steadfastly protected his identity. He had two changes of status and viewed both as externally imposed to meet the unrealistic concerns of others, a perception that avoided any unsettling reassessment of self at a time when he was biologically besieged. He defended his self-image by distortion: For example, he interpreted a series of interviews with the social work intern as scheduled so he could help her learn about the home. His social functioning improved as soon as the demands on his besieged system were eased. Second, despite the upward fluctuation in his comfort level when burdens were lifted, his general trend appears to support the Lieberman-Tobin picture of terminal decline.

> Shortly before his seventy-ninth birthday, John McGreevy entered Mountainside, pressed by his children and protesting every step of the way. They were upset because he was "holing up in his apartment" and because he often forgot and left the oven on. They chose Mountainside because it was close to his relatives and friends. He resisted because living at Mountainside violated a deeply ingrained perspective—in his youth, the nuns at Catholic school had motivated

their pupils by pointing out that they would have to
compete in a Protestant world.

The nuns' admonition had the desired effect. Mr.
McGreevy worked hard: He began as a messenger in
a large corporation, continued his business education,
and eventually rose in its managerial ranks. He looked
back on his working years with satisfaction. He was
an active member of the corporation's organization for
its retired employees and especially enjoyed the telephoning privilege the company provided its former
personnel, which enabled him to keep in close touch
with his grandchildren.

His basically genial personality must have warred
with a nagging sense that at Mountainside he was in
the camp of the enemy. The ensuing ambivalence expressed itself in mixed behavior: He richly enjoyed the
weekly outing when the Mountainside men went out
to lunch; he tweaked the bluenoses in the house by
announcing that he had been to visit his brother and
had drunk two sidecars; he kept candies for the nursing assistants who made nightly rounds through the
boarding unit and especially liked a black woman he
described as "Mrs. Mac-something—definitely Gallic"
(her name was Smith); and he infuriated the boarders
by clumping in to lunch just when the silent grace
was underway.

The Protestant residents were not immune to cohort bias either. They all had been of voting age when
it was rumored that to elect Al Smith president was to
put the Pope in the White House. Some of that may
have lingered to lend an edge to any conflict surrounding the mealtime prayer.

John McGreevy's enduring sorrow was the death of
his wife fourteen years earlier. He missed her companionship very much and often said so. Despite his ambivalence and his loneliness, however, the setting's
location served him well. Almost every day he strolled
to town and was greeted by familiar faces.

The first time I interviewed him, he had been at Mountainside three years and was eighty-one. His linen was immaculate and he was neatly dressed, but his fly was unzipped and the earpiece of his hearing aid dangled. He was an affable conversationalist. The administrator was viewing him darkly because he had left the water running, causing damage to the ceiling below. Nevertheless, his memory for both remote and recent events was good and he fully grasped the feelings of his fellow boarders about his cane-thumping entries during silent grace.

A few months later, the director of nursing reported that he had returned from a walk so spent that the nurses notified his physician. She speculated that he had had a small cerebral accident: He seemed more silent and less organized afterwards, and the administrator observed that he was late to meals more often. When I interviewed him at this time, I again found his earpiece dangling, but I also noted, "Talks fairly well though wandering."

A few months later, his tablemates complained, "He doesn't belong here." He was "bad tempered" and "slamming the butter around," and they were campaigning to get him transferred to the nursing unit.

Eight months after our first interview, they were still complaining. The administrator reported that Mr. McGreevy's physician son, who had always stopped to chat, now hurried past her door. In the meantime, his daughter-in-law was tidying his room and making sure that fresh linen was always available.

When I visited him, his conversation was dominated by a Catholic-Protestant polarization that he phrased in ambivalent but conciliatory terms. His success in the corporate structure arose from his ability to get along with people and it was hard for him to be disagreeable even in the "enemy's" lair, although he was beginning to show an uncharacteristic testiness with his peers. He related that he had been trying to balance his checkbook and had succeeded at last.

A year after our first interview, transfer to the nursing unit was threatened. What was especially noted was his unsteadiness, his shortness of breath (he frequently puffed as he stalked down the hall), his uncharacteristic bad temper, and other general signs of strain. A little earlier, I had scheduled a series of weekly interviews for him with a social work intern, feeling that they might be supportive and that, at the least, he would enjoy them. He did, but now he was having trouble keeping us straight. (We were both tall women.)

His family and physician assented to staff's demand that a transfer take place as soon as a private room became available. Unfortunately, this occurred when he was away on a holiday, and he returned to find his belongings—and his beloved telephone—moved to the nursing unit. He was enraged and verbally assaultive for two full days. Then, after a long talk with his daughter-in-law, he systematically apologized to each member of the nursing staff.

Two weeks later, he explained to me that his transfer had been necessary to reassure his oversolicitous brood, although, he added, he did not suffer the physical or mental impairment of many of his fellow patients. By this time, he was enjoying his private room, his personal phone, and the attentions of the nurses. He had many visits from his former neighbors in the boarding unit, town friends, and members of his family.

A year later, he was doing well in the nursing unit but had had an episode of cerebral insufficiency that had reduced his energy level further. He died three months after his eighty-third birthday.

The familiar surroundings played a large part in the comfort of John McGreevy's last years. This is consistent with continuity theory. In his framework for continuity theory, Atchley (1989) contends that the major task of the very old is the maintenance of an acceptable and consistent self in the face of late life's challenges. He says that older persons do this best when they are supported by what is familiar—predictable persons, known settings, and customary strategies. Change is stimulating and adaptive but easiest to flow with if it is change within a familiar domain, such as one's world view or vocation, and if it can be linked to experience or learning that has gone before. Atchley emphasizes that whether something is familiar is a personal judgment, affected in part by cultural expectations. Mentally healthy older persons have strategies for the preservation of an acceptable self, such as reinterpretation, selective avoidance, and the abandonment of some of the psychic baggage that served them in the past. Atchley contends that continuity theory is not applicable to the "pathologically aging." Without memory, everything is strange to them and their world, being unpredictable, is in danger of being chaotic as well.

In retrospect, it seems unlikely that Mr. McGreevy could have been completely happy anywhere in the absence of his wife. Although her death preceded his by seventeen years, he continued to say, "I miss my wife." As the product of a less ecumenical age, he could have been expected to have reservations about a Protestant home for the aged, but going to a Catholic facility would have required moving away from his town, his parish church, his many acquaintances, his children, and his brother.

In a semisuccessful effort to resolve this, he employed one of Atchley's linking techniques: He mentioned the changes in the church itself and quoted a Jesuit, who endorsed his going to Mountainside but cautioned him against his use of a derogatory name for the sponsoring sect. The priest pointed out that this was like the old days when Protestants called Catholics "papists." Since the example he cited underlined the past discourtesy of Protestants, this was a somewhat ambivalent rapprochement, but it was a way of coming to terms with the transition.

He was able also to reinterpret events to make them more congruent with an acceptable self-image. He attributed his coming to Mountainside to his children's worry because he burned a pie and his transfer to the nursing unit to their "oversolicitude."

His lifelong skills with people came into play, even when his increasing irritability worked against them. Four of his fellow residents named him in response to the salience question "Name five people who live here"—his score was double the average. His peers were angry at his daily assaults on their silent grace and they wished him banished when his declining functioning reminded them that they, too, were aging, but they did not abandon him as they sometimes did other transferees.

His morale score, taken at a time when transfer to the nursing unit was three months away, was 19, at the lower end of the upper range. He answered "If you could live where you wanted, where would you live?" with the "Right here" response. Recall that the "Right here" response indicates that the respondent perceives the setting as the best alternative realistically available.

Despite the fact that he was failing at this time, he enjoyed a high social resource score. On self-care skills, he functioned marginally for a boarder but he made up for it in social outreach. The spontaneous comment of my staff informant was, "Enormous!" He had another important social asset as well—a son who was a prominent local physican. With these resources, his transfer could be precipitated only by visible physical decrements—his unsteadiness, his shortness of breath, and the manifest shrinking of his reserves. His family was able to insist on a delay of transfer until he could have a private room.

The same social assets, a physician son and a family willing to accept responsibility, had much to do with his being able to continue his daily visits to town until his transfer to the nursing unit. He was protected by his familiarity with the neighborhood and by the many persons who knew and watched out for him, but any other resident so unsteady would have been restricted for safety's sake. This calculated risk kept him contented, even if it did worry the nurses, who often saw him totally expended after his walk.

Some residents ended their stays at Countryside and Mountainside the way they intended; others did not. Chapter Three described four common career patterns. The next section will examine them more closely in terms of the ultimate outcome and the individual's role in achieving it.

The Completed Career: Proper Exits and Forced Departures

Of the 116 residents, three were lost to the study, one is still alive, and information about their completed careers is available for 112. (See Resource A.)

Two of the "lost" respondents were "younger" patients who sustained themselves through the frustrations of chronic disability by "nursing home hopping." A forty-seven-year-old paraplegic received his spinal cord injury years earlier when a youth fired a random shot from his Christmas rifle. A series of unsuccessful skin grafts kept him on his stomach for weeks at a time. The other "younger" respondent was a sixty-four-year-old woman, alert and well spoken but with a maddeningly unresponsive body. Both had higher energy levels than the older patients and both took pains to distinguish themselves from what they perceived as their doddering peers. The woman's roommate, an alert eighty-six, wheeled into the hall to escape her radio. The man, a hobbled lion, railed against the "crockery" around him but added ruefully, "What will I be like when I'm as old as them?" Both were difficult for staff. He remained at Countryside three years and she less than one; for both, their stays were single episodes in a series of moves. The Countryside director of nursing, Winnie Mason, was singularly patient and compassionate with their complaints and frustration, although less so, perhaps, with the woman, who was older and denying her neurologically based incontinence. The man had no choice but acknowledgment: There were the wounds on his buttocks.

The third "lost" patient was a woman in her mid-seventies, sad and confused but very protective of her more dependent roommate. The two used to sit side by side in the Countryside lobby, watching people pass by. Her morale score (4) was very low. Her delusion that her son-in-law wanted to kill her made it impossible for her daughter to keep her at home. In a metaphoric sense, she may have been correct since he probably was distressed at the toll her night wandering took of his wife. When the daughter and her husband moved to another state, they found a nursing home for her nearby, and her death was reported two years later.

Of the four common career patterns, the most desired was *board-*

ing home–based, when the resident either died while still a boarder or moved to the nursing unit within the last two months of life.

Fourteen percent achieved this goal, sometimes fortuituously and sometimes as a result of personal grit and strategy. Mr. McDevitt dropped dead when strolling back to Countryside after a long evening with an Irish friend. The woman that Mamie Stover christened "the Creep" spent only two months in the nursing unit because a bed was not available sooner. Elizabeth Reynolds illustrates a more deliberate route to the desired end.

> She entered Mountainside at eighty-six when her son-in-law elected early retirement and the family, with whom she lived, was contemplating a move. She acknowledged being further influenced by the death of her oldest friend, a woman whose last years were clouded by gentle confusion. She enjoyed her children greatly and did not wish to burden them.
>
> In the home, she set about learning the norms and quickly became a valued member, named by eight of her fellow boarders when they were asked to mention "five people who live here."
>
> Over the years, however, she became increasingly unsteady and in response, she narrowed her range. She even refused the trips to the family's summer cottage because she felt insecure on the sand. In spite of this, she remained quietly in command.
>
> Her morale score, always in the middle range, edged downward and at one point, she said she could not answer the "gloomy questions." (This did not affect the scoring because only the positive answers were counted, but it did reflect rising distress at that time.) Her social resource score remained high, but it dropped several points. In the last year of her life, she was more silent at the table than she had been but attentive still to the needs of others.
>
> In the end, she became very weak. Her fellow boarders knew she was ill but supported her silence. She firmly resisted transfer until the day she could not

walk from her room. Barbara Archer brought a wheelchair to her door and asked, "What would you do if
you wanted to go to the bathroom?" She bowed to
that. She died five weeks later, missing her ninety-fifth
birthday by less than a month.

The secretary said she knew Mrs. Reynolds was going to die when she gave her an oil painting that hung
in her room. Both women were cat lovers and the picture featured a large orange tabby.

Elizabeth Reynolds appears to have died of cancer, which must
have been a long-standing illness, but she neither complained nor
invoked physicians, whose labeling would have made transfer inevitable. She was very explicit about her desire to stay in the boarding unit and she took pains to avoid falls and other accidents that
might have provided the occasion for transfer. She was mentally
alert, she was determined, and she had a great deal of social credit
to draw on.

A second successful survivor manifested some of the snappish
qualities that Lieberman (1975) identified as helpful to old persons
dealing with crises. Lieberman listed these as magical thinking,
viewing oneself as the center of the universe, and a pugnacious
stance. When experiencing illness, this resident displayed all three.

Evan Brewster's ability to avoid patient status was
striking in view of the battle he fought with cancer.
He was a table host and a respected member of the
group, but he possessed the egocentric framework and
the capacity for complaining that Lieberman (1975)
identified with survival.

He assessed medical and nursing personnel in
terms of their support to him. He was sharply critical
of persons who avoided him when he was in isolation
because of an infectious disease and spoke highly of a
nurse who visited him without taking the precaution
of gowning.

He was able to fend off unwanted intrusions. After
talking apparently contentedly and at length, he re-

fused the morale scale. His eyes fairly glinted as he snapped, "The doctor says I shouldn't do interviews!"

At the same time, he related with glee how he and another resident had put down a third man who had boasted of his local connections. The other resident had asked the offender when he had come to the area. When he responded, "1940," the interrogator retorted that Mr. Brewster had come at birth.

Mr. Brewster became crustier as the pileup of medical crises and treatment failures became harder to bear. The director of nursing even quit weighing him because his weight loss was upsetting him. He entered the nursing unit a month before he died.

Mountainside residents with boarding home–based careers were older and remained longer than their Countryside counterparts. Their average age at death was 87 as opposed to 82 for the Countryside boarders and their average stay was 10 years, as compared to 3.4 years for Countryside. Sponsorship may account for the difference: Countryside boarders came in order to end their lives in medically endorsed surroundings; Mountainside boarders came to spend their late years in a less demanding setting.

A second career was *nursing home–based:* The residents who followed this pattern arrived as patients and remained patients, dying either in the home or during a brief terminal stay at the hospital. Of the four groups, this was the largest, constituting 41 percent of the whole.

The age differential between Mountainside and Countryside persisted but narrowed: Both patient groups lived longer than their boarding home–based fellow residents. The mean age at death of these Mountainside patients was 90.6 while that of their Countryside peers was 88. Their average stay at Mountainside was nearly 6 years (5.97) and at Countryside, 4.5, but in each case a few individuals remained a very long time.

Residents with nursing home–based careers fell into two groups: those who entered because they were ill and those whose confusion prevented their remaining safely at home. The boundary between the two groups blurred. Sometimes the physical iilness that brought patients to the home entailed brain damage, and with time and confinement, most of the merely mentally impaired also became frail and unsteady.

Ernest Magyar and John Wesley typified those who were ill. Dr. Magyar's morale score was low (9) at entry and, with some wavering, rose to medium (16 and 15) the two years before he died. John Wesley's scores began at 17, dipped following his wife's death, improved, and finally tapered down toward the end when even to talk was a burden. At a midway point, he commented that he felt he had overcome loneliness. He added, "I realize it is five years since Meg died."

If they were intrusive wanderers, the mentally confused were soon to be found in wheelchairs with "postural supports" that held them fast. With the footboards of the wheelchair raised, they could "walk" within a limited range. If this seemed undesirable, there were gerichairs, which were difficult for even an able-bodied person to move. These persons, who might otherwise have bathroomed themselves, appeared to become incontinent sooner, and wheelchair-bound patients also became unsteady, thus providing ex post facto justification for the use of the restraints.

> No wanderer but typical of the less-alert group of nursing unit patients, Kaethe Fried was already wheelchair bound, incontinent, and confused when she arrived. She had been in another home but Mountainside was closer to her daughter.
>
> She looked like a small Dresden figure, with her blue eyes, shining pink cheeks, and hair pulled up in a knot. In her girlhood in Hamburg, she had learned English from her father's business visitors, and when she arrived at Mountainside she still spoke it well but sometimes switched languages in midsentence. This led to difficulty with the nursing assistants who often did not know what she wanted. In time, she lost her English altogether but not her love of music. By that time, staff knew her preferences better and there were fewer conflicts.
>
> One young nurse who spoke German was very pro-

tective of her. When we were scoring Mrs. Fried on
norm conformity, we came to the item about bathing
routines. The nurse indicated that Mrs. Fried was
"ready, willing, and cooperative." In surprise I exclaimed, "But she hits and scratches!" "Oh, yes," said
the nurse, "but only because she's afraid and doesn't
understand." So much for the objectivity of raters.

Mrs. Fried fared well in the setting. There were other patients
who had more troubled careers, but even those received good physical care.

If the boarding home–based career was the wished-for outcome,
the expected one was the *symmetrical career*. In this, the individual entered the boarding unit and then, as the infirmities of age
increased, transferred to the nursing unit. People generally choose
facilities offering two levels of care in order to ensure this
continuity.

The 22 percent of the residents who experienced this progression
were the oldest and remained the longest. At Mountainside, their
average age at death was ninety-two and at Countryside, eighty-
nine. Of eighteen Mountainside residents in this group, only three
remained less than five years and several others approached twenty.
Two Countryside residents stayed more than ten years but the other
four died much sooner.

Their stays were symmetrical only in the sense that they spent
time in both units. Residents whose placements were precipitated
by early signs of cognitive decline tended to move through the
boarding unit more quickly than the others. The boarding units
were designed to support persons whose failing energies were no
longer up to the burden of keeping house and those who were
uneasy about living alone, not the cognitively impaired. Countryside was slower than Mountainside to transfer the mentally frail to
its nursing unit because its location and the compactness of its
boarding unit made surveillance relatively easy. Both homes had
waiting lists for their nursing units and this was a disincentive to
fill them with those already resident.

Helen Revere's career at Mountainside illustrated the foreshort-
ened boarding unit stay of the mentally impaired. She had a pleas-

ant social facade and, with her well-proportioned figure, erect carriage, and handsome white hair, she looked like the older woman in a fashion magazine.

> She managed fairly well for about a year after her husband's death, but when her housekeeping began to slip, her older daughter encouraged her to enter Mountainside's boarding unit. She remained there for fourteen months, sustained by her inoffensive manner and her daughter's prompt response to any crisis.
>
> The crises arose when she thought her things were being stolen. (Often the "missing" article was in full view.) Her nocturnal restlessness and her belief that there were men in her room had caused difficulty even before the precipitating event occurred: a fainting episode accompanied by increased confusion. She was transferred to the nursing unit shortly before her eighty-second birthday and remained there seven years.
>
> At eighty-two, she was soft spoken and courteous even when she appeared guarded and anxious or angry as she often was at that time. She had periods of agitation succeeded by drowsy withdrawal when exhausted staff members increased her medication. As she paced in her wheelchair, narrowly missing feet and brushing the nurses' station, a young nursing assistant sighed, "We'll just have to medicate her down to a vegetable!" The medication level dropped, however, with the arrival of a new director of nursing who had reservations about the use of medication for behavioral control.
>
> Mrs. Revere was quite aware of her effect on the nurses. Once when I retrieved her from the nurses' station, urging her not to "bug" them, she announced with resolution that they would "just have to stand it."
>
> Another day the nurses and aides were talking, oblivious to her pacing presence. She slipped out of the

restraining soft ties, and the next time she passed them, she was pushing the wheelchair, which was festooned with a big gauze bow, and smiling playfully at their startled expressions.

At other times, her anger was unmistakable. Once as we passed a glass door, she remarked that she could kick it through, quite plainly meaning that she would like to. She was very responsive to respectful attention, however, and whenever possible, the social work student or I walked her, trying to use up some of her fearful energy. After the arrival of the new director of nursing, I often found her in the wheelchair but without the soft ties.

When she was eighty-four, she scored 10 on the morale scale, just above "low" for that setting. She responded to "If you could live where you wanted, where would you live?" with "I'd live right in a nice little one-shack house." She answered most of the items fairly directly, but when I asked her to name "five people who live here and five people who work here," she became indirect and tangential. She named no one. On the mental status questionnaire, she missed nine of the ten items, which suggested a high level of organicity.

Four years later, she looked leaner and had become skillful at weaving the wheelchair in and out without hitting anyone. My notes read, "She used to crease the nurses' station; now she threads her way adroitly—perhaps less angry rather than a better driver." My first effort to test her failed, but when I caught her on a "good" day, we ploughed through the morale scale. She tended to lapse into word salad occasionally, but on the whole her answers "fit." Her morale score had crept up a few points (13). She was quite clear about where she would live: "Not here." Some of our problems in dealing with the test appeared to come not from a lack of comprehension but from expressive difficulties. She responded to "How much do you feel lonely, not much or a lot?" with "No, I haven't loved anybody," then, after a pause, "Restless." She became better focused as we progressed.

She often sang softly to herself, but when people tried to engage her, she responded with nonsense speech, a mixture of clear words and neologisms. She seemed good tempered, but she no longer related to others as much as she had in the past.

At this time, her elder daughter and son-in-law were visting her weekly but no longer taking her home. Her younger daughter, reported to have been closer to her, had withdrawn when she entered the home and did not visit.

Three months before her death, I was unable to test her. A nurse commented, "Utterly undemanding. The others avoid her." She died at eighty-nine following a cerebral thrombosis.

Mrs. Revere's striking feature was the durability of her core personality. Even in her situation as a tied person who could be "medicated down," she kept a certain dignity; even when she was angry and mistrustful, a basic courtesy remained; even when she was thoroughly demented, she retained an element of playfulness. At the same time, she illustrates the futility of overplacement: Her stay in the boarding unit was relatively short and troubled. Helen Revere's whole course was a slow but steady slide.

John McGreevy presents a different pattern. His cognitive functioning, borne down with the strain of trying to keep up, responded to relief from pressure when he went to the nursing unit.

The most interesting of these residents were those who first entered the nursing units and then managed to move back and forth. One of these was Robert Farmer.

When Robert Farmer was eighty-four and had been organizer of bridge games and Scrabble in the Mountainside boarding unit for more than a year, he had a morale score in the middle range (14) and a relatively high resource score. All of this ended abruptly three years later when he awakened one morning, uncoordinated and unable to put on his socks. He returned to the nursing unit.

Life was never as good again. When he was tested at eighty-eight, he was gaunt and physically feeble. Asked if he missed his farm, he replied, almost in a whisper, "I miss everything." His morale score was again 14 but the comments that accompanied his replies belied it. To the item "My health is about the same, better, or worse than that of most persons my age," he replied, "About the same," but added, "I'm going downhill fast." At another point, he said, "I don't like that kind of question—it exposes my weakness," and he described himself as "a wreck of a man." His resource score plummeted to 22, and the following year, when he was eighty-nine, his morale score dropped to 10, the beginning of "low." His replies came slowly. On one question, "If you could live where you wanted, where would you live?" he simply froze. When he came to the item "I see enough of my friends and relatives," he laughed abruptly and without mirth. Nevertheless, it was Father's Day and a few hours later his son came to take him out. I wrote in my notes, "I think he is depressed rather than confused."

He was a smiling, dignified figure the following year when grandchildren, sons, and a sister gathered to celebrate his ninetieth birthday. At ninety-one, he was still scoring 10 on the morale scale but his comments were even gloomier. He described his health as "worse" than that of other persons his age and when he came to "I am as happy now as when I was younger," he replied, "I don't know how to answer that." There were long silences.

Stimulation was provided by an ill-matched roommate who liked Masterpiece Theater and the symphony while Robert Farmer preferred baseball. Since both were mildly hard of hearing, the decibels on their warring TVs rose.

Throughout his stay in the nursing unit, he had had one faithful friend, his old bridge partner from the boarding unit. She came to his room each evening and kissed him good night. By the time he was eighty-nine, however, both were in the nursing unit, and when he was ninety-one, both were terribly frail. She had a broken hip. When I once pushed their two wheelchairs so they could face each other, there were small glances of greeting and she smiled. Three days later, she died.

The next summer, at an in-service training, nurses and aides expressed the opinion that he was aware but was depressed and had given up since his friend's death. I could not break through to test him that year, but he did smile after worship service when I told him how nice he looked in his suit. Six weeks later he died, just after his ninety-second birthday.

Like Robert Farmer, Dr. Carol Wolfe was able to exchange patienthood for the more acceptable status of boarder. If she had died the day she moved to the boarding unit, her career would have been considered a happy one. As it is, she illustrates the uses and limitations of past status and current resources, the overriding role of physical illness, the importance of viewing the completed career before making judgments, and the uncertainty that lingers even then.

Until her Parkinson's disease intervened, Dr. Wolfe had been the anesthesiologist at the hospital on whose staff most of Countryside's physician-owners served. The retirement of her housekeeper and a subsequent fall forced her to enter the home at sixty-six.

The role transition from physician to patient was painful. Accustomed to nurses who obeyed her commands, she was now dependent on nursing assistants who resented her demands. Her roommate was Greta

Hansen, who mistook her underwear for her own. The most acceptable companion she could find was Mrs. Flowers, sixteen years her senior and in an advanced stage of the same chronic disease. Two weeks after she came to Countryside her morale score was 5.

A number of events soon made her life more tolerable. One of her daughters left her husband and returned to the area, bringing her little girls. A retired physician began coming to read to her, included Mrs. Flowers, and gradually expanded "Dr. Wolfe's Reading Group." Soon she had gathered a small coterie of the more alert, who became members only on her invitation. She was in a drug study that required her to be transported at regular intervals to a large teaching hospital, where her role as a physician was gratifyingly reaffirmed. Unlike most of the other patients, she had money under her own control and she deployed it to secure small outings away from the home. Two months after admission, her morale score had risen to 11, and it remained there when the test was repeated nine months later.

At Countryside, a primary requirement for becoming a boarder was being able to climb the stairs. With practice, she passed the "stair test" and escaped to the relative privacy of the boarding unit. Life improved. Sixteen months after her admission, she was in good spirits, living in the boarding unit, and making her own arrangements to go to the hospital for cataract surgery.

Then a number of things went awry. There were shifting accounts of what happened. Reportedly liquor mixed poorly with her medication and she returned from an evening out and was ill. She was transferred to the nursing unit for greater supervision. Then "something physical happened"—she had a sudden onset of confusion. She became restless and upset and aware that she was forgetting things. She was dispatched to a private psychiatric clinic and died

there eighteen days later, a month before her sixty-
ninth birthday.

Dr. Wolfe's status as a physician made it easier for her to negotiate her way to the boarding unit, but it maladapted her for a
residential career. Physician-to-nurse patterns of communication
may take the form of terse orders in the operating room, but they
are dysfunctional in the nursing home when the physician becomes
a patient. The director of nursing, Winnie Mason, explained the
difference once when she overheard Dr. Wolfe telling a nurse to
bring her a glass of fruit juice: "You don't tell a nurse. You ask an
aide." Her attempts to keep her self-image constant were not effective in that setting.

Before Dr. Wolfe died, many of her hopes had been snuffed out:
Her daughters wearied of her demands, as the staff did, and set
limits, nothing miraculous and lasting came to her from the drug
trials, and she could not really come and go because she could not
drive a car. In the end, she saw Mrs. Flowers, who suffered the same
illness, become helpless, drooling and no doubt relieved to escape
life on her eighty-fifth birthday. Spence (1986, p. 114) has commented that for an acceptable life, people must be able to shift to
new targets when their expectations are thwarted. For Dr. Wolfe,
there were few targets left. The point of agreement in all accounts
was, "Something physical happened."

In the last years of her life as in her death, Dr. Wolfe's status was
anomalous. The same uncertainty surrounds her categorization in
this study. Does she belong among the residents who had symmetrical careers—she died within three weeks of her psychiatric hospitalization—or does she belong in the fourth category, among the
exiles? There is no evidence that Countryside intended to take her
back and neither is there evidence that she had a voice in her
transfer.

The fourth career was the nursing home–based career with
transfer, and the *exiles* were those residents who left the home and
died elsewhere. These fell into two groups: seventeen who outlived
their funds and were forced to find a facility that would accept
payment by Medicaid and thirteen who left for other reasons. Together they constituted 26 percent of the residents. The mean death

age of the twenty-seven whose death dates are known was eighty-eight.

Because more than half of the Medicaid movers died within six months of transfer, it is tempting to suggest that their deaths were hastened by the forced move. With the exception of one seventy-three-year old, however, all of the Medicaid movers were in their eighties and nineties. There is no statistical support for the belief that they died significantly sooner than the other movers or than their peers who remained at the homes. There is a substantial literature on the subject of transplantation shock, but this sample is too small to contribute to it (Borup, 1982; Coffman, 1981; Horowitz and Schulz, 1983; Kowalski, 1981; Pablo, 1977).

Most of the Medicaid movers were transported by grim-faced and unhappy relatives. When kinship was more distant, the task may have been easier. Mrs. Gladwin was moved by her niece and Mr. Beasley by his nephew. One man chose between his mother and his aunt, who were twin sisters. Two months after he moved the aunt, his mother, ninety-one, died at Countryside, while the aunt lived six years longer.

Families may have been more willing to let their members make the Medicaid move if they seemed unaware of their surroundings. Only five of the seventeen Medicaid movers could have been described as even "relatively alert." In this they differed from the other movers: Only four of the thirteen who moved for other reasons were confused. The dichotomy between Medicaid movers and other movers suggests that the latter were more purposeful, but this was not always true: They were a mixed group.

Two Countryside residents went to church homes of their choice, where each lived to an extraordinary old age: Miss Northern, at once so passive and so demanding of her pastor, died at ninety-nine, and Elfreda Dormeier died a month after her one-hundred-second birthday. For Mrs. Dormeier, going to her church home meant returning to her old community, where former neighbors visited and there were residents she knew. From Countryside's nursing unit, she went directly to the church facility's boarding unit, where she remained a boarder for three of the next eleven years.

Two boarders truly "returned to the community." Grace Rogers gave Countryside the "try" her physician recommended and afterward went home. She came back seven years later, gravely ill, and died within eleven days. The other was Mamie Stover, who joined her daughter, to her joy and the relief of all.

Indignant at being transferred to Mountainside's nursing unit, Myrtle Weatherford moved to another facility and became a patient there. Another boarder, confused and in need of supervision, went to a larger facility with an intermediate care unit. When she left, a lifetime of family photos was discarded, as well as the paper napkins, bits of thread, and scraps of paper that crowded her drawers. She died five months later. For her and for others, personal intent was less evident. Two went to acute care hospitals and were discharged to other nursing homes, and Dr. Wolfe died in the psychiatric facility. In short, some moves were happy; more were not.

The Preservation of Identity

Leo Tolstoy's dying Ivan Ilych remembers that he was once "little Vanya with a mama and a papa" (1981, p. 93). It is this continuity, but more—an acceptable adult identity—that the individual is trying to cling to through a rapidly changing existence, partly pragmatically for the preservation of place, but more deeply as a bulwark against chaos. Without a continuous self, there is no stable point from which to assess and respond to a world in flux. A stable self is the starting point for all other relationships and meanings.

When Kaufman (1986) interviewed sixty alert, middle-class, urban elderly individuals, she found them engaged in a process of continuous reconstruction. They reworked old themes and integrated current circumstances to support a viable and "ageless self" that would enable them to cope with change. Their sense of identity was broader than the sum of their social roles: There was an inner self that had been there through it all.

In a second study, she speaks of stroke patients' search for "anchors of predictability" and their efforts to integrate the disruptions in body image in order to achieve a continuous sense of self (Kaufman, 1987).

Most of Kaufman's urban elderly were still living independently in the community, but the stroke patients in her second study had been "medicalized," which made them vulnerable to redefinition by others. The residents of Countryside and Mountainside, especially the patients, shared this vulnerability in different degrees. The patients were under continuous staff surveillance and dependent on those watchful others for intimate day-to-day care. The normal processes of identity negotiation were tipped in staff's favor, and the patients were under pressure to accept staff's definitions of who they were.

Swann (1987) describes how persistently individuals train those around them to give them self-confirmatory feedback—how sedulously they seek interaction partners who do and avoid those who do not. Swann and his associates studied other populations, presumably none of them chosen for their advanced age or institutionalized status.

In semiclosed worlds, however, like the nursing units, individuals with limited mobility find avoidance difficult. They find it hard also to retrain their more powerful others. Their stigmatized status deprives them of the almost automatic reaffirmation that helps people outside maintain a sense of sameness. It would seem that they have three alternatives, each with its costs: They can negotiate a modified self more compatible with the expectations of the environment, they can cling to a secret self in the face of daily disconfirmation, or they can escape into psychosis. Nevertheless, Lieberman and Tobin (1983), using institutionalized populations, affirm—as Swann (1987) and Kaufman (1986) do—the extraordinary power of people to sustain a steady self. The issue becomes how they do it.

Lieberman and Tobin provide test results that show that their institutionalized subjects differed from their community controls in depending more upon the past for self-validation. The institutionalized had a shifting cast of interactive others, whereas the elderly respondents living in the community had familiar friends, neighbors, and helpers who were cultivated for their confirmatory views or at least might be brought to hold them.

Mountainside and Countryside patients and boarders had continuing contact with outside others, but those outside others were freer than they were to withdraw and thus were in a more powerful position in their social exchanges. All the residents were living closely with others but patients, because of their need for personal care and their limited mobility, were at greater risk of having their identity maintenance processes overwhelmed by others. Those losing their capacity for recall could not even turn to the past for validation unless they told themselves stories, and they could then be accused of lying, which added one more humiliation to their lot. Under the circumstances, what is remarkable is the persistence of personal style.

As long as the predictable patterns distinctive to the individual are accompanied by recognizable affect, the personal style is more than a complex of deeply grooved responses similar to the wiggle of a worm. When persons who were very impaired responded to items in the morale scale with words that were their own and with affect that was culturally validated, they were in some measure self-reflective and therefore fully human. When their responses were in keeping with long-held values or ways of thinking, they were manifesting the persistence of a personal style. An age that glorifies fetuses as "little people" is curiously quick to dismiss the impaired elderly as "vegetables" or "crockery." A patient can be unaware of who he or she is but still be conscious of feelings.

> Rebecca English, who presented as an incontinent crying baby tied in a chair, nevertheless responded to the morale scale item "I have a lot to be sad about" by replying, "My father and mother are gone and I have only my sister and my sister's daughter. That's all I have." She reacted also with consideration for her roommate, stopping the noise she was making when I pointed out that she might awaken her. She scored seven errors on the mental status test, indicating organicity. Although she produced her birthdate, she could not calculate her age.

The best way to observe this persistence of self is to follow a known individual's descent into confusion. At some point, of course, a person is not fully alive but rather caught up in a process of dying that may last minutes or months. The foregoing does not suggest that becoming demented is either an inevitable or a regular feature of normal aging; nevertheless, it does sometimes occur. One of the advantages of a longitudinal study like this is that researchers could observe some persons who moved from clarity to confusion over a period of time.

The remainder of this chapter is divided into two sections. The first deals with residents' preferred identities and the second looks at the persisting core and the loss of self as the individual moves into dementia.

A Hierarchy of Identities

Charmaz (1987) has drawn up a hierarchy of preferred identities based on her interviews with fifty-seven persons with chronic diseases, who rejected identities founded on invalidism and tried to keep a valued self. Most of her subjects were between forty and sixty, so some of her categories were less accessible to the elderly residents of Mountainside and Countryside.

The Supernormal Identity. These disabled individuals judge themselves by the standards of the conventional world and feel they must work harder and perform tasks better in order to succeed. For residents at the two homes, the "conventional world" was that of older retirees living in the community, a less competitive environment than the "normal world" of the still employed that challenged Charmaz's younger chronically ill. There were few opportunities for a normal competitive life at Countryside, but a handful of Mountainside boarders drove cars, took courses, participated in peace and civil rights demonstrations, and played continuing roles in their churches.

Agnes Chase followed this active course for a number of years, but John Penfield discovered its limitations. He had exercised leadership in the wider affairs of the sponsoring sect, so when he came to Mountainside, it seemed only natural that he should serve on the local group's committees. A new generation was running things, however. He remarked wryly, "They listen to you and then disregard what you say." Also, since most of the younger members worked in the daytime, the meetings were held at night, and eventually the requirement for night driving terminated his participation.

For most of the boarders, the main concern in preserving their identity was not to be identified with the patients.

The Restored Self. These individuals hope to become again the persons they were before the illness. Three Countryside residents rejected the statuses their physicians had assigned them and returned to community living, although perhaps, in slightly modified arrangements. For most, this hope was not realistic, not only because of health or mental status but also because previous living arrangements had been folded up behind them rather quickly by persons who assumed they would not be needing them, and thus they had no place to return to.

> Although Jim Gaines, the forty-seven-year old, knew that spinal cord injuries did not heal, the restored self he dreamed of becoming was that of a marvelously athletic paraplegic sending his wheelchair up the well-concealed ramp to his home, operating his motorboat, and driving his car with hand controls. When he was feeling well, he practiced with iron dumbbells to develop the upper-arm strength he would need. When he was forced to spend weeks lying on his stomach waiting for his grafts to heal, however, the vision wore thin. When he left, hope was flickering again, and he went to a rehabilitation hospital for another go at breaking out.

Because all the pathologies of the elderly are blamed on old age and old age itself is viewed as a terminal disease, it is almost as hard for the patient as for the staff to imagine a return to a higher level of functioning. Minimal efforts were made to maintain or improve function. Countryside nurses agreed there was one exception, Mrs. Bennett, who rehabilitated herself.

> When Clarissa Bennett entered Countryside at eighty-two, she was ready to die and fended off staff efforts to help her. "I lived alone too long," she said afterward, adding that it had gotten worse every year.

At some point, she changed her mind. She got herself out of bed and set about recovering her mobility. She had no wish to return to the community; "I am more independent here," she said. But she took control of her life and made for herself the measured existence she desired. She associated with a few residents as alert as herself, enjoyed an occasional hand of bridge, looked forward to her two favored visitors, and depended as little as possible on staff. Although she relied on her wheelchair, she practiced walking daily.

A Contingent Personal Identity. These individuals settle for a less valued self because of the intrusiveness of the illness, but they have guarded hopes for something better.

Charmaz points out that the individual can distance the confronting physician but it is harder to deal with an intimate who rips down the web of hope. The patients were confronted by "realists" every day.

In her excited flurry of activity when her daughter was returning with her little girls, Dr. Carole Wolfe saw for herself the prospect of a life "outside." In her dream she would babysit the little granddaughters, stay overnight sometimes, and perhaps even find a place for herself in her daughter's household. This hope was squashed when her daughters "set limits." She experienced a final disconfirmation—she invited her cousins to visit, only to be told by her elder daughter that she was "too old to make plans like that." The cousins came but spent their time with the younger women.

The Salvaged Self. This is a valued affirmation of self-functioning within undeniable limitations.

Dr. Ernest Magyar said with great serenity, "My wife loves me." This was validation by another. Many patients expressed thankfulness that they still had their minds. A few found useful roles even within the nursing units, most notably Marcy Mae White, who played the piano and led the wheelchair exercises. At Countryside, an old Viennese sat by the door and watched for wanderers as a service to the nurses. In the Mountainside boarding unit, there were many resident leadership roles—table hostess, flower arranger, maker of announcements, reader—and some contesting over them. But some boarders and most patients had no such options. Charmaz says that sometimes just being taken seriously is a continual struggle. This is the dilemma of the patient and to some degree even of the boarder. For example, when Henry Hobart's first love at Mountainside died, her family invited him to sit with them at the funeral. He was deeply touched at this acknowledgment of the relationship, but, he remarked sadly, "Our children did not want us to marry."

The Lasting Essence

It was Dr. Carole Wolfe who observed that some were at Countryside because their minds had gone and some because their bodies had gone—and those who were confused seemed to suffer least. Nevertheless, no alert resident ever expressed a desire for this end.

When life has gone on too long, many of the very old say they would like to die. Ramona Everly's "good Presbyterian God" had taken away the music that she loved, the eyesight needed for reading, and finally, the energy required to complete the simplest act of living, and still He would not let her go. Hers was the lament of Job. At ninety-seven she composed her ending for Henley's "Invictus."

> But, oh, I wish the road might end,
> The gate might open wide,
> My weary heart to read the chart
> That says, "Welcome! Come inside."
>   (personal communication, 1985)

Many would have applauded the sentiment but although they wished to die, they were not ready to give up their wits. Most felt dying with their minds intact would be a triumph over time—and many achieved it. The loss of the mind seemed to mean a final degradation that would somehow spread and spoil the self they had created through so much of a lifetime. What they had achieved would be contaminated by what they had become.

They failed to see in the demented how much of the essential self remained when the part that remembered, planned, and calculated was taken away. Much of what is perceived as personality change is merely the behavior of an individual operating with different data and a shrunken repertoire.

If residents were impaired when they entered, there could be only speculation about what they might have been like in the past. At both homes, however, there were those whose long tenure provided first-hand histories of the aging self. Two illustrate the persistence of a personal style. One was a Mountainside resident who was much in command at the beginning; the other was a Countryside patient who, although depressed and delusional on arrival, trailed an adventurous past.

> Sarah Coleman demonstrated remarkable consistency despite the confusion, the mental impoverishment, and the visual impairment that engulfed her near the end of her life.
>
> At ninety-one, she was a table hostess, troubled only by the unsteadiness that had led to a series of falls. She had many friends, had only recently stopped gardening at the home, and attended Sunday services and a prayer meeting at her church in the community. She no longer went out at night.
>
> Many years before, she and her husband, a YMCA secretary, had befriended an Iraqi student. They had no children and she often spoke of Ali as her "adopted son." He had given her much pleasure the year before by motoring a substantial distance to surprise her on her ninetieth birthday.
>
> She commented that her income was adequate to her needs "unless I get sick and am in the nursing home several years." She wanted to die before her health, her wits, and her money ran out.
>
> When she was ninety-two, her morale score was in the middle range (16), though she declared that death

was thinning the ranks of her friends. At ninety-three, she had less energy but continued as a part-time table hostess. She continued to be well informed and, at this time, she voiced her concern about the rising prices that were eroding the incomes of old people like herself.

A series of falls brought her to the nursing unit at ninety-four and when she was retested at 96, her morale score had dropped to 12. She related a small disagreement with a staff member and commented that she had to be aggressive in defense of her interests and her rights. Her social facade was intact but her recall had slowed. She skillfully changed the subject when she could not retrieve a name. At ninety-seven, she ruefully declared, "My mind's not as good—I'm slipping," and later, "It's a lonely age."

At ninety-eight, she conceded irritability: "I get angry. If I didn't, I wouldn't have much zest for living." She was less alert and was having visual misperceptions due to failing eyesight, which gave rise to staff suspicions that she was delusional.

At ninety-nine, her morale score, which had risen in the interim, dropped to 11. She seemed confused and mistrustful. My notes allude to "half-formulated concerns relating to helplessness and death or being sent away associated with poverty," and later I noted she was "more delusional when upset."

A boarder, who had known her many years, expressed the opinion that she was unaware of the death two days earlier of a long-time neighbor from the boarding unit, but she did know. She reminisced about the woman and spoke of the days when they had watched television together on her friend's large screen.

That same day, a patient fell and there was a great flurry as the rescue squad arrived to take her to the hospital. Sarah Coleman watched with agitation, expressing the fear that they would take the woman away as they had "poor Mae." ("Poor Mae" was the long-time neighbor in the home who had died.) I stayed close to her and assured her they would bring the woman back after X-rays at the hospital. She quieted then, but afterward she wanted to be taken to her table to wait there alone.

When I returned the following June, she seemed to be experiencing physical discomfort, and at night, she sometimes cried out. (John Wesley, always alert to sounds, said he had thought he heard a baby crying.) This final time she was too incoherent to test, but two statements were very clear. First, she said, "I wish this would not go on so long," and again, her brow clouding, "What will happen to you? You don't know anyone here." She seemed very troubled as she said it. When I assured her I would be all right, her brow cleared.

She died that August, two weeks before her hundredth birthday.

Sarah Coleman did not outlive her money but she did survive her health and her wits. Several things were striking: She was aware of her memory failure, and at ninety-eight, she showed awareness of the mobilizing role of her own anger.

Most of what staff members perceived as her "crazy" talking occurred during periods of high anxiety. For example, when I took a centenarian for a wheelchair walk in the garden, she was much concerned and expressed the view that it was too cold and windy. The administrator called me in to hear how "crazy" she sounded because she did not believe I understood how confused she was, but what was not observed was how quickly the anxious flood of words stopped when she saw the woman return. The same phenomenon occurred whenever she was exposed to too many stimuli, as when the woman fell, the nurses ran to her side, there was much phoning, and the rescue squad rushed in.

She displayed a steady concern about not having enough money, which might necessitate her having to leave the home. She perceived staff efforts to reassure her as merely placating. Once, when she had mentioned these fears several times, I reminded her that she was a client of the Santa Claus Society and would always be taken care of. At this point, she told me that her begonia, which she had previously described as a gift from a friend, was from her caseworker from that organization.

Long after she was assumed to be totally confused, she grasped the responses of the people around her. Her conversation, for example, made it quite clear that she understood that the staff thought she needed new dresses but that she was reluctant to spend the money. She continued to be attentive to the needs of others, which gave rise to worries when she did not fully know what was happening to them. Considerateness was, in fact, a quality Sarah Coleman not only practiced but appreciated in others. Of her husband's grandmother, she reported that the woman, dying in winter, expressed regret that the men would have to dig a grave in such weather.

The director of nursing, who liked her, was especially acute at picking up her concerns and also the awareness that still remained. She knew, for example, that the care of her hair was important to her and often tended it herself, thus acknowledging a cherished attribute of self.

The Commander presented a quite different picture. As an old explorer, he had a well-established public identity but at Countryside his greatest resource was his physician brother.

> The Commander had been on the waiting list for an apartment in a western state, but by the time he came to claim it, pathological age changes had taken place and he was turned down. He responded explosively. His friend on the spot, an old surgeon who had accompanied him on expeditions, called his brother, who told him to tranquilize him and put him on a plane. This provided the base for much that followed.
>
> His brother placed him in a boarding facility, where he lay on the floor, explaining to the staff that the oxygen level was better there. (He had been an aviator since before World War One and was reluctant to give up flying. His brother told him that with his

pacemaker he might not get sufficient oxygen at the higher altitudes.) This explained his preoccupation with oxygen but not to the satisfaction of the administrator of that boarding home, who demanded the Commander's removal.

Countryside was more tolerant. A large oxygen tank stood by his bed, a concession to his delusional system. A week after his arrival, he had a morale score of 13, but the testing had been difficult because he was preoccupied with a scheme to become a "pinch-hitter" pilot. He thought older flyers—he was then eighty-three—might be employed as stand-bys.

To the morale scale item: "How much do you feel lonely—not much or a lot?" the Commander replied, "I feel lonely when I'm not flying."

To the morale scale item "I sometimes feel life is not worth living," the Commander said, "Yeah, if you can't trust people. . . . When your friends lie to you, then it's tough. When somebody tells you, 'That's nothing' . . . and you know it is."

It took more than two and a half hours and two tries to complete the twenty-one-item test. He missed nine of the ten items on the mental status test. The one item he got right was his birthday: He struggled with it but when the wording was modified to "When should they bake the cake?" he came up with the correct answer. For the most part, however, he was preoccupied with vibrating propellers, submarines, and air pressure.

He refused to eat. When Countryside had its Labor Day picnic, he sat looking morose, so I took a plate and, with the nurses' permission, began to feed him. He accepted the food but forgot to swallow unless reminded.

A few weeks later, I found him cheerfully nursing a can of beer. He seemed more alert. A chubby aide came in puffing with signs of exhaustion—his brother had ordered more exercise and she had been assigned to accompany him on his jog. He had been an athlete and even at eighty-three, with a pacemaker, he suffered under close confinement. As his physician, his brother ordered the staff to turn him loose on the grounds, and, as next-of-kin, he assumed responsibility for the risk. He eliminated most medication. The turnaround was striking.

When we repeated the morale test he had taken just four months before, themes of flying and perfidious friends occurred but, on the whole, he sounded better. He described his recent depression in terms of having been "doped" and explained that he was weak because of his mental state. "I didn't want to live," he said. His morale score (12) had not risen but the change in affect was marked.

Given more freedom, he settled down. The home no longer assigned an aide to accompany him as he stalked the grounds. Basically he had a sunny disposition and—unless pushed—was inclined to please.

A few weeks later, there was a tremendous storm and he was in his element. The maintenance man had "tried to lash the awning with a string. . . . He couldn't spit in the wind. . . . He'd never been around the Horn." He had wanted to go out to show them how to secure the awnings and was distressed when staff members would not let him out in the gale.

The following year, he was transferred to the boarding unit at the urging of his brother and with the misgivings of the staff. With the private room, however, he did much better. He ate alone: He liked the society of men but not the company of women unless they were young and pretty.

A year and a half later, he was returned to the nursing unit after a trip to the hospital, but this time they put him in a small private room and the transfer was acceptable. He was having more physical problems but still taking long walks.

Retested at eighty-six, he had a slightly higher morale score (16). He was more alert now and a new theme ran through his remarks—resignation to the inevitable restrictions of age. He expressed satisfaction with his present residence as the best he could get if not a millionaire and not young, but he would have liked to go back to the bleak, dangerous land that had been the scene of his explorations.

In response to the morale test item "Life is hard for me most of the time," the Commander said, "Life is easy. I can't do what I want to do. According to my age, I'm doing all right."

From time to time, his stoicism faltered. To the morale test item "Things get worse as I get older," the Commander replied, "They can't get any worse than they are—they're about the best they can get at my age. I wouldn't be here if I was younger."

He blocked on the dark questions, calling them "dumb questions" or saying he could not answer them.

In the years that followed, his cancer was responsive to neither surgery nor radiation but he remained active.

He was a favorite with the staff even though inservice trainings had a way of winding up with the current problems of managing the Commander. As he presented more physical dysfunction, the nurses were required to intervene more often and if he experienced their intervention as intrusive or restrictive, he balked. Then they would send for his brother to resolve the impasse—they came to dread his brother's vacations. The nurses reported that he respected physicians, but when I asked about nurses, they replied that the only nurse he respected was Florence Nightingale.

While everyone else worried about his prostatic cancer, he was concerned about his failing eyesight. By ninety, he was displaying more anxiety about many things. To the morale test item "I am afraid of a lot of things," the Commander replied, "I don't trust anybody, not even you." When the interviewer asked, "What are you afraid of?" the Commander responded, "Anything that might happen."

His morale scores were dropping again. He worried more about his health, his hearing was poorer, and there were increasing signs of mental impoverishment.

At ninety-one, his lowering energy level was making him easier for staff to manage. The recreational therapist noted that he had become "more reasonable." This trend continued as at ninety-two he was quieter and there was a more fatalistic note. His underlying stoicism came through in responses to test items. For example, to the morale test item "I am afraid of a lot of things," the Commander replied, "I try not to be. It doesn't do any good."

Asked if he was happy, he said, "As happy as I hope to be," but underneath, there was a strain of contentment, which showed in his answers to the morale test item "Life is hard for me most of the time." The Commander said, "As long as I have a place to eat and sleep and the food is good, I enjoy it."

He was quite clear in stating that Countryside was his home. He no longer referred to the distant land he had once explored or to flying, his wistful and wishful themes in the past. He seemed to have come to a harbor of compromised desires.

The next year, he was very frail and ill. His brother thought he did not know him but I thought he knew the director of nursing, for when she spoke to him and touched his arm, he smiled. Six weeks later, two days after his ninety-third birthday, he died. In the end, he just slept his life away.

The same qualities that led the Commander to spend years of his life on a frozen frontier in the company of other adventurous men made him difficult for nursing personnel to cope with, but these qualities also enabled him to adapt. His physical reserves fended off dying but made him restless with confinement. If not fenced in, however, he was willing to go along.

Military life had accustomed him to lines of authority that were hierarchical: When he did not like what a floor nurse or nursing assistant was proposing, he did not argue with her but went to the director of nursing. When most other names eluded him, he remained quite clear about the name of the administrator.

He had an ingrained norm against complaining: He tried not to protest against the inevitable, even when it hurt. At the same time, he was outraged at the untrustworthiness of his surgeon friend, whom he believed (correctly) had "doped" him. He was strongly committed to mateship, the comraderie of men: Your friends were supposed to be loyal.

How well he would have fared without his physician brother is another question. In the balance between personal competence and environmental press and resources, the performance of the vulnerable individual depends greatly on the setting's support and lowered demands (Lawton, 1989; Lawton and Nahemow, 1973). Countryside was remarkably flexible in its dealings with the old warrior: Other homes might have medicated him or sent him to a psychiatric facility before anyone had time to discover that he was more docile with a lighter rein. His brother and the nurses pushed and nudged him into a safe and quiet port like so many tugs. They let him live and die with his personal identity intact.

Part Three

ADAPTATIONS TO A CHANGING CLIMATE:
WHERE WE ARE NOW
AND WHAT WE CAN DO

When I went to Countryside for the very last time, the old explorer lay dying. The Commander was very quiet now, with only the smallest flicker of a smile when the director of nursing took his hand. He had had the curious gentleness of the old athlete, but he had been a handful for the nurses. In the past, in-service trainings at Countryside had often centered around how to cope with his fierce will. Today, new currents were flowing and the topic for the training session was burnout. The reason soon became clear.

In many respects, Countryside had never looked better. A little earlier a bright young activities director had been conducting pet therapy. She placed a small dog in the arms of a woman long withdrawn into some gray hinterland of private depression. The woman smiled with pleasure now as she stroked the puppy. This was the home where once the director of nursing had said that all the very old wanted was to be kept clean and comfortable and well fed. The new director of nursing had gone beyond that. Staffing seemed active and good. As I walked through the halls, one thing struck me: The proportion of bedridden and demented patients had grown.

At the in-service training session, I looked at the circle of faces. Why were they so depressed when plainly they were doing better? To cut the gloom, I began with a question: "If you could have any kind of patient you wanted, what would be your ideal patient?"

There was a moment's silence. Then an earnest young nursing assistant replied, "A hundred Commanders!" He wasn't dead yet, but already they were missing the feisty old explorer. He had given them trouble but he had interacted with them as few of those well-tended bodies could.

During the decade, the two homes had changed greatly and so had the population mix, the regulatory demands, and the economic climate. Chapter Nine describes these three factors, which affect all homes for the aging today, and tells how Mountainside and Countryside responded to them. These homes, so different in the beginning, became more alike as they adapted to the same conditions.

Chapter Ten examines the institutional forces that challenge elderly residents as they try to maintain acceptable selves in these settings today and the barriers that make it so difficult for homes to change. The chapter then turns to the three areas where incremental change should begin—the management of incontinence, dementia, and staffing. The failure of homes in these areas is devastating to all the residents, including those who are neither incontinent nor demented but are distressed by what they see. The chapter concludes by asking whether the current fervor for reform is not proposing to solve yesterday's problems tomorrow.

For the incurably practical, Chapter Eleven looks at what individuals can do while waiting out the glacial process of major change. The structural factors, studied earlier for their transformation of Countryside and Mountainside, are reexamined now for their effect on those most deeply concerned with making things better. Those in the system—administrators, families, physicians, nurses, social workers, and other staff members—are paralyzed by belief in their own impotence (Wiener and Kayser-Jones, 1990), but each has the resources to act right now.

CHAPTER NINE

The Spiral of Change:
Political and Demographic

Countryside and Mountainside illustrate well the early development of proprietary and sectarian homes. Mountainside was intended to serve aging members of its sponsoring sect while
Countryside's founders hoped to combine the provision of service
with making a profit. Their buildings reflected their evolution. The
large Victorian mansion where Mountainside's boarders lived over-
shadowed its small modern nursing unit. Countryside's use of a
dozen upstairs rooms for its boarders indicated the boarding unit's
status as a postscript to its nursing section. The fire code no longer
permitted their use for patients.

During the study period, the two homes faced the same three
challenges: the rising age of their residents, the proliferation of regulations, and the increased cost of doing business. As Robert Kane
(1985) noted, private not-for-profit homes and for-profit homes were
beginning to look more alike as they responded to the same conditions. By the study's end, the greater difference appeared to lie not
between Countryside and Mountainside as proprietary and sectarian
homes, but between them and the giant chains. They were not competing with the latter for patients—as Scanlon (1988) reports, the
United States is underbedded—but rather for lower costs, and in this
Mountainside and Countryside were disadvantaged.

Arling, Nordquist, and Capitman (1987) have suggested that these
corporate behemoths achieve their edge by providing a standardized

low-cost level of care tailored to Medicaid demands and permitting economies of scale that smaller individual facilities, competing for private-pay patients, cannot achieve. As non-Medicare, non-Medicaid facilities, neither Countryside nor Mountainside fit the regulatory template very well and thus they were doubly disadvantaged, both in purchasing and in meeting the demands of the monitors.

In adapting to an older clientele, increased regulation, and a climate favoring bigness, Mountainside and Countryside made changes in their physical plants, policies, and staffing and, in the case of Countryside, in ownership as well. In these, they followed national patterns.

There were also idiosyncratic changes. Some arose from local conditions, such as the increasing value of real estate around Countryside and local shifts in the labor supply. Time itself contributed to other changes—the departure of staff members and the deaths of residents.

The dynamic interplay rules out a tidy discussion of single causes. For example, the aging of the residents had implications alike for staffing, state regulation, and the costs of delivering care while the higher rates may have been one of the factors leading to the later entry and the older population to be found in the homes. After mentioning three staff departures, this chapter will look at the major change-forces and the homes' response to them.

Three key figures moved from central positions. At Countryside, Ernest Miller and Winnie Mason withdrew from active management. Mr. Miller had been the prime mover at Countryside: He saw the potential of the property, organized the group of physician-buyers, and gave the facility its day-to-day leadership. The home was a convenience for the physicians at his hospital, and, as an experienced hospital administrator, he was strongly responsive to the medical point of view. Together with his director of nursing, Winnie Mason, he set the climate at Countryside. For her part, Winnie Mason was strongly committed to comfort care as opposed to what she viewed as the unrealistic goals of rehabilitation for this population. She left, but he did not totally sever his ties.

At Mountainside, the important departure was that of the earlier director of nursing. Her emphasis on even-handed enforcement lent a certain inflexibility to an otherwise warm and friendly style. It was she who had worked so hard to press Margaret Wesley into the patient mold. Her replacement, Beth McGann, reduced medication, restraints, and incontinence, a not-unrelated triad. Barbara Archer remained as administrator, ensuring continuity in the face of other staff changes.

An Older Population

Ten years after the study's start, the average age in both homes had risen. The entry age did not advance as rapidly as the cross-sectional average, indicating that to some degree this represented an aging in place of persons already there. This rise was part of a national trend and not unique to these two homes.

Overall, the average age of the residents in both homes increased by slightly more than two years between 1974 and 1984. The change, from 83.59 to 85.66, was significant (t test -2.12 df 226.67 $p > .0175$). The difference was unevenly distributed. At Mountainside, the mean age in the nursing unit went from 87.2 to 89.6 and at Countryside, from 83.2 to 84.7. The two boarding units showed similar advances: from 82 to 84 at Mountainside and from 81 to 84 at Countryside.

The differences in entry ages was much smaller. The overall change between 1974 and 1984 was less than half a year (from 81.19 to 81.63). The shift was slightly greater in Mountainside's nursing unit (from 83.9 to 84.65) and in Countryside's boarding unit (from 79.8 to 81.67). The entry age in Countryside's nursing unit actually edged downward from 81.45 to 81.28 but the standard deviation dropped, suggesting greater homogeneity.

Averages can easily obscure the distribution of ages within a group. Esther Hing employs a method of analysis that gets around this. In emphasizing the increasing burden of care, she reports that the proportion of patients eighty-five and older in nursing homes grew from 40 percent in 1977 to 45 percent in 1985. Because these nursing home patients need substantially more help with activities of daily living, such as bathing, dressing, and eating, and because 58 percent have difficulties with bowel and bladder control, this older group requires more nursing and personal care. She adds that even when age was held constant, the 1985 patients required more care than those included in the 1977 National Nursing Home Survey (National Center for Health Statistics and Hing, 1987). Even among the well-functioning community elderly, eighty-five is generally considered a watershed (Suzman and Riley, 1985).

Hing's approach can be applied to Mountainside and Countryside residents, using 1974 and 1984 data. Overall, 51.6 percent were eighty-five or over in 1974 and 57.7 percent ten years later. At Countryside, the over-eighty-fives rose from 44.4 percent in 1974 to 52.7 percent in 1984. Mountainside began with a larger proportion of these oldest residents, 61.5 percent, and this rose to 63.2 percent. Countryside experienced the greater burden because its patients outnumbered its boarders.

The weariness that an older, frailer caseload can engender was illustrated by the comments of staff members at an in-service training session at Countryside in 1984. They agreed that they were dealing with a quite different population, one that made the most willful, difficult, and complaining but interactive patients of the past seem interesting and desirable. They were providing physical care to many persons who lacked even a rudimentary capacity to respond.

What they were lamenting was not so much the overwork as their frustration at an endless task they could never complete to their satisfaction. They spoke of moving as rapidly as possible through the work that had to be completed during the shift—and not being satisfied with what they had done. One of the nurses commented that in the past she often had taken some of the patients out of doors on pleasant days, but now there was simply never time enough. The others assented.

At this point, the home was more richly staffed than the state required. The difference lay in the fact that an increasing number of patients depended upon others to perform for them all but the most vegetative functions.

If a home exceeded staffing standards but found its personnel distressed because they could not meet the creature needs of their patients and still have time to provide psychosocial nursing care, questions must be raised about the adequacy of those regulatory standards and the priorities they set.

The Proliferation of Regulations

Regulation of nursing homes increased sharply during this period (Morford, 1988). Behind the more detailed demands and more vigorous enforcement lay two concerns: cost containment and the quality of care. The rules addressing cost containment did not affect Mountainside and Countryside directly because neither home sought Medicare or Medicaid certification. There were two other sources of regulation, one voluntary and the other not: the Joint Commission on the Accreditation of Healthcare Organizations and the State Department of Health.

In the early 1970s, Mountainside was certified by the Joint Commission. This gave the home a credential to hang on its wall, but, more important, the site visit by the nurse inspector stimulated the staff. The changes she suggested were accepted readily and nothing but good emerged from the experience. Nevertheless, when the time came for reaccreditation, the home did not apply. Rising costs ruled out the site visit. ("There's nothing concrete we have to show for it." said Barbara Archer, clipping grocery coupons.) The board's more pressing concern had become curbing costs that might force a rise in rates for the residents.

The second source of standards could not be sidestepped, however. This was the State Department of Health in its licensing capacity. Foregoing Medicare and Medicaid reimbursement freed both homes from regulations designed to control costs to the taxpayer, but they were still accountable for those that addressed professionalization, protection, and patients' rights.

Over time, staffing improved: Both homes added social workers and activities directors, and aides became nursing assistants, better equipped for the work they were doing. The changes licensing explicitly required were made.

> When continuing education was mandated for assistant administrators, Ernest Miller took Winnie Mason and Gayle Dockert, his assistant, to a two-day workshop for nursing home personnel. This was the first time either had attended such an event. Participants

were told to organize discussion groups in their facilities and report back at the next meeting.

Excited but apprehensive, the two women gathered
the most likely residents around a table and suggested
they talk about foods they had enjoyed cooking. To
their astonishment, the residents responded eagerly.

Two sessions were required. When the residents assembled the following week, they were served coffee
cake made by a recipe one of the patients had described. Winnie Mason and Gayle Dockert returned to
their workshop flushed with success: The patients
were pleased and all had gone well.

As memories of the workshop faded, however, the
press of work took over and routine was restored.
Nothing like it happened again, until years later when
the home had an activities director.

The episode typifies the fate of many quality-of-life innovations.
When mandated, they are implemented, but they never seem as
"real" to staff as the daily haircombing, bathing, and toileting routines. If not specifically required, they are soon lost, dismissed as
"frills" in the face of staff turnover and absenteeism. At Countryside, some of the opposition was ideological—the nurses' bias
against rehabilitation and the physicians' distaste for government
interference—but most seemed grounded in the day-to-day difficulties of delivering care.

By the late 1980s, there were striking changes in the staffing,
some in response to rising state standards and some self-initiated by
individuals with new goals of career development. Winnie Mason's
successor as Countryside's director of nursing was engaged in an
external degree program in nursing administration. Many of the
earlier aides displayed real concern for their patients, but they appeared to see themselves primarily as women earning money for
their families. The new nursing assistants, on the other hand, expressed distress because they were unable to meet their own professional standards.

For the homes, the purpose of in-service training and new patterns of staffing was to meet a requirement. The inspection process

fed into this by focusing on reports, charts, and lists. Mountain-side's new social worker was hired to provide the case records the surveyors demanded—any other input was seen as secondary. Emphasis at the in-service training sessions was on the sign-in sheet and documentation of the trainer's credentials. Because off-duty staff had to be paid for training time, one administrator suggested that sessions be kept to thirty minutes.

If regulations designed to increase professionalization were dismissed as inflating costs needlessly and those intended to enrich residents' daily life were considered frills, rules aiming at patient protection might be expected to have the support of all constituencies. Residents ranked safety norms high. Management was concerned about institutional liability, and the nurses were aware of their own vulnerability to suits, especially after an insurance agent addressed a nurses' organization to which many of Mountainside's registered nurses belonged.

Nevertheless, the response was not unmixed. For example, after a hot spell had been coupled with several deaths in the state, each facility was required to have a written plan for handling heat emergencies and appropriate equipment to implement it. The latter was spelled out in minute detail. The concept was commendable but, at the time, it was hardly greeted with enthusiasm.

Some of the regulations appeared to purchase a specious safety at the cost of resident autonomy and even of patient welfare. The more defensible of these related to medications, the more damaging to the prevention of falls.

Had Mountainside's boarders been in their own homes, no one would have questioned the contents of their medicine shelves, which held such over-the-counter items as mouthwash, aspirin, and milk of magnesia. After a trip through the boarding unit at Mountainside, however, the inspector admonished the administrator and she, in turn, implored the boarders to keep their home remedies out of sight, at least when the inspector was on the premises. Later it was proposed that a lock be placed on each resident's medicine cabinet. Apart from cost of installation, this evoked visions of endless crises over lost keys.

At Countryside, where many of the boarders did have unreliable memories, there was a different problem: Could the aide remind them to take their prescribed medications without raising questions about the appropriateness of their placement? The two populations were different but they were held to the same rule.

Substantial savings could have been effected if the homes had been permitted to purchase stock supplies of certain widely used medications. As it was, approximately twenty-five bottles of a well-known laxative, each labeled with its owner's name, stood in the cabinet near the nursing station at Mountainside—to the pharmacist's profit and the patients' cost.

More serious was the issue of restraints. Regulations and legal liability in this area tend to be contradictory, conservative, and not necessarily in the patient's best interests. Neither was institutional practice.

Wandering and intrusiveness undoubtedly were factors, but staff members employed soft ties and "postural supports" as restraints chiefly to keep confused patients from rising and setting out precipitously, risking falls and fractures. Not every confused patient was tied, but almost anyone was who had once had a serious fall. Many very old people are unsteady, some medications increase the unsteadiness, and there are also spontaneous fractures—that is, the bone breaks, causing the person to fall. Being tied for long periods also increases unsteadiness. Fear of citations and suits runs high. The original director of nursing at Mountainside commented that by the time ties were necessary, most patients were ready to accept them. Her successor, Beth McGann, was less certain. When a 103-year-old woman had cracked a shoulder blade in a fall, Mrs. McGann lamented the necessity of restraining her. She said, "They become crazy when they are tied in a wheelchair." The patient in question was a bird-like figure, generally alert and very distressed at the indignity of the ties.

The issue was complex. Fractures took patients on a difficult journey that often left them regressed even when physical recovery was complete. Because neither Mountainside nor Countryside was certified for Medicare, patients usually went from the hospital to a Medicare facility for rehabilitation before returning. Often when they came back, they were tied. Harriet Hoagland illustrates the problem.

At ninety-three, she presented as a moderately confused, sometimes difficult patient in need of watching
because she wandered. Nevertheless, she was eloquent
in summing up her situation: "Nothing's nice when
you're old." Of her husband's death, she said, "There
ought to be some way you could go together." She was
equally articulate when her freedom was impeded.

Her daughter was upset when she found her tied
and said she would assume responsibility if they
would not restrain her mother. A fall subsequently
broke Harriet Hoagland's hip and sent her on a sad
odyssey to the hospital, a Medicare nursing home, and
then another facility while she awaited another bed at
Countryside. Four months later, she was back, now
tied, dispirited, and more confused than she had been
before.

In a review of the literature about physical restraints, Evans and
Stumpf (1989) cite studies suggesting that bed rails and ties increase
the danger of falls. The injuries occur when patients attempt to
escape their bonds. Nevertheless, tying a frail elderly person is such
an uncomplicated solution that it has retarded the implementation
of the multiple safeguards that would be required to take its place.
Nothing else reveals more clearly the degree to which protocol is
dictated by fear of citations and suits as opposed to the best interests
of the patient.

New York State nurses report that if the patient is not tied when
the second fall occurs, they are cited by licensing authorities. At
the same time, they can be cited also for the inappropriate use of
restraints (Comments, 1985). This not only places them in an
untenable position but blocks the development of better nursing
practice.

Regulatory double-binds like these feed the natural paranoia of
the operators in a climate that is often adversarial. What staff
members believe to be the "gotcha" attitude of inspectors leads them
to engage in what Wiener and Kayser-Jones (1989) call defensive
work and to report what they think the examiners will find acceptable (Buckholdt and Gubrium, 1983).

Day and Klein (1987) have pointed out that there are two models
of regulation—the compliance model, which coaches and negotiates
and resorts to the law only when cooperation is not forthcoming, and
the deterrence model, that ferrets out and punishes wrong-doers. The
first assumes that operators are ignorant; the second implies that they
are unprincipled. In England's compliance model, licensing authorities often act as consultants. In the United States, violations are noted
but the regulators are not encouraged to tell the facility how to
remedy them.

The complaint about facilities is that they concentrate on the
minutiae necessary to get through inspections without relating to
the humanistic intent behind the regulations. The complaint about
the regulations is that they are operationalized in terms of small,
countable details. The complaint about the inspectors is that they
issue citations without taking into account more basic concerns like
patient autonomy and the retention of function. Regulators might
well respond that this is the only way they can operate in a legalistic
business society.

Many operators would join Schur (1980) in saying that the regulation and monitoring have not raised the quality of care but have
driven up its cost. This would be endorsed as wholeheartedly by
Barbara Archer, whose home was never intended to make a profit,
as by Countryside's owner-operators, whose facility was always
meant to.

During this period of increased regulation, both Mountainside
and Countryside did improve the quality of care and staffing. That
their costs went up may have been due less to the imposed standards
than to an economic climate that favored bigness.

The Economic Context

A recurrent theme among residents was, "If the money holds
out."

> Alma Foley said that she was sometimes awakened by
> pain when the medication wore off, but she no longer
> lay awake at night worrying about running out of
> funds and having to go to a welfare home. She had

enough money of her own for another year. In addition, she was now a client of the Santa Claus Society
so she was free of the haunting fear.

Four days later, she died as she had wished, in her
sleep and before her funds were exhausted. The Santa
Claus Society had given her great peace of mind, although she had never had to draw on its resources.

Other patients, some less alert than Mrs. Foley, expressed the same
sentiments, but few had the comforting reassurance the Santa Claus
Society gave her.

While residents were worrying about rates, the administrators
and their boards were concerned about costs. New regulations made
it harder to transfer patients when they switched to public assistance. Wages were going up and the patients they were getting now
required more services and used more supplies. As a consequence,
rising costs shaped the development of the two facilities throughout
the study period and beyond.

Between 1974 and 1984, both homes had increased rates about 240
percent. At the beginning of 1974, Countryside patients were paying
$168 to share a double room. In July of the same year, this crept up
to $189. By 1981, the same room cost $308 and by 1984, $420. For
boarders, the rate for the least expensive room rose from $94 in early
1974 to $109 later that year, to $180 in 1981, and to $230 in 1984.
Mountainside residents experienced equivalent increases: from $175
for patients in double rooms in 1974 to $357 in 1984 and $434 in
1987. Mountainside boarders paid $49 for the least expensive room
in 1974, $103 in 1984, and $133 in 1987.

In their struggle with costs, Mountainside and Countryside were
smaller homes in a climate favoring bigness. The trend was toward
larger facilities, multifacility ownership, and huge corporate
chains. Throughout the 1970s, there was a rise in the number of
beds, with the average bedsize for homes with twenty-five or more
beds going from just under seventy-four in 1969 and eighty-six in
1973 to slightly over 100 in 1980. By 1980, proprietary homes ac-
counted for 68.7 percent of the beds and their beds outnumbered
those in nonprofit homes three to one (National Center for Health
Statistics and Strahan, 1984, pp. 3–4). Between the national nursing

home surveys of 1977 and 1985, the chain-owned homes increased from 28 percent of all homes to 41 percent. Their average bedsize per unit (101.5) was larger than that of the independent proprietary facilities (68.1) (National Center for Health Statistics and Strahan, 1987, p. 4). As buyers of supplies, Mountainside and Countryside were disadvantaged in competition with the chains.

Countryside's solution reflected the times. A number of factors may have influenced its physician-owners to sell what had been a very profitable property: There was increasing outside regulation of health care facilities; the home had been an adjunct to their private practices and now many of them were retiring; some of the original owners had already been replaced by their widows. All were enriched by the sale, especially since they took the mortgage and since the new owners had declined to purchase the extensive grounds, which included waterfront property ripe for development.

Although the real estate proved to be exceedingly valuable, the new owners, a family that already owned a facility in another state, tailored their decision to the times, too. They invested instead in a third home—and thus moved into multifacility ownership. The surrounding acres, a part of Countryside's past, had become a luxury when the area urbanized.

Ernest Miller and his successor had arrived at nursing home management by different routes. Miller entered the field when little formal training was available or required. He began with a small doctors' hospital that grew into a community medical center. As a hospital administrator, he took over management of Countryside and picked up credentials as they were required. The new administrator studied business administration at an eastern university. As son of the owning family, he was catapulted into management in his twenties and initially operated the home under his father's license.

In a community where old families tended to view residents as newcomers for the first twenty years, Countryside's old owners might have regarded their successors as "outsiders" and waited for standards to fall, but they were motivated to pull for their success because they held the mortgage. Had the new proprietors failed, the old owners would have had the burden of restoring and reselling the property. Ernest Miller remained attentive to their progress.

As part of a three-facility chain, Countryside now was able to enjoy some economies of scale while Mountainside remained a small buyer. Barbara Archer joined administrators of other non-profit homes in cooperative buying, but this solution was limited by the lack of uniformity in their purchases. For food, she turned increasingly to institutional suppliers.

Mountainside's second problem affected its boarding unit, which needed new blood to replace the first generation of peer leaders. The twentieth century had produced a healthier, more affluent group of elderly persons who remained in the community longer. Many were willing to shed the headaches of home ownership and maintenance but reluctant to exchange their houses for a single room and shared bath. To serve this group, Mountainside built a row of five small apartments. For a couple, these were not more costly than one of the better rooms in the boarding unit and they appealed strongly to those wanting more privacy and less group living. The apartment dwellers took their main meal in the boarding unit but prepared their own breakfasts and lunches.

The apartments' construction was a boon for the patients. The chosen site was just across the garden from the nursing unit, and every day patients wheeled to the dining room windows and settled down for hours of happy viewing as the work progressed. In a proper world, the builders would have torn them down and started all over again to the applause of their audience.

Mountainside tailored its second series of physical changes to the tastes of the new elderly. When the old mansion was originally converted into a home for the aging, most of the bedrooms were a moderate size and a few even suite-like, but in addition the odd Victorian contours lent themselves to a number of quite small rooms, all without private baths. Some were distinctive in character, with a bit of a fireplace, a circular window, or some other special feature. Rates for these rooms were set so low that their occupants might live comfortably on their Social Security checks while enjoying all the appurtenances that went with life in a mansion. These rooms were especially attractive to those members of the sponsoring sect who had spent their lives doing good or scholarly works instead of making their fortunes.

As the decade progressed, standards changed. There was a waiting list for beds in the nursing unit and many persons were eager for the better rooms in the boarding unit, but the small bedrooms lost their appeal for the newer applicants. They wanted bigger rooms and private baths. Rising rates made the little bedrooms a bargain only in comparison to the big ones. About this time, the elevator began manifesting age changes: When the weather was very cold or very hot, it often refused to budge. The board decided to embark on a program of general remodeling, to enlarge the small rooms.

The outcry was immediate. Although the small rooms had become difficult to rent, their current occupants anticipated rising rates. A bargain was struck with them: They might continue to pay the same low rate for their enlarged rooms until a smaller room became available. Then they would have a choice between the better room and the lower rate. Residents who were members of the sponsoring sect protested against "such luxury" and quickly referred to the expenditure, but everyone settled down to the excitement of construction, which entailed many temporary moves while rooms were being remodeled.

In the end, the residents expressed satisfaction. Some of the fine Victorian molding that had been lost to make the many small rooms was restored. Most rooms had private baths and all were larger. The sturdiness and modernity of the new elevator proclaimed its dependability: No longer did any elderly resident living on the third floor have to resort to the stairs on a hot summer's day. (The only enthusiastic stair climber was Faith Fairchild. At one hundred and two, she elected to walk at least one flight for exercise before taking the elevator.) Agnes Chase, still in the boarding unit but experiencing some confusion, viewed her transformed room with misgivings. She expressed pleasure in its handsome design but had difficulty grasping that she should close the windows when she turned on the new air conditioner that came with it.

Prudence Reardon made the most poignant statement. In the six years since her husband's death, she had continued to keep his bed beside hers. She said she experienced a shock when she walked into her new room and saw one bed all alone.

The economic climate was making subtle changes in the composition of the peer group, affecting both whom the home was willing to admit and the age at which boarders elected to enter. The Mountainside boarding unit had always drawn some local persons of more moderate means who wished to remain in the area. Now it appeared that the home was reminding these applicants about the cost of later care and they were not pursuing their applications. Both parties had reason to be chary—the individuals because when illness struck and dying was long delayed, they were likely to have trouble meeting the costs of nursing home care; the home because the state was now frowning on the eviction of patients simply because they had exhausted their funds and were forced to apply for public assistance.

Entering the home at a more advanced age husbanded individuals' financial resources but resulted in their having less energy to invest in the life of the home. The bigger rooms meant fewer of them, which shrank the reservoir of potential leaders. The few residents in their mid- to late seventies were not inclined to take on tasks in the home because they were still engaged with family, community, and travel. The strong peer leaders of the past had been healthy persons in their eighties. Near the study's end, a relatively young couple took one of the apartments at Mountainside to use as a base for their travels. They were the daughter and son-in-law of John and Sarah Penfield, who had been founders and afterwards peer leaders.

Other economic changes affected Mountainside through its work force. In the first place, each rise of the minimum wage reverberated through the payroll as the home endeavored to keep the pay of its beginning nursing assistants ahead of that of its tray girls. In the second, the structure of female employment was changing. In the 1970s, the home had been able to hire nurses and aides who lived nearby. As retirement and widening work opportunities shrank this pool, the county welfare system provided another. As part of its program to promote independence for recipients of assistance to families with dependent children (AFDC), it was encouraging these women to seek training as nursing assistants. Unlike their predecessors, this group arrived with systematic job training but little general experience in the work force. They caused some shocks in the staff work system when they failed to call in sick or otherwise missed work on short notice. A year later, however, those who remained appeared alert, businesslike, and at least quasi-professional. Health care facilities of all kinds were experiencing difficulty getting professional nurses so this was not unique to Mountainside but reflected the low pay for care of the elderly and the expanded opportunities for women elsewhere.

In the beginning, Countryside and Mountainside differed because one was proprietary and the other sectarian. In the end, both had been buffeted by the same economic, regulatory, and patient-age pressures. The difference in the field now lay in size.

Countryside resolved this by becoming part of a chain, effecting economies from bulk buying. Mountainside was forced to ensure that its residents met the full cost of their care. Altruism had to make way for survivorship: Mountainside could serve its residents by providing better care but it could no longer subsidize them by simply foregoing profit.

Although some of the new regulations improved Mountainside and Countryside, others simply increased their costs. The state's rules were influenced by Medicare and Medicaid, which viewed the nursing home as a minihospital, an attitude that was irrelevant to what both homes did best.

Organized around its boarding unit, Mountainside was most effective at supporting late-life living for the healthy and alert old old. Emphasis on passing nursing home inspections could only subvert attention from this task. To maintain a viable nursing unit, Mountainside had to accept some patients from the hospital and the community, but its infirmary's intended function was maintaining its residents as long as possible in the boarding home and giving them assurance of a safe conduct at the end. A study by Cohen and his associates (1989) of six prepaid managed retirement communities suggests that these settings use their nursing units more for short recuperative stays and less for lengthy final transfers. This is close to Mountainside's boarding home–based career, which was achieved by 14 percent of its residents. To extend this pattern further, both residents and staff would have to view the boarding unit as the expected habitat for most of the frail elderly, and state licensing regulations would have to accept the use of walkers by alert but unsteady nonagenarians.

Oriented to its nursing unit, Countryside was now receiving a number of slowly dying patients, persons whose needs were different from those of the hospital patients discharged to Medicare facilities for rehabilitation. Its other residents were benefiting from the new activities and stimulation and, if their numbers had been greater, they could have provided balance to the work day of staff members, who tend to remain brighter if their time is not totally devoted to the care of inert but still-breathing bodies. There must either be this balance or else funding and licensure must adjust to a new kind of patient load. In the meantime, it appeared that the merely senescent were being displaced by those whose dying took a long time.

The professional care needs in settings like these are less medical than nursing and social (Kaufman, 1980). Neither home was a plantation with absentee ownership, and it was the sins of the latter that the regulations were intended to curb. This mismatch between rules and setting increased the cost and discomfort. As Vladeck (1980, p. 207) said, "To the extent that nursing homes resemble hospitals, they are deflected from providing a pleasant place for frail and isolated old people to live."

CHAPTER TEN

Toward Better Endings

After Mrs. Flowers's death, her daughter was asked, "What could have made things better?" She replied: "Treating the far-outs and the not-so-far-outs-but-not-with-its as if they were actually saying something. . . . I suppose I'm saying, 'Treat them as if they are *all intelligent human beings*'" (personal communication, 1976).

Mountainside and Countryside were not homes where sick old people lay in squalor, untended. Residents and their families rarely complained about the food, the physical arrangements, or even the quantity of service. There was general acceptance that this was the best alternative realistically available. When 103 residents were asked where they would live if they could live where they wanted, 47 percent replied, "Right here." Most of the other answers were nostalgic. Nevertheless, there were some very low morale scores and most of these were concentrated in the nursing units. At the first testing, there were thirty-one low scores (9-0) and, of the eleven lowest scores (2-4), ten belonged to patients. Mrs. Flowers scored 2.

Much of this ebbing morale could be attributed to what Stanley Cath (1965) has called the "assault on the omnicon," a cumulative loss of much that was significant in the personal cosmos. The homes cannot be faulted for deprivations rooted in the larger social system or in the nature of biological aging itself, but they did contribute to the "excess disability" (Brody, Kleban, Lawton, and Silverman, 1971) of residents in their nursing units.

216

Researchers dealing with diverse populations agree that a major task of the elderly is preserving an acceptable self in the context of change and death (Lieberman and Tobin, 1983; Kaufman, 1987). Maintaining one's self-image is a concern at any age, but in late life the challenges become quantitatively and qualitatively different. They are greatest when there is an abrupt discontinuity with all that has gone before. The ensuing behaviors are defensive. What Mrs. Flowers's daughter was deploring was the attack on those defenses.

The institutional assault on the self is not so much the act of thoughtless people as a structural property of the situation. This chapter will deal first with some of those built-in factors and the barriers to their change. Because morale is lowest in the nursing units, it then will look at three areas that figure prominently in the nursing home's assault on the self: the management of incontinence, dementia, and staffing. Finally, it will close by examining institutional reform in the context of changing patterns of entry.

Institutional Givens

While individuals' social resources and the way they deployed them influenced the course of their residential careers, there were impersonal forces within the setting that also helped to determine the shape their careers would take and the quality of the experience. These addressed categories, not people: the patient as patient only, the boarder as boarder. Idiosyncratic elements entered only when norms were bent for this one or strictly interpreted for that. Among these structural factors were (1) staff expectations, (2) peer norms in the boarding units and staff controls in the nursing units, (3) administrative preoccupation with inspections and suits, and (4) concern with costs.

Certain staff expectations were so widely shared they gained the force of policy. There were two reasons why patients rarely became boarders: first, the chronicity of their impairments; second, the assumption that patienthood was irreversible. Even in those cases when there was functional parity, staff members found it hard to conceive that a patient might sustain gains long enough to justify the effort required for rehabilitation. Therefore, the climate in the nursing unit favored retention. When no one but the patient ob-

jected, the patient's protests were taken as evidence of poor judgment and he or she was likely to remain. When individuals collaborated in their own patienthood, staff members did not view this as
a pathological response, requiring active intervention.

> Furious at her recovery, Ramona Everly, then eighty-
> nine, refused to leave the nursing unit when she re-
> turned from the hospital. She resolved to remain
> where death could find her without difficulty. Staff
> acquiesced although she could have functioned in the
> boarding unit for at least a few of the remaining ten
> years.

Only boarders admitted for acute illnesses or posthospital con-
valescence were expected to get better.

> Although Evan Brewster struggled with cancer
> throughout his eight-year residence, he was able to
> remain in the boarding unit except for short stays
> when he returned from the hospital. He earned social
> credit as a table host, he was a boarder with a car,
> and he was not inclined to challenge traditional
> arrangements.

While staff expectations governed the perception of patients in
ways detrimental to their care, boarders sometimes experienced the
tyranny of peer controls. At Mountainside and Countryside, effective peer controls diminished with transfer to the nursing units.
This is not to say that patients did not complain about one another
but only that they generally had to enlist the assistance of staff
members to make their complaints effective. In the boarding units,
however, the peer group had sufficient cohesion to make their sanctions stick.

> Countryside boarders exiled to the periphery of their
> group the woman Mamie Slocum labeled "the
> Creep." They insisted that a place be set for her at a
> separate table. While the others ate together or, when

feelings ran high, in separate armed camps, she dined alone. Her crime was raising for them all the specter of senility. Her morale score was 4 out of a possible 21 and she was a picture of mute misery.

When Gretchen Elder's noisy lamentations bothered her fellow Countryside boarders too much, they were able to effect her transfer to the nursing unit by presenting a common front. They did not change her behavior but they caused her great distress. She literally got on her knees to beg that she not be transferred.

At Mountainside Elka Miller, whose hiatal hernia compelled her to eat slowly, was punished by successive table hostesses who refused to dismiss the group until she finished. They inflicted as much discomfort as possible under the guise of courtesy, invoking the norm of polite delay to punish the sin of dawdling. The group exhibited quiet impatience—and supported the sanction. When Evan Brewster became her table host, he was less silent in his criticism. Elka Miller and another boarder drew his ire. In describing the way he treated them both, Miss Miller said, "My nerves—I get very tense inwardly!" This was a man whose behavior was generally endorsed by the group.

Peer pressure exists everywhere, but peer pressure in a residential setting occurs in close quarters and thus can be unremitting. This is not to minimize the intense intrusiveness in the nursing unit, where the patient is never out of sight.

In the boarding units, where their level of personal accountability was low, nurses could react to falls with first aid and empathy without putting a defensive account in the record and physical restraints on the victim. In the nursing units, the overriding emphasis was on preventing accidents and incidents that could result in fines, loss of license, and possibly suits against the home. The nurses thus exercised high controls because they were held professionally and legally accountable for the safety of a fragile population. This control was apparent in their response to falls and led to practices inimical to patients' self-esteem. Foremost among these was the use of physical restraints, which the literature suggests may actually increase the likelihood of the falls they are intended to prevent (Evans and Stumpf, 1989). Falls call for investigation and preventive approaches on a wider scale (Tinetti and Speechley, 1989; Tideiksaar, 1989) rather than blaming and tying the patient, but these tend to be bypassed once the individual incident has been described as an aberrant event beyond the control of staff. A rash of falls in one of the homes did lead to an in-service training.

Nurses acknowledge that some patients might maintain their mobility longer if they were not restrained, but they point out also that the threat of citations and suits is too great to risk. For nurses, the threat is both professional and personal; for administrators, it is primarily institutional, although they may well feel their jobs are on the line.

Administrators today express the view that they are victimized by an adversarial system more intent on catching them out of compliance than on helping them meet standards. While practice varies somewhat from state to state, federal policy requires inspectors to avoid a consultative role, like that played by their counterparts in Britain, and to content themselves with giving citations for violations (Day and Klein, 1987). This keeps administrators focused on getting through the next inspection. Patient care must compete with this and with their effort to stay within the budget. Wiener and Kayser-Jones (1989) point out that defensive work lowers standards by diverting attention from patient needs. They suggest that permitting inspectors to provide constructive criticism would improve the atmosphere without increasing costs. (In its report, *Losing a Million Minds*, the U.S. Congress's Office of Technology Assessment [1987] complains about the present blending of enforcement and consulting functions, but this is in opposition to all the accounts this writer has heard in the field.)

Although families and alert residents cannot help homes pass inspection, they could lessen the fears about litigation by sharing responsibility with the homes, but facilities find it hard to relate to families in this role. Staffs are wary in their dealings with them: They prefer clear role division lest there be some unbalancing of the tight social order, some infringement on their system of controls. In their survey of the literature, Smyer and Frysinger (1985) found that families were usually seen as "service recipients, rather than as active collaborators." The system's preoccupation with the demands of state inspectors as opposed to the wishes of patients and their families makes plain to residents their own impotence to influence the course of their care.

The high level of institutional totality in the nursing units serves the near-military "inspection readiness" nursing staff strive to maintain—presumably it would look bad if visitors found that a bath had been delayed until afternoon because a frightened patient had been resistant. More important, it also forwards the effort to contain costs.

Institutional totality, with its "batching" of patients, its adherence to routines, and its press to uniformity, enables a small staff to provide bed-and-body care to a large number of patients. Nursing homes standardize their human material for one purpose only, to deliver as cheaply as possible care that is by its nature labor intensive and expensive. They cannot provide personalized service or privacy without increasing costs. But it is individualization that affirms the resident's unique and continuing identity and standardization that denies it. The lack of privacy mitigates against the intimacy that fosters supportive human relationships, and it accounts for some of the isolation that patients experience in such close quarters.

For Mountainside, keeping costs down was a daily struggle that could never be ignored. Every rise in rates created a threat that reverberated between boarding and nursing units. Although Countryside aimed at making a profit, its original physician-owners were local residents. In many instances, they were dealing with individuals who were their long-time patients, their neighbors, and even their friends—they had no interest in causing them needless distress. Nevertheless, there was probably no response that the nursing assistant on a lightly staffed night shift could make to the patient who complained about waiting for a bedpan except the one she offered, "There's an incontinence pad under you. Just let yourself go." That reply was experienced as a direct assault on the adulthood of the ninety-four-year-old woman who had requested the bedpan.

In summary, the major barriers to normalizing life in the nursing units were the preoccupation with regulations and liability and the cost of providing care. Status generalization served staff members by justifying the restrictions these priorities dictated and by reducing the need to personalize care. By creating a *generalized aging other*, they freed themselves from doubts and decisions. As useful as this was for staff, it had its costs for patients. The management of incontinence and dementia was particularly damaging to residents' self-esteem. Even those who were neither incontinent nor demented were affected because they saw around them what they feared they might become and they sensed staff's feelings of contempt for regressed patients. If change is to be incremental, it should begin here.

Incontinence: Rivers of Regression

One of the residents at Mountainside spoke of "those poor things in wheelchairs with their urine bags." The urine bags and catheters soon went. They provided external control but at the cost of possible infection, so the problem of incontinence remained.

At the study's start, four Mountainside patients were indisputably incontinent and two others possibly so. The definition was clear-cut: "incontinent beyond infrequent accidents, as indicated by special provisions for incontinence being routinely made, such as an incontinence pad on the individual's wheelchair seat." Nocturnal enuresis and occasional "accidents" were not counted because the conditions of patienthood—bed rails and soft ties—made them almost inevitable.

Nevertheless, there were differences between raters. One of the marginal individuals was scored incontinent in 1974, not incontinent in 1978, and incontinent again in 1979. This may have reflected changes in the patient or the change of raters. The other might better have been described as "on her way to incontinence." Urine was found in her bed and it was unclear whether she had wet the bed or bumped into the bedpan. The decision rule dictated accepting staff's assessment. There appeared to be a reluctance to describe any alert resident as incontinent and a tendency to expect incontinence in the confused.

Only 15 percent of Mountainside's patients were incontinent, which is well below the national average. The 1985 National Nursing Home Survey found slightly more than half of the country's nursing home patients to be incontinent of bowel or bladder or both (National Center for Health Statistics and Hing, Sekscenski, and Strahan, 1989). Countryside came closer with 46 percent. It is not clear whether this was because Countryside's patients were more disabled or whether it was easier to know individual voiding patterns and "catch" patients in a smaller facility. At Mountainside, there were fewer puddles and other evidences of daytime incontinence after the new director of nursing, Beth McGann, introduced an incontinence chart that led staff to toilet marginal patients sooner. When all the patients in the study cohort were grouped together, less than 36 percent were incontinent. There was no reported incontinence in the boarding units.

These Mountainside and Countryside patients fit the descriptions of other incontinent nursing home patients: Most were confused and most were either immobile or immobilized (Ouslander and Uman, 1985; Resnick, Yalla, and Laurino, 1989; Ouslander, Kane, and Abrass, 1982). Although 88 percent of the incontinent were confused, more than a third of the confused were not incontinent. Every confused patient who was incontinent was also immobilized—either bed-bound, in a gerichair, or tied. Of the confused patients who were not incontinent, most—ten—were not restrained, and two were. This raises questions about which came first, the incontinence or the restraints. For example, when I asked whether Mrs. Winthrop was incontinent, the nurse replied, "Only when tied." Mrs. Winthrop knew when she had to go to the bathroom but she had trouble communicating this from the gerichair. When not restrained, she found the toilet herself.

Neither home smelled of urine. This was achieved by changing incontinence pads promptly and by leading confused patients to the bathroom at regular intervals. At Countryside, two aides pushed a cart piled with pads on its regular rounds. There was little systematic effort to treat incontinence or to prevent its occurring; instead both homes addressed its consequences. This paralleled Mitteness's (1987) observation that the community elderly dealt with the wet underwear instead of seeking a cure they thought impossible. But much, probably most, urinary incontinence is amenable to intervention (Willington, 1980; Resnick and Yalla, 1985; U.S. Congress, Office of Technology Assessment, 1985; Burton, 1984).

The incontinence industry has blanketed the country's nursing homes with the adult equivalent of diapers, simplifying nursing care and removing the incentive for better assessment (Starer and Libow, 1985). In reviewing the charts in a teaching nursing home, Starer and Libow found that 90 percent of the incontinent patients had no diagnosis relating to their urinary problem. (Only one had had an extensive, in-depth study.) Nurses reported the incontinence in their notes, but only 10 percent of the physicians mentioned it in their records.

Patients share the therapeutic nihilism of their physicians. In her community study, Mitteness (1987) found that many of her respondents were prisoners in their apartments because of fear of an "accident." One-third had never mentioned their problem to their physicians, assuming that this was a normal part of growing old and that their doctors could not do anything about it anyway. Nearly half of those who did consult physicians received either no response from them or a dismissive reply.

While incontinence's cost in laundry, labor, and disposables runs high, Schnelle, Sowell, Hu, and Traugher (1988) suggest that nursing homes may have little incentive to intervene because for many of them, promoting continence would be more costly. Because of poor mobility, most patients would require staff help with toileting. Studies indicate that many homes save money by not changing their patients every time they wet. The rehabilitation program itself would not be cost free. At present, marginal care tends to be noted only when its effects have visible sequels, such as skin breakdown. The Schnelle study is limited because the only intervention his team employed was behavioral: Candidates for urinary rehabilitation were prompted, rewarded for requesting toileting assistance, and toileted, first at one-hour and then at two-hour intervals. They achieved a 71-cent reduction in laundry costs per patient per day but a 68-cent increase in aide labor. The authors suggest that medical intervention in addition might have reduced the frequency of voiding.

Incontinence has more than economic consequences. The triad of unsteadiness, confusion, and incontinence feed upon one another. Immobilizing the patient increases the unsteadiness, deprives the individual of orienting exploration, and ensures incontinence in patients like Mrs. Winthrop, who have trouble communicating their need for assistance when they are tied. Many might find the bathroom because the capacity for motor learning sometimes lasts longer than effective oral communication. Regulatory trends toward the reduced use of physical restraints may therefore ultimately result in a more mobile and drier nursing home population.

What no one has proposed is striving for night dryness, chiefly because staffing is so low on late shifts, but bedwetting raises the specter of shamed childhood and sometimes provides the first break in the dam. The emphasis on costs and feasibility obscures the deeper human consequences of failing to preserve or restore continence whenever possible. Underlying this is the assumption that the confused are beyond embarrassment, which is not true.

> Margaret Goudie's niece was pushing her wheelchair past the nursing station when the nurse stopped her and asked her to bring additional nightgowns for the patient. The nurse explained that she had been changed three times during the night and she had gotten all her gowns soaking wet.
>
> From the wheelchaired depths came an indignant voice, "No, she didn't," said Margaret Goudie. "Someone else did it."

"Someone else did it" was the perennial response of confused and incontinent patients when confronted with a puddle. Their denying the act indicated that they knew incontinence was stigmatized. To assume that they did not experience distress is to dismiss all their behavior as both "organic" and meaningless. In their Rhode Island nursing home study, Jackson and her associates (1989) found that relatively alert but incontinent residents engaged in more than their share of disruptive behavior. They attribute this to their "humiliating and frustrating experience."

A consensus statement from the National Institutes of Health urged more attention to incontinence in both nursing and medical curricula (U.S. Department of Health and Human Services, National Institutes of Health, 1988). In the meantime, pressure for intervention must come from administrators and nurses, who believe this is an important standard for their homes to meet, and from licensing authorities, who still have the power to ask why no treatment was provided and no referral was made.

Because patients are discounted as incompetent to judge their own needs, they cannot influence the incontinence-management process, although some exceptional patients may be able to get schedules bent to meet their own toileting requirements. Because families are dependent upon the facility for services they themselves are unable to deliver, social exchange theory suggests that as individuals they, too, will be unable to influence incontinence-management practices. As articulate members of the public, however, they have been able to arouse regulatory concern about the abuse of restraints. Despite an incontinence industry and some physicians contented with things as they are, they may be able to stir up equivalent concern about the neglect of incontinence as well. At present, they lack force because they too believe that the loss of urinary control is an inevitable part of aging.

Dementia: The Stigmatizing Disorder

At some level, the assumption of inevitability is also made about dementia. The ubiquity of dementia in the nursing home exceeds its prevalence because those afflicted tend to be the most visible patients. At Countryside, the profoundly confused were grouped around the nurses' station close by the principal entrance from the parking lot. Nurses cluster these patients together so they can watch over them. Alert patients in both homes tended to remain in their rooms and emerge only for meals, entertainment, or a breath of air on the patio. For the most part, boarders entered the nursing units only on business or to visit a friend. Status generalization did the rest.

According to the 1985 National Nursing Home Survey, 43.4 percent of residents have senile dementias or other organic brain syndromes (National Center for Health Statistics and Hing, Sekscenski, and Strahan, 1989). Estimates in the literature run from 40 to 75 percent, with a general consensus that about half of all nursing home patients are moderately to severely impaired (U.S. Congress,

Office of Technology Assessment, 1985, 1987; Rovner and Rabins, 1985; Reisberg and Ferris, 1982; National Institute on Aging Task Force, 1980; Jenike, 1986; Katzman, 1986). The variation reflects differences in definition and measurement.

The two study homes illustrate the difficulty. Mental alertness in such a setting is dynamic and not a simple aggregation. Some patients with dementing illnesses had a steady downward course; the mental status of others fluctuated, depending upon medication, health factors, and the imminence of death.

Measuring at a particular point in time might have circumvented the difficulty, just as the use of a standard instrument might have increased the reliability. The first round of testing at Mountainside and Countryside began with Goldfarb and Kahn's "Special Ten," a mental status questionnaire (Kane and Kane, 1981). This upset so many of the more impaired patients that it was abandoned and residents' scores on the Activities-of-Daily-Living (ADL) type items in the social resource inventory and their ability to name "five persons who live here and three people who work here" was substituted.

According to this rough measure, 95 percent of the boarders were relatively alert. The two exceptions were "the Creep" and a gentle Englishwoman who often read the same page again and again. By the same criteria, 59 percent of the patients were relatively less alert. This figure does not do justice to the variation in their day-to-day functioning nor to their ability to extend themselves in response to outreach. Only seven of these patients were unable to complete the morale scale when it was read to them. They did not always know where they were but they did know how they felt. Staff members, for their part, were not impressed with these patients' lucidity: It is hard to respect someone you have to lead to the bathroom.

No resident in the study cohort was labeled as having Alzheimer's disease because when they had entered the home, the prevalent diagnosis for confused patients was cerebral-arteriosclerosis; Alzheimer's disease was still classified as solely a presenile dementia. Cerebral-arteriosclerosis was compatible with the then-prevalent view that most senile confusion was due to cell death caused by clogged arteries unable to carry enough blood to the brain. This was believed to be a normal consequence of living too long.

By the mid- to late 1970s, the literature was presenting a different picture and the new knowledge began to affect local labeling practices, sometimes with untoward consequences. Researchers seeking funding projected a sharp rise in the incidence of Alzheimer's disease based on the general graying of the population. Relatives' support groups emphasized the intractability of the victims. Newspapers described them as violent and difficult to control. Everybody forgot that these frail, elderly patients had been with them all along but with a different label.

In the mid-eighties, two patients were admitted to Mountainside with the new diagnosis. After an in-service training on Alzheimer's disease, staff complaints about this pair rose sharply. The patients had not changed but perceptions of them had.

> One was a tall, gaunt seventy-eight-year-old engineer, whose speech was difficult but whose distress was plain, much of it relating to his puzzlement. He could not understand the restraining geriatric chair: He indicated that it was keeping him in and that he wanted help getting out. He was puzzled also about why his family could leave and he could not. His son had moved into a decisive, paternal role, and his wife now turned to this other man for guidance.
>
> He soon learned that I would come when he beckoned. I read headlines to him, talked with him, and sometimes pushed him where he could watch TV, which held his attention. I don't think he grasped the headlines or followed the talk but he responded to the companionship.
>
> The way staff handled this patient was revealing. Although he was confined to the gerichair sometimes, this was by no means a twenty-four-hour proposition. The director of nursing, Beth McGann, was present in the morning, and although he was a wanderer, she was opposed to restraining him unless the nurses were too busy to supervise him. The nurses and aides on the early shift were the ones who had to breakfast, bathe, and dress patients and marshal them for lunch but

theirs was the shift that let him enjoy his freedom most often. On the other hand, evening staff members were busy, too, when they were putting patients to bed, but even when they were not busy, they tended to keep him in the gerichair. At the same time, some of the nurses were extraordinarily patient: One approached him a number of times with his medicine but never forced him, although she very much wanted him to take it and the hour was late.

Even without the Alzheimer's label, the category of confused patient is encompassing and only persons who are very attentive can see beyond the status. A more common response is to attribute the distress or anger to the confused patient's organicity. This forecloses any further examination of the circumstances that may have contributed to the response.

When the individual had acquired social credit before the dementing process was identified, a more differentiated personality was perceived and this provided some protection against categorical discrediting, at least by those who had known the person before. Both Sarah Coleman and Agnes Chase had been well established as boarders and Sarah Coleman continued alert during her first years in the nursing unit. Despite several years of increasing confusion, Agnes Chase remained in the boarding unit until a stroke compelled her transfer. Those years were sometimes tempestuous but probably the best that could be expected, considering her high energy level and impetuous temperament.

Keith Kenyon illustrated how much longer functioning could be sustained when support was forthcoming, but his story also shows some of the limitations of that support.

When Keith Kenyon entered Mountainside at sixty-five, his occasional forgetfulness appeared to be an artifact of his bereavement. He was very active, often house- and baby-sitting for his sons who lived in nearby states. His car was his special pride and he put it at the service of all. He conducted a reading group for the patients. His tablemates liked him.

Over the next thirteen years, his memory loss increased. At seventy-one, he avoided a family celebration because he knew he would have trouble with the names. He was still driving but he had had a series of small accidents. Through it all, he remained friendly and helpful.

Two years later, he was mourning the loss of his car. He had set out to visit his son, lost his way, and wound up in another state. He returned ignominiously after the police sent for his family. The administrator did the driving now but took him on her errands, respecting his need to help. He continued to read to the patients, who sometimes had to help him find his place. His fellow boarders also prompted and protected him.

When he was seventy-five, Barbara Archer saw small burn holes in his clothing and took charge of his cigarettes, dispensing them and reminding him to smoke outdoors. He was aware of his memory loss, unhappy at not being able to be more useful, and still mourning his car.

When he was seventy-seven, his confusion had become profound. Boarders complained about his outbursts and once he wandered away and was returned by the police. What precipitated his transfer from the home was his taking butts from the ashtray in the nurses' coffee room—they feared he might set himself on fire. Because he was relatively "young" and active, the nursing unit could offer him neither the protection nor the space he needed. He was transferred to a home with an intermediate care facility. He left a wake of uncertainty and sadness behind him because he had been well loved and in the end, the home could not meet his need.

More remarkably, though, he had not only managed to remain in the boarding unit thirteen years, but he had continued to contribute to the group life long after much of his cognitive capital had been spent. His

warm, nurturing personality had triumphed over the
disease. He suffered many small defeats but throughout he maintained a sort of rueful honesty about his
memory loss.

There are homes with special care units for confused patients in
which, ideally, their physical design provides safety without the
frustration of continual restraint, but neither Mountainside nor
Countryside was large enough to offer this kind of care.

Diagnosis and segregation can come too soon. Keith Kenyon and
Agnes Chase benefited from the good years in the open setting,
where both were seen in the context of their full residential careers.
Others were not so fortunate. Competing with the relatively alert
and without an institutional history, these others received the perfunctory processing and casual disregard that arose from their being
viewed as mindless and therefore absent and somehow less than
fully human. (This is typified by two nursing assistants working
over a patient and talking to each other as if they were dealing with
an inanimate object.) These dementing individuals were seen as
entropic, drifting downward to an uninteresting sameness. Because
they are incapable of remembering, patients like this are viewed as
also incapable of feeling real distress, the kind of distress that
arouses the empathy of others.

Two quite different studies illuminate the process. Drawing on
field observations of family caregiver support groups and the news-
letters and other documents of ADRDA, the Alzheimer's Disease and
Related Disorders Association, Gubrium (1986) broadened Mead's
conception of mind as something that the individual creates in
interaction with others in a process that gives rise to awareness of
self. Gubrium saw mind as also the creation of others, in these cases,
caregivers acting as the individual's agents. He observed that much
of the caregivers' dialogue related to whether there was indeed a
"hidden mind," whether the loved one was really there inside his
body but somehow unable to articulate or to reach through. There
often came a point when a caregiver, aided by others in the group,
recognized that there would be no miracle cure to free the hidden
self because that lucid self simply was not there. Gubrium referred

to this as the "demise of mind." At this point, the caregiver was freed to move to closure.

Gubrium's work derives support from the study of a quite different population: the severely developmentally disabled and those caregivers, not always parents, who have meaningful relationships with them (Bogdan and Taylor, 1989). These persons' definitions of the disabled person lead to his or her inclusion in the human circle. These caregivers underline the humanness of the handicapped individual by attributing to that person more mental activity than is readily apparent. They see the handicapped person as "locked in a body . . . limited in its capacity for communication." They are attentive to indications that the other is thinking, feeling, and willing, seeing him or her as a distinctive personality. These writers were aware of Gubrium's work and cite it.

Bogdan and Taylor's work provides clues to improving care in facilities like Countryside and Mountainside because staff members there need to see even the very impaired as fully human. To achieve this, they themselves must be perceived as more than interchangeable units and the work situation must be restructured to make their task easier.

The Aide as Caliban

Countryside and Mountainside were fortunate in their staffing. They experienced only in attenuated form the problems of aides' absenteeism, turnover, and culture clash that are endemic in the nursing home industry. They were not entirely trouble free, however, as was attested by small buried episodes of hasty hands and tart tongues that mostly escaped the nurses' attention. Nevertheless, what has generally been described as an aide problem might better be seen as systemic because the interface between the nursing assistant and the patient expressed most of the breakdown.

The factors that made the situation better in these two homes were idiosyncratic. Both facilities had access to pools of workers whose primary language was English. Although both homes had bad days when someone failed to show up, neither facility was minimally staffed as a matter of policy. The decision for marginal staffing is easiest made in distant corporate headquarters far removed from the chaos, stress, and patient discomfort it can engender on the floor. This leads to the third factor. Those making the decisions and those carrying them out in Mountainside and Countryside were operating face to face. Even after the purchase of Countryside by a family expanding into multiple holdings, a member of that family was the administrator. Mountainside's administrator lived on the grounds, ate breakfast and supper with the boarders, and worked in an office within constant sight and sound of the patients. The proximity of the two administrators signaled strong personal involvement in the functioning of the home.

The root problem common to all facilities is the need for a plentiful supply of inexpensive labor to provide hands-on care. The restructuring of nursing education through the community colleges has made it possible for returning housewives who wish a service career to qualify for the more rewarding roles of licensed vocational nurse or registered nurse. This leaves as a potential work force women who need the money and do not have the option of substantial training, which ensures a needy crew.

Kerschner (1987) wrote about the "$3.75-an-hour factor" and proposed raising the reimbursement rates on the condition that the additional funds be used to increase the wages of aides. Some industries, such as agriculture and coal mining, have been able to raise wages by increasing the productivity of their workers through mechanization, but in the care of frail elderly people, there is no substitute for human hands.

The system compounds its labor pool and cost problems by denigrating the aide through its medically oriented value system. The minihospital model does not meet the need of patients for a supportive environment because it demeans the very persons who deliver most of their care. Like Caliban, the aide is perceived as a mindless performer of menial chores even though the tasks themselves are seen as essential. The insult is built into the very structure of the system and hardly helped by the attitudes of the media, patients, families, many administrators, and even the victims themselves (Bowker, 1982).

Much has been made of the cultural and caste-like cleavage between staff and patient, but a similar gulf exists between the professional nurse and the aide or nursing assistant. At the shift change, departing nurses in both homes briefed the nurses who were arriving, but no systematic effort was made to include the nursing assistants, as it was assumed that the nurses would transmit to them as much as they needed to know. This exclusion was important, not so much for the missed content as for telling them they were not expected to think.

At Mountainside, the caste differences were indicated by the name tags nursing personnel wore: The nurses' said "Mrs." or "Miss"; the aides gave only their first names. This made *aide* akin to *maid*. The aides gave their elderly patients the same symbolic treatment: They called most of them by their first names even when the nurses said "Mr." or "Mrs."

Bowker (1982) says staff members who are dehumanized by their administrators can hardly be expected to be humanizing in their relationships with residents. He proposes that top-level staff members demonstrate the primacy of the work by their own willingness to perform any needed task, that they be accessible to all personnel, and that they provide support groups to help aides deal with work stress. In both of the study homes, the directors of nursing worked beside aides when needed.

Waxman, Carner, and Berkenstock (1984) concluded from their survey of 234 aides in seven nursing homes that turnover was not significantly influenced by wages and benefits, the quality of the homes, or even job satisfaction. Turnover appeared to be associated with a management style that was centralized, tightly organized, and possibly seen as authoritarian. The aides they interviewed were rarely involved in such decision-making events as the patient care planning conferences.

Tellis-Nayak and Tellis-Nayak (1989) describe the two worlds of the nursing home aide. Neither serves her well as she moves between the chaotic and depriving private world in which she lives and the demeaning work world where management treats her with barely veiled contempt. The authors speak of the "determined strivers," who ultimately leave because they have worked their way up, and the "disaffected endurers," who stay because they see no way out. Both groups are distanced by a management that is unconcerned with their problems. They sense the hypocrisy in all the talk of caring. The patient endurers survive by insulating themselves emotionally from their patients and the job. All of this makes unremarkable Pillemer and Moore's (1989) findings of self-reported and observed patient abuse. What most patients want from staff is consideration and respect.

It should be added that researchers exhibit their own disinterest when they sandwich a short staff training session between pre- and post-tests but make no provision for follow-up. Their experimental interventions are often designed to improve staff attitudes, but homes rarely replicate these demonstrations, although, in view of the turnover, it might be a good idea.

Barbara Archer recognized the relationship between salaries and self-esteem when she raised the wages of Mountainside aides each time the minimum wage went up. The tray girls received the minimum wage and she felt it would be insulting to aides to have the wage gap between them narrow. She knew the symbolic importance of even a small wage differential.

The home's first task is to attach employees to the job. This includes reducing staff turnover and unplanned absences. The employee who leaves gives patients a sense of instability and unmanageable change unless, indeed, that person's departure is a hoped-for event. The unplanned absences contribute to the work overload and burnout of other staff members and are disturbing to patients who sense the stress and get less than optimal care. Some facilities exchange unplanned absences for predictable ones by allotting each employee a pool of paid days; whatever is left the employee can use for extra vacation. Planned absences are easier to deal with.

A second task is to enhance employees' interest in the resident. Training, formal and informal, should have as its goal the development of problem-solving skills that will reduce the irritants they encounter in caring for patients and thus make their work experience more gratifying (Edelson and Lyons, 1985). Asking them about the patient will make them more observant. Developing their charting skills is difficult but rewarding because it forces them to consider what they are observing and doing, while simple check-off forms encourage a mechanical response more related to what is expected than to what has occurred. The use of their notes in day-to-day planning would give meaning to the process.

A final set of tasks would address the needs of the nursing assistants as workers and individuals. Homes too small to offer promotions within the ranks can support those who wish to pursue extra training by scheduling their hours so they can attend class, by lending them books and journals, and by giving them opportunities to relate their work to their studies. These employees will leave when they graduate, but a reputation for furnishing encouragement to scholars will help in recruiting other determined strivers, short stayers perhaps but a leaven to the system.

Finally, management should take into account their aides' other world and make the services of the social worker available to them for assistance with some of the crises of their lives. The social worker is a more appropriate resource than either the administrator or a nurse counselor because the social worker is not in the chain of command. This makes the social worker a less threatening figure and also keeps the supervisory function uncontaminated by the counseling relationship.

Are We Planning to Solve Yesterday's Problems Tomorrow?

In the fifteen years covered by this study, there was ample confirmation of the national trend toward older populations in residential care settings. Not only did the age level rise but as a consequence the energy level of Mountainside's peer leaders fell, and Countryside's patients were older and sicker.

These changing demographics raise questions about the direction of reform. Residents' councils have proved to be more interested in the menu than in larger issues of life in the home—in part, perhaps, because there are no larger issues that they have been encouraged to discuss. The proposals for patient involvement in treatment decisions, for greater freedom from chemical and physical restraints, and for patient interviews as part of the inspection process can all be circumvented or negated, but they are valuable in making the patient more visible as a person. Salience itself thus becomes a social resource. If the patient is more visible to all, it becomes more costly to ignore her: The caregiver's performance is now under scrutiny, with both the promise of approval and the threat of censure.

This current attention to residents' quality of life (Bearon, 1988) and autonomy (Hofland, 1988) parallels a similar concern with the self-determination of other categories of persons formerly regulated "for their own good." Lagging a little behind the other movements, it may either suffer from the pendulum swing or profit from society's observation that a little liberty was not catastrophic. Growing experience with the "rights" movement has illustrated the complexity of the issues. On the one hand, there are the autonomy games and deceptions and, on the other, improved ways of providing optimal feasible freedom for individuals at different functional levels.

For the nursing home patient, many of the barriers to self-determination are grounded in the medical model, which perceives the good patient as a compliant figure benefiting by the care of professionals who know best. The nursing home as minihospital seems likely to persist because convalescing patients are thrust into the system by earlier hospital discharge and because others are seeing it only as a last resort, entering only when all other resources are exhausted and they are very frail indeed. What may emerge are separate skilled nursing facilities—some specializing in convalescent care and others based on the social model for those who are simply older and frailer. Some will be specifically designed for the demented and others will offer a more stimulating environment for the mentally alert. To accept the social model for these latter groups, it will be necessary to accept also the naturalness of death, because it is our fears that have led us to place our old people in restrictive environments with uniformed personnel at the ready, standing by to fend him off.

In the meantime, each planner should have the following posted above his or her desk:

> In the future, our residents will be older and frailer.
> Some will be alert and some will not.
> Our task is to serve each according to his needs, which
>   may be as much psychosocial as physiological.
> We can do this only if we respect our patients and
>   ourselves.

CHAPTER ELEVEN

Things to Do While Waiting for Reform

No one ever set out to run a bad home, but a lot of good people are working in homes they would hate to enter as residents.

Regulation has won its victories but they have been slow in coming and few persons are satisfied with the situation as it now exists. Professionals burn out or flee the system, families feel helpless, patients and nursing assistants endure.

The futility of waiting for governmental action was demonstrated in the 1980s when Congress spent most of the decade trying to push reform past a White House that was philosophically opposed to regulation. When legislators finally took matters in their own hands and enacted the Omnibus Budget Reconciliation Act of 1987 (OBRA), the Department of Health and Human Services managed to delay its implementation until late 1990 and even then industry opposition was raising questions about its total, tidy, and timely enforcement. Moreover, reform does not always achieve its objectives. No sooner is a new mandate put in place than an economic or political consideration or a previously latent demographic factor arises to confound it.

This chapter will review three intractable forces that have infected the system with learned helplessness. These lead into a discussion of the plight of administrators and steps they can take to bring sanity to their impossible situations. The chapter closes with suggested strategies for professionals and families. In writing Chap-

ter Eleven, I draw on current contacts in the field as well as on my
earlier observations at Countryside and Mountainside.

Converging Structural Factors

The unpredictability that generates the sense of learned helplessness pervading the system arises from the interaction of three structural forces:

1. A changing residential population that neither reimbursement
    nor the rules have caught up with.
2. The consolidation of the "industry" under huge corporate
    chains. The facilities these chains control are standardized by
    central offices and any innovation must be justified by the "bot-
    tom line." The large corporations are driving many of the non-
    profits and other independent homes to the wall, since these
    smaller units cannot compete with their economies of scale but
    are subject to the rules designed for them.
3. A regulatory apparatus that seems unable to control either its
    own growth or the facilities it seeks to regulate. The regulators'
    efforts to rope in the rogue elephants of the industry compel
    them to issue a flood of requirements experienced as arbitrary
    and give their dealings an adversarial character.

The findings of the National Nursing Home Survey support the
impression of nursing home personnel that today's patients are
older and more impaired (National Center for Health Statistics and
Hing, 1987; National Center for Health Statistics and Hing, Sekscenski, and Strahan, 1989) but they are also younger and sicker.
Increasing community support and prospective hospital payments
account for the paradox.

In-home supportive services and home health care are skimming
off many of the old old, frail but alert, who made up much of the
population of homes for the aged when residential care was less
costly and fewer community services were available. Before Medicare switched to prospective payment (DRGs), hospitals found it
profitable to keep many of their young old patients until they were
well enough to go home. Under prospective payment, they are reim-

bursed according to diagnosis, not length of stay. Consequently, hospitals make as much money and incur fewer costs if they discharge Medicare patients early.

When Shaughnessy and Kramer (1990) compared nursing home populations before and after the introduction of prospective payment, they distinguished between traditional homes that provided maintenance and high-Medicare homes that offered rehabilitation and convalescent care. The populations of both changed greatly between 1982 and 1986. Medicare homes were getting patients who needed much more nursing care and traditional homes were receiving patients who required much more personal care and supervision.

Medicare payment for rehabilitation in the nursing home ends abruptly when the patient ceases to make significant progress. Its funding does not allow for the fact that many of the very old need to have their rehabilitation provided in smaller doses over a longer period of time (Becker and Kaufman, 1988). When this payment stops, the Medicare home transfers the person either to one of its own Medicaid beds or out to another facility. The traditional homes are receiving Medicare "push-outs," who are making greater demands on their staffs without a proportionate increase in reimbursement. Thus Medicare changes are reverberating through the system, affecting even homes that do not accept its patients.

The second intractable factor is the consolidation of the health care industry under a few large chains, as noted in Chapter Ten. The chains' economies of scale occur not only in the purchase of supplies but also in the deployment of personnel. The big chains can centralize certain management services, such as purchasing and accounting, while allocating some professionals to more than one facility in a locality. The independent facility must meet the same mandates for staffing with fewer resources. As Stoesz (1989) points out, the chains aim at severe standardization within Medicaid limits. Because they bring a high level of sophistication to skirting these requirements, state regulations are finely prescribed to prevent their evasion. Independent facilities must conform to the same rules although their strength lies in their ability to respond to individual needs rather than to pare costs by reducing choice. Thus they are caught in a sometimes costly web of control geared to giants.

The third seemingly intractable condition is the resulting regulatory climate. This is experienced by administrators and nursing staff as even more oppressive than rising costs and staff turnover. In the nearly two decades since the Senate's subcommittee on long-term care lamented the flagrant abuses and the failure of enforcement (U.S. Senate, 1974), regulation has become a force to be reckoned with. Congress's recent OBRA has limited the use of restraints, dealt with the quality of life, mandated professional social services in any facility with 120 beds or more, required certification and continuing education for nursing assistants, and prescribed a hierarchy of penalties short of closing (U.S. Department of Health and Human Services, 1989). (Regulators have always been reluctant to close poor facilities because this has meant relocation of the elderly residents, so these lesser penalties are more likely to be invoked.) These are only more recent measures. Although OBRA's requirements relate specifically to Medicare and Medicaid certified homes, facilities like Mountainside and Countryside feel their impact because most of their provisions are incorporated in state regulations.

Regulation has improved staffing, but the emphasis on documentation has undercut many of its benefits by taking time away from implementation. According to Buckholdt and Gubrium (1983), when planning and charting become reactive to paper-oriented inspection processes, the intended functions of communication and client-oriented planning become secondary. Manuals are written with nursing philosophies spelled out and emergency plans are developed, but there is not the slightest evidence that staff members have been encouraged to read them.

In an effort to reduce the redundant paperwork and relate inspections to real patient care, the federal government's Health Care Financing Administration introduced a new survey process in 1986 (Balcerzak, 1985). Instead of checking the facility's written policies-and-procedure manuals each time, surveyors were instructed to tour the home, observe treatment processes, interview the residents, and then make judgments about compliance. The substitution of output criteria for input measurements was supposed to reduce the burden on homes and at the same time produce more meaningful compliance (Morford, 1988).

With all of this, there was no guarantee that inspection would strike less dread into the hearts of administrators and nurses.

Workers in the field tell me that the effect of attempts to simplify the survey process have been additive: Cautious inspectors follow both the new procedures and the old.

A major complaint has been that the survey process has been adversarial rather than consultative. Although there are provisions in the guidelines for exit conferences and further reviews, these were proposed to negotiate agreement on what the deficiencies were rather than to provide consultation about how the home could remedy the problem (Health Care Financing Administration, 1989).

The survey process has ended some abuses, but it also has introduced negative consequences of its own, such as records that conceal rather than reveal the realities of patient life. Presently some administrators are so preoccupied with the next inspection and the quarterly report that patient care is conducted on an ad hoc basis with little real planning, monitoring, or supervision. Their concern often seeps through the setting, disrupting the rhythms of service delivery and giving ordinary routines a defensive character.

To Administrators: Suggestions for Your Psychic Survival

Administrators are the most beleaguered persons in the system because they are expected to meet incompatible goals and must depend on everyone's help to do it. They must (1) pass the next inspection and avoid costly citations, (2) keep costs down, and (3) provide quality care.

The for-profit sector does not make goals two and three any easier by changing them to "making a profit for the company" and "providing a marketable level of service." "A marketable level of service" must be standardized enough to be cost effective and packaged well enough to attract private-pay clients.

Administrators receive suggestions from everyone. In the freestanding for-profits, these come from owners; in the chains, corporate managers, and in the nonprofits, boards. Anyone interested enough to serve on a sectarian facility's board is likely to have strong feelings about the image the home should project. In lowcare areas, like Mountainside's apartments and boarding units, residents are in every respect capable of voicing their views. Those patients who cannot often have relatives who complain for them.

No one ever became an administrator because he or she was seeking a quiet life.

Because you as administrators are so central, I will address you directly, knowing full well that many of the things I suggest will be familiar to you. There are many things you can do to restore sanity to your systems.

Foster a strong, unified peer group among your residents. Social exchange theory provides a guide to working with those who are alert and well. Such residents need gratifying roles that will enable them to earn social credit. The boarders at Mountainside who had happy, sheltered old ages were those who arranged the flowers, made the announcements, organized the sewing group, gardened, served as table hosts and hostesses, and otherwise came out ahead in the processes of social exchange. Exchange relationships bind individuals together into functional groups; a strong peer group manages many of its own maintenance tasks. Even though waves of anxiety and misinformation can sweep through such a group quickly, it tends to be self-healing and reequilibriates more easily because it has natural channels of communication and support.

The difficulty is that today's older residents have lower reserves. They are entering congregate settings only when they or their families feel that their need to save energy outweighs the threat to their independence. To the extent that they hold back from leadership on this account, tailor demands to their strength. To the degree that they are influenced by the larger society's low expectations, disregard their misgivings and thrust autonomy on them. Each resident has a helping role to play. Finding it will contribute greatly to contentment.

In the long run, a cohesive peer group reduces complaints and demands. For example, a resident committee that is encouraged to meet with the dietitian and the cook, provided with information, and asked to poll other residents about their preferences within a defined range is less likely to complain about menu limitations designed to keep their own board rates from rising.

Matters are not so easily managed in the nursing unit, where costs career, accidents occur, surveyors give citations, and short staffing and absenteeism contribute to all these problems. Nevertheless, there are steps you can take:

1. *Check staff turnover.* Turnover costs money, wastes training time, and increases the likelihood of "incidents."

2. *Prevent theft and property loss.* Things are misplaced, taken by confused patients, or stolen by staff. Some misplacement is inevitable when so many persons live in close quarters and laundry services are shared. In addition, confused persons often mistake other patients' things for their own or help themselves casually like boys in an apple orchard. Alert patients need a locked drawer so they can keep snacks and other small items safe. This gives them some sense of control in a setting in which they have very little. Failure to provide this small security betokens a basic mistrust of their capacity to manage even so small a kingdom.

Petty theft by employees demands your immediate attention. Its neglect suggests to patients and their families that this is an unsafe place and that management does not control its staff. There are things you can do. A speedy response to reported loss is unlikely to result in many retrievals but it communicates to both patients and employees that management takes these losses seriously. Other measures take longer because the causes of the problem are more deeply ingrained, in the society if not in your facility itself. The roots of this thievery are disquieting because they appear to lie in the cleavage between caregiver and patient that results at least in part from the structural racism within many health care settings.

Address the basic alienation between white middle-class patients and poor, ethnically different staff members. In-service training can help modify the attitudes of nursing assistants toward their elderly patients, but your best tool is a nondiscriminatory hiring policy.

In planning your educational approach to staff attitudes, remember that the elderly do not always give up their biases easily and patients are often rude to minority staff members. Because we as professionals are middle-class, we fail to recognize the values and mannerisms of patients that may be foreign to those from different milieux. Help your nursing assistants understand their elderly patients better so they will not be needlessly offended by them. They need to perceive the uncertainties and losses that lie behind patients' demandingness, so they can experience them as human beings who have participated in life experiences that they, too, can grasp.

Examine role assignment within your staff. Many times the racism of patients appears to be supported by the hiring policies of the setting itself. If all the African-American, Latino, and Filipino employees are nursing assistants and all the nurses and clerks are white, the castelike division makes it hard for ill-paid help to relate to the sanctity of property belonging to either patients or facility. Consider promotion within the ranks. Thanks to a community college, administrative encouragement, and her own efforts, Mountainside's former laundress is now a licensed nurse on the staff.

Finally, stabilize the work force. This reduces theft because the worker who stays establishes some bonds with the setting and the people in it. The transient employee is stealing from strangers.

3. *Reduce absenteeism.* I have followed the fortunes of a large nursing home during much of the last decade. Most medication errors, patient falls, and other events that brought the threat of regulatory action involved nurses or nursing assistants from the registry. Called on short notice to fill a vacancy, they did not know the patients and the patients did not know them.

A number of factors contribute to absenteeism, including problems at home. At the same time, good relationships with fellow employees tend to bind the worker to the job. You can encourage group cohesion by assigning compatible partners to common work areas and by organizing teams to achieve together. A nursing assistant's absenteeism then becomes an act of disloyalty to peers, not an offense against an impersonal organization.

4. *Integrate inspections into the regular work cycle.* The best preparation for surveys is good patient care, which cannot be provided when attention is skewed to this single event. Concern rises when the calendar suggests that inspection is likely. It deflates with relief when the survey has passed. The employee reminded about records when inspection seems imminent soon learns that the purpose of record keeping is to avoid a citation. Defensive recording defeats the real purpose of charting, which is to ensure continuity of care. Positive recording suppresses problems, but problems exist. Showing that they were recognized and dealt with is more effective.

See that staff members at all levels understand what the requirements really are and their purpose—why they are important to patient care and required by the state. These rules are a useful tool for you because they have the impersonal force of law: You are not

thrusting them down staff members' throats; you are trying to help
them comply. The performance of nursing assistants places an inor-
dinate burden on supervising nurses if they do not grasp the regulatory context of treatment. This is particularly true when
behavior verges on patient abuse.

> In a large public facility, a patient threw her breakfast
> dishes on the floor. Exasperated nursing assistants
> placed the woman on the floor and commanded her to
> pick them up. Supervisory staff reported the incident
> as the law required and suspended the offenders. What
> struck them was that the aides had not grasped that
> this was patient abuse in the eyes of the law. System-
> wide in-service training followed.

5. *Temper the adversarial climate.* Being "nice" will not change
the regulations, but reducing staff defensiveness and counterthreat
will lower tension for all parties.

Although surveyors have been instructed to emphasize patient
care above paper compliance, they continue to gather written evidence as assiduously as before because they fear being challenged
and unable to make the deficiency statement stick. This is an understandable response to the guardedness they encounter when staff
members feel they are on trial. The exit interview becomes an occasion not so much for clarification as for rebuttal. Energies would
be better spent on plans of correction.

What Professionals and Families Can Do

While administrators struggle with costs and licensure, many of
the professionals who might improve the homes distance themselves instead. According to Wiener and Kayser-Jones (1990), professionals working in these settings are immobilized by their own
sense of impotence. Neither staff members nor families are helpless
but when they abdicate, as many do, they contribute to the disorder
that plagues the system.

Foremost among these are physicians, who often transfer their
patients once they have gotten them placed. Physicians' avoidance

has been attributed to the meager rewards and low status associated with practice in these settings, to their lack of training for work with the chronically ill elderly, to the depressing sounds and sights, to the frustrations of dealing with chronic disease, and to the threat of their own aging (Kayser-Jones, 1981). A more likely cause is their sense of powerlessness. They issue orders without certainty that they will be properly carried out (Wiener and Kayser-Jones, 1990). They depend on nurses too overburdened to supervise the paraprofessionals who do much of the work. This is distressing to persons dedicated to giving protection and care.

Nevertheless, theirs is the ultimate signature and the necessary assent. They are external to the system but essential to its operation, and they are in a position to take a stand. There are two things physicians can do:

First, they can set aside a regular time to visit and an appropriate time for the nurse to call. This will not free them from all interruptions, but once it is institutionalized, it will reduce day-to-day irritations by introducing some predictability into their relations with the home.

Second, they can educate the staff by example, by bedside instruction, and by in-service training: They can demonstrate good practice and simple courtesy by addressing patients directly when they examine them, they can enlist the nurse as a partner by explaining some of their goals and their rationale; they can speak at one of the home's in-service trainings. Since these sessions tend to be brisk and pro forma, not much will be learned at the time but physicians who assist will gain salience for staff at all levels and thus ensure greater attention to their wishes and to the needs of their patients. Finally, physicians who listen thoughtfully to the nurses and are not too irritable when they call win both loyalty and devotion. This may be their best gift to their patients—the nurses then know them as "Doctor X's patients" and treat them accordingly.

When physicians' visits are perfunctory, they communicate to the staff that their patients are of no account to them either and thus contribute to the general disrespect they find so distressing. Everything the physician does has an impact on the setting.

Although physicians are powerful in these homes because most of the rules, borrowed from the hospital, have been written for

them, the most important individuals are nurses. Directors of nursing control the staff and set the tone; they are managers, clinicians,
and educators; they can protect the owners from angry relatives and
litigation.

Wise administrators conserve their directors of nursing. They free
them to spend time at the bedside—the activity for which they studied nursing. They see that they do not have to make frantic phone
calls for replacements when somebody calls in sick or carry the main
burden of writing reports that can be assigned to others. They respect their breathing space as well as their professionalism. There
are two reasons for this. One is to preserve an asset: Turnover in this
position is disruptive. Another is to keep the director of nursing on
the floor, which greatly improves patient care. When directors of
nursing give patient care, they make the point that the task is important, so important they are willing to do it themselves.

Like the physician and the director of nursing, all licensed nurses
are in powerful exchange positions: Their presence is mandated by
law and certain acts, such as the distribution of medications, can be
performed by no one else. Their professional performance is diminished when short staffing transforms their task into one of just
getting through the shift.

Licensed nurses can reduce the staff turnover that makes their
work so difficult by treating nursing assistants as team members
rather than as menials. If the assistants do what the nurses say but
do not understand it, they can neither anticipate nor follow through
without another order. Nurses can improve the quality of the nursing assistants' observations by questioning them about patients and
listening to their replies. They can expand their understanding by
including them in the patient care planning conferences. Every licensed nurse can be an educator. The bedside instruction nurses
provide their nursing assistants is more important than their formal
in-service training because it occurs in the work context and cannot
be dismissed as something they are supposed to be told but not
necessarily required to do.

Even the devalued aides are not totally without power, because
turnover is costly and upsets the system. More than anyone else, they
can contribute to residents' immediate comfort if they are given time
to do so.

Because a nursing home is just that, members of the nursing staff do not have to establish their identity, but social workers do. Many of the persons called social workers in these settings have not been social workers at all. Because owners were merely meeting a requirement, they often selected as social service designees nursing assistants or secretaries who could interview families enough to fill in forms. When more credentials were required, they contracted for consultation by professional social workers. The consultant spent too few hours to relate to the home and its residents or to work well with staff. Most of the consultant's time was spent instructing the designee and signing off for her. Even the college-educated designee with a social science background was not fully equipped for the task: She was not socialized to the profession itself or to its code of ethics, she could not present professional standards, and she was too dependent on the owner to move beyond his or her immediate vision and develop a program. This suited owners who wanted as little change as possible.

The Omnibus Budget Reconciliation Act of 1987 helped, but not a great deal, when it described a "qualified social worker" as "an individual with a bachelors degree in social work or two years experience in a health care setting working directly with patients or clients or similar professional qualification" (U.S. Department of Health and Human Services, 1989, p. 5343). Among social workers, the practitioner with a B.S.W. is considered a professional social worker, but an M.S.W. is the preferred degree for this position.

Social workers' first task in these settings is to enhance their social credit by demonstrating what they can do. Their credit rises when they relieve the kinds of pressures they have been specifically taught to deal with—those presented by difficult families and angry, anxious, or depressed patients—when they help patients receive their financial entitlements, when they deal with red tape, secure speakers, negotiate referrals, organize family councils and patient groups, and prove helpful through the survey process.

Social workers sometimes annoy others with their reformatory zeal, but when they have established their skills, their advocacy for clients becomes more acceptable. Then they are free to introduce new programs and make other changes: Management will let them enhance care as long as it does not cost money. Since in-service training is mandated for the nursing assistants, social workers can join nurses in improving the aides' communication skills and sensitizing them to the psychosocial aspects of care. Most other professionals are happy to turn families over to the social worker, especially when the families are complaining.

The other professionals in the setting—dietitians, physiotherapists, occupational therapists, and activities directors—are recognized for their expertise. They can use their visibility to communicate standards of care by demonstration. For example, dietitians can remind staff of their patients' individuality and continuing capacity for choice by taking into account their preferences. They can ask the birthday patient what kind of cake he or she likes, and then they can make sure that everyone knows that this is the cake the patient chose. The range may be narrow, but to consult patients at all makes a statement about their human worth.

Families, too, have more power than they know to humanize the setting. Their importance as informants is recognized in the OBRA requirement that the families or legal representatives of three patients be interviewed by surveyors as part of the inspection process (Health Care Financing Administration, 1989). Despite the threats—"If you don't like it here, why don't you take your mother home?"—few homes are going to take action: Adult children and spouses who can articulate their complaints are entirely capable of going to the ombudsman if there is evidence of reprisals.

Families can advocate effectively for their patient. As a first step, they should increase their own visibility. They should approach staff members with their concerns while they can still discuss them calmly and be clear about what they want. To complain without presenting a feasible alternative is merely to harass an already overburdened staff. If their complaints are serious, they should keep notes so they can be precise about dates and details when they pursue them through other channels.

Family members can make the family council the effective instrument it was intended to be. Because the placement of a parent or a spouse is a painful event, few families attend the council meetings. Those who do often relate in a wheel-and-spokes fashion to the staff member facilitating the meeting, voicing only specific concerns about their own patient. Instead, family members should use this opportunity to nurture system change with positive reinforcement for good things done. In doing so, they are not only acting for their own patient but also helping to humanize the setting for others.

Research Agendas

As part of its OBRA implementation, the Health Care Financing Administration contracted to have the Research Triangle Institute in North Carolina develop a single resident assessment form that could be updated whenever there was a change in the patient's status. States were allowed to devise their own versions but these had to include the minimum data sent (MDS). This standard form was intended to replace the multitude of forms currently required to meet the demands of federal, state, and other authorities and thus reduce paper work. The MDS provides data for research and monitoring. It makes possible comparable findings across studies and helps policy makers track population changes more quickly than the National Nursing Home Surveys.

Even now, many of the trends are clear. Accepting these, research can address the population mix but policy will have to consider the findings within the context society is able and willing to fund.

Research should look at the following elements of nursing home care.

1. *The younger, sicker hospital dischargees.* What institutional and community provision would expedite their return to more independent living?

One concern would be to determine whether iatrogenic effects are prolonging their dependency. Another would be to test different programs of support and challenge. These DRG orphans may need a greater range of psychosocial interventions to enable them to take advantage of the physical rehabilitation currently offered.

> One Countryside resident spent the remaining fifteen years of her life as a patient because she was so frightened by her fall and solitary hours on the floor that she refused to try to walk with her newly pinned hip.

There was no evidence that her fears had been addressed by any means except exhortation.

2. *The alert but physically frail older persons in congregate care.* What combination of physical environment, intellectual challenge, and social supports can prolong their social functioning?

Do present regulations banning walkers in the boarding units press these individuals into a higher level of care prematurely? Would modifications in stairways and bathrooms help? The writer visited a home for the aging in Madrid where the elevator was inaccessible to residents but very wide stairs with low risers encouraged them to walk.

Most Mountainside and Countryside boarders struggled against transfer and some were able to delay it long after others would have been moved. What are the costs or gains to other residents when a home keeps failing members in the boarding unit longer?

3. *The relatively alert patients with chronic disabilities or terminal illnesses.* How can staff better support their autonomy and their preferred personae?

4. *The cognitively impaired.* What kind of physical environment and programs best preserve mobility, continence, and morale?

Many nursing homes are adding special care units for Alzheimer's patients. Some merely adapt existing wards while a few provide the additional safe space needed to meet the needs of physically active but very confused persons. What factors distinguish the better special care units from the others? What are the criteria for transfer to the special care unit? When should the patient be returned to routine nursing care? Would it be practical to combine an inpatient program with day care—either from the resident's home or from other units? How do costs compare?

5. *Differential staffing.* Are there ways to achieve cost effectiveness without sacrificing standards of care?

The hospital dischargees need heavy staffing with an emphasis on skilled nursing care and rehabilitation. Other resident groups may need the availability of nursing services but much more in the line of personal care (nursing assistants) and psychosocial intervention (social workers and activity directors). What combinations are optimal?

6. *Ways to stabilize and improve the work force.* The labor intensity of long-term care makes it unlikely that wages for its foot soldiers will ever be comparable to those of policemen, firemen, or retail clerks, although in many respects the demands are the same. Improvement will have to come within the setting. Now that continuing education for nursing assistants has been federally mandated, more attention needs to be paid to making it effective. Special programs for bilingual aides could be tested. Cohen-Mansfield (1988) and others have addressed the problem of absenteeism. Much more is needed.

7. *Ways to promote safety without restraints and to encourage continence.* Many studies have introduced short-lived programs that have proved their worth and vanished. In their battle with costs, administrators have not appreciated the gains enough to continue them at the facility's expense. One of the most famous of these experiments increased patients' adjustment by giving them control over visitation, but the experiment was terminated at the study's end. The investigator scrupulously reported the regression that followed (Rodin, Timko, and Harris, 1985). Findings like these have raised questions about the ethics of one-time interventions.

The studies should continue. They put the patients again in the position of being givers, a role most have lost. As residents assist the interviewer or join the group, the balance of social exchange is redressed for a little while. The contribution of these studies to staff is twofold: The importance of their work becomes manifest when researchers swoop down to question them or to interview their patients, but better still, even the temporary gains their patients make show them what can be done when there is the will to do it.

We who are interested in the elderly, we, too, could use that will. And lest we fear what lies ahead of us as we ourselves grow older, it is comforting to note that many residents at Countryside and Mountainside never lacked the will to act on their own behalf. They lived in superior settings and had the support of families and staff but they also helped themselves. They negotiated the terms of their own old age.

As I write, Jean Blackwell, the last member of the cohort and Agnes Chase's fellow campaigner, now ninety-four, lives in Mountainside's nursing unit, her energy level grown low. She dedicated much of her life to others through three careers—teaching, social work, and the ministry—and in giving, she gained. She practices intentional poverty: Her only luxury is a journal. Physical activity gave her the strength to do what she wished far into late life. Until a few years ago, neighbors said they often saw her jogging to the park; more recently, she walked every day. Her good intellect grapples with the currents of the times. She has never been an easy person and it would be disappointing if she became one now. She eschewed the comfort of conformity and managed to live on her own terms: Like many of her fellow residents, she negotiated a good old age.

RESOURCES

RESOURCE A
Attrition During the Study

**Table A.1. The Thinning of a Cohort: Subject Attrition
at Mountainside and Countryside.**

	Mountainside		Countryside		Total	
	Number of		Number of		Number	Percentage
	Boarders	Patients	Boarders	Patients	Still There	
1974	24	27	14	51	116	100
1975	17	31	6	44	98	85
1976	15	24	5	22	66	57
1977	14	16	1	11	42	36
1978	13	15	1	8	37	32
1979	11	15		6	32	28
1980	11	11		6	28	24
1981	10	10		6	26	22
1982	8	5		6	19	16
1983	6	4		4	14	12
1984	5	3		4	12	10
1985	4	2		0	6	5
1986	3	2		0	5	4
1987	3	2		0	5	4
1988	2	1		0	3	2
1989		1		0	1	1
1990		1		0	1	0

Because more than three-quarters (78.48 percent) of Countryside residents were patients at the start as opposed to slightly more than half (52.94 percent) at Mountainside, attrition was much faster at Countryside. In 1984, the remaining four cohort members at Countryside died, and my visits to that home ceased.

Forty-one Mountainside residents (80 percent) and forty-four Countryside residents (68 percent) died in the home. (This does not include one woman who returned to the community, remained there seven years, and only came back to Countryside for the last eleven days of her life.) Twenty-one Countryside residents left; eleven transferring directly to Medicaid homes, five to the community or awaited-for placements, and five to hospitals for treatment. Of these, three were lost to the study and their death dates were unknown. Nine Mountainside residents moved; six to Medicaid homes and three to facilities providing intermediate care, which was not available at Mountainside. In 1990, one Mountainside subject was still living in the home.

Some individuals who entered the homes after the study cohort was closed are discussed in the text, but these do not enter statistical calculations. Of the 116 residents, eleven were unable to complete the Philadelphia Geriatric Morale Scale in 1974 and one was unwilling. Norm conformity was not scored for two Countryside residents because they were so near comatose as to make the concept irrelevant.

RESOURCE B
Instruments Used in the Study

Of the four instruments, three were developed expressly for this study. These were the norm sort, the norm conformity evaluation, and the social resource inventory. The fourth was a standard instrument, the Philadelphia Geriatric Morale Scale.

I employed the norm sort only once, at the study's start. Its findings guided the design of the norm conformity evaluation. The other tests were repeated in 1973–1974, 1978, 1979, 1980, 1981, 1982, 1983, and 1984, providing a series of individual scores for each resident.

Norm Sort

In each unit, residents and staff members were given four norms to rank in order of importance. Chapter Six discusses this instrument and its two underlying assumptions: There are four types of norms and residents and staff members value them differently. The findings not only made it possible to distinguish between staff and peer norms but also indicated the group solidarity and fragmentation within the setting. The norms employed in the instrument were gathered by field observation and interviewing.

There are separate but equivalent versions for the Mountainside and Countryside boarders and a single version for the two homes' patients because the settings themselves differed. This is illustrated by the second norm for boarders. Mountainside boarders often went away for the day and therefore the cook needed to know whether they would be dining in; Countryside boarders could elect to eat either in their own lounge or in the general dining room downstairs, so staff needed to know where to set places for them.

Mountainside Boarding Unit

1. Guests should sign out when they go out.
2. Guests should notify staff when they expect to miss a meal.

3. Guests should not discuss unpleasant subjects (such as sickness) at the table.
4. Guests should make a well-groomed appearance that will not discredit their fellow residents.

Countryside Boarding Unit

1. Guests should accept the help of staff to protect them from falls.
2. Guests should remember to tell Helen where they will be taking their lunch.
3. Guests should not say things that hurt the feelings of other guests.
4. Guests should make a well-groomed appearance that will not discredit their fellow guests.

Mountainside and Countryside Nursing Units

1. Patients should respect the safeguards the nurses provide for their protection, such as bed rails and soft ties.
2. Patients should take their medicine promptly when the nurse offers it.
3. Patients should not take more than their share of staff attention at the expense of other patients.
4. Patients should not act silly, making visitors think this is a place for crazy people.

In each instance, (1) is a security norm, (2) a maintenance norm, (3) is an internal tension management norm, and (4) is an external image management norm.

Norm Conformity Evaluation

Separate but parallel instruments were prepared for each unit. Each listed in succession (1) a maintenance norm, (2) a security norm, (3) an internal tension management norm, (4) an external tension management norm, (5) an internal tension management norm, and (6) a maintenance norm. Residents were scored by staff members. For the relative scoring of patients and boarders, see Chapter Six, page 131, and for the association between social resource and norm conformity scores, see page 135. The different versions in the two homes are dealt with in Chapter One, page 9.

Mountainside Boarders

1. Meals
   a. Appears promptly. Posts note when expects to be absent.
   b. Occasionally inconveniences tablemates or waitresses by arriving late, finishing last, or expecting unusual service. Notifies staff orally when expects to miss a meal—or fails to do so altogether.
   c. As often as twice a month, makes late, disruptive entries, holds up others with slowness, wants special service, or forgets to notify staff when missing a meal.
2. Sign-Out
   a. Always signs in and out.
   b. Occasionally makes both entries on return—or forgets them altogether.
   c. Forgets to sign out more than two or three times a month.
3. Not Pushing Oneself Forward
   a. Avoids front row, does not often volunteer opinion in group situation, never "takes over" unless asked by staff. (Exception: acknowledged group leader acting with peer support. Criterion: no complaints.)
   b. Sometimes offers unsolicited opinion and occasionally contests for leadership. (Criterion: complaints from other residents in addition to the challenged leader.)
   c. Mistakes group cues and tends to try to take over, speaking for group and sometimes striving to assume duties of staff.
4. Decorum
   a. Accepted by fellow boarders as a well-spoken, appropriately dressed representative of their group, not necessarily a leader, but one they would feel comfortable claiming as a member.
   b. Dress and/or manner elicit occasional comments to the administrator by other boarders or hints to the offender.

   c.   Dress, manners, or demeanor elicit active eldering by
        members of peer group.
5. Being Considerate
   a.   Never has TV or radio audible beyond own room.
   b.   Occasionally has radio or TV too loud at night or makes
        other noise so that administrator or neighbors have to
        hint.
   c.   Blaring TV or radio in disregard of neighbors, plainly
        audible after 10 P.M.
6. Room Maintenance
   a.   Keeps room "picked up" and tidy, requiring no special
        service from housekeeping staff.
   b.   Clean but untidy, requiring some attention by others (but
        not on a regular basis) and/or careless about public rooms.
   c.   Frequently careless about own room, requiring extra at-
        tention of others on a regular basis (allows dirty laundry
        to accumulate, for example) or the person's untidiness in
        public rooms (for example, shared bathrooms) is sufficient
        to cause complaint.

Countryside Guests

1. Meals
   a.   Prompt. Tells staff in advance if there is to be a change in
        dining routine.
   b.   Occasionally inconveniences staff by forgetting to report a
        change in plans or by demands for special service.
   c.   As often as once a week, upsets staff work routines in one
        of the following ways: late for meals, forgets to notify
        about change in plans, demands special service on short
        notice.
2. Bath Safety
   a.   Arranges to have a staff person standing by when getting
        in and out of tub or shower.
   b.   Sometimes forgets to get staff help for getting in and out
        of tub or shower.
   c.   Either dodges staff supervision of bath safety by bathing at

unscheduled times or evades supervision by avoiding bath until reminded.

3. Interpersonal Conflict

When a guest does not like another guest,

   a. Tolerates him or her when present and avoids him or her when possible.

   b. Complains and attempts to involve staff; occasionally makes sharp, critical remarks.

   c. Pursues conflict: makes hostile remarks, attempts to get staff and guests to take sides, and/or interferes with other's use of the common areas (for example, by switching TV channels or preempting seat).

4. Appearance and Demeanor

   a. Makes well-groomed, "sensible" appearance so that other guests tend to include him or her when outsiders are present.

   b. Appearance and social behavior sometimes inappropriate so that guests tend to avoid him or her when they have visitors.

   c. Appearance and behavior create impression of senile confusion so that guests either "explain" or tend to invoke staff help in avoiding resident.

5. Being Considerate

   a. Attentive to the needs and feelings of others: including others in conversations, being helpful to patients (in ways approved of by staff), and watching out for newcomers.

   b. Sometimes insensitive to others, as shown by noisy TV or radio, demands for service by others, noisy complaints, talking when others are watching TV.

   c. Inconsiderate of others: demands to be taken first, "overflowing" into others' territory, moving others' possessions, interrupting.

6. Room Maintenance

   a. Keeps room "picked up" and tidy, requiring no special services from housekeeping staff.

   b. Clean but untidy, requiring some attention by others (but not on a regular basis) and/or careless about public rooms.

   c. Own room requires extra attention on a regular basis and/

or untidiness in public rooms sufficient to cause
complaint.

Mountainside Patients

1. Medication
   a. Takes medicine promptly without argument.
   b. Takes medicine but must be coaxed or watched.
   c. Has refused or spit out medication. Sometimes it has
      seemed best not to press compliance and/or he or she has
      successfully "cheated."
2. Safeguards
   a. Accepts restraints and boundaries provided for safety—
      such as bed rails, soft ties, or staff-set limits such as
      "within sight" or "on grounds."
   b. Accepts safeguards but sometimes tests them and/or
      protests.
   c. Climbs out of bed despite bed rail, attempts to undo soft
      ties, and/or must be supervised constantly lest he or she
      disregard boundaries and stray.
3. Table Behavior
   a. Except for the effect of tremors, behavior (conversation,
      manner of eating, and so on) makes him or her an accept-
      able tablemate for any other patient.
   b. Table behavior precludes seating with the most alert
      patients.
   c. Regressed table behavior elicits complaints and/or avoid-
      ance by most other patients, so that there is a seating
      problem.
4. Decent Appearance
   a. Presents a neat, "decent" appearance and observes at least
      the surface proprieties (even though staff may have to help
      with dress). Alert patients with visitors are not embarrassed
      by appearance or behavior.
   b.. Occasionally unaware that appearance is unsuitable
      (moist, unzipped, or uncovered) and/or approaches vis-
      itors inappropriately so that some staff oversight is re-
      quired and some complaints are made.

    c.   Constant staff oversight required to achieve a "decent" apearance, and alert guests with visitors are embarrassed or feel the need to "explain."

5.   Attention

    a.   While pleasant, does not demand attention to a degree resented by roomate. (Resentment would be indicated by direct or indirect complaints.)

    b.   Through the use of charm, complaints of pain, or persistent demands, contrives to secure extra staff attention, resulting in notable neglect of roommate or arousing resentment of roommate. (Personnel cannot enter the room without paying attention to him or her.)

    c.   At least one reshuffle of roommates has been required because of difficulty that appears related to monopolizing staff attention. (If patient is in a single room, note reaction of other patients in general.)

6.   Bathing Routines

    a.   Ready, willing, and cooperative with staff routine.

    b.   Complies, but only with diplomatic staff handling and with some verbal protest.

    c.   Bath consistently presents a problem, circumvented only at the cost of staff time and patience.

Countryside Patients.

(This is identical with the version for Mountainside patients except that item 5 is different.)

5.   Interaction

When person does not like another patient,

    a.   Tolerates the patient when present, quietly avoids him or her and only on rare occasions (with good cause) requests staff intervention.

    b.   Frequently complains to staff about annoying patients (when avoidance would be possible) and has hostile verbal exchanges upon moderate provocation.

    c.   As often as once a month, strikes out, trips, kicks, or engages in loud, hostile interchanges on low provocation.

Score 3 for a, 2 for b, and 1 for c.
>   High Norm Conformity   = 18
>   Medium Norm Conformity   = 17–14
>   Low Norm Conformity   = 13–6

Staff norms are 1, 2, and 6. Peer norms are 3, 4, and 5.

Social Resource Inventory

This measures resources the individual brings to his or her social exchanges: the ability to do without the services of others, persons the resident can rally on his or her own behalf, and special rewards to bestow. This was scored by staff members for each resident. For more about the social resource inventory, see Chapter Four, pages 72–75.

A. Internal Human Resources
>   1. Cognitive and Self-Care Skills
>>   a. Dress
>>>   (1) Needs help dressing
>>>   (2) Dresses self but without supervision would put on soiled clothing or wear mismatching items or have slip showing. Must have help with assembling laundry and arranging repairs. Others must shop for resident.
>>>   (3) Dresses self, procures and cares for clothing. (For shopping, requires only such help as transportation.)
>>   b. Personal Hygiene
>>>   (1) Incontinent beyond infrequent "accidents." (Special provisions for incontinence are routinely made—such as an incontinence pad on wheelchair seat.)
>>>   (2) Sometimes soiled or untidy (fly unzipped, clothing misbuttoned or food-stained) and/or occasional "accidents" or nocturnal enuresis.
>>>   (3) Nails clean, neatly groomed (without undue efforts by the staff), bathes on own initiative or (if

bath must be scheduled for the convenience of others) willingly.

c. Food

    (1) Does not assume responsibility for own arrival at meals (someone must hunt for, fetch, or remind person most days) and/or requires substantial help with feeding.

    (2) Others must assume some responsibility for appearance at meals (lest resident be late) and/or is an untidy eater, requiring bib and/or some help in feeding. (Does not forget meals, however, and knows when he or she has just eaten or is about to eat.)

    (3) Assumes responsibility for appearance at meals (notifies staff if expects to miss one), is prompt, and eats acceptably.

d. Procurement

    (1) Takes no responsibility for procurement of personal supplies, such as toothpaste, toilet articles, or newspaper. (Even deficits must be noted by other people.)

    (2) Notes and reports deficits but takes no active role in procurement. ("I have no Kleenex.")

    (3) Arranges procurement of personal supplies, such as stationery, stamps, toilet articles, and newspaper and sees that they are paid for.

2. Social Outreach

a. Outreach

    (1) Avoids interaction, responds only when addressed, spends much time sitting and staring—or makes constant, repetitive demands on an infantile level (as opposed to true communication).

    (2) Participates in and sometimes initiates conversation (beyond mere passive response).

    (3) Corresponds with or telephones persons outside or, lacking friends or relatives outside the home,

reads the paper and follows news on TV or radio.

b.   Particularization

(1)   Can name fewer than three fellow residents (by first, last, or customary names or recognizable nickname).

(2)   Can name as many as three but fewer than six fellow residents and/or employees.

(3)   Can name more than five fellow residents and/or employees.

3.   Health and Physical Mobility

a.   Mobility

(1)   Bedridden, wheelchair-bound, or requires walker or arm—or confusion necessitates an escort.

(2)   Walks in community unescorted (beyond institution grounds).

(3)   Drives own car or uses public transportation unescorted (if taxi, can summon it).

b.   Health Care

(1)   Needs health care he or she cannot manage alone, such as procedures ordinarily requiring the services of a nurse.

(2)   Needs supervision of routine medication, special diet, and/or help with prostheses (including hearing aid).

(3)   Manages own routine medication (insulin, aspirin), prostheses (dentures, hearing aid), and special diet. (Diet may be provided by the kitchen but resident is aware and does not cheat.)

B.   External Human Resources

a.   Outside Significant Others

(1)   Infrequent visitors or none.

(2)   At least one regular visitor. (This would ordinarily entail at least monthly visits except in the case of actively involved out-of-state visitors who frequently call or write and who may visit less often.)

(3)   Visitors who take the resident away for meals,

overnight visits, or shopping trips and other outings (or provide exceptional services if physical condition precludes going out).

b. Inside Significant Others (Residents have been asked to name five residents. Staff members have been told to name three residents "you would miss.")
    (1) Named by fewer than three other residents or staff members.
    (2) Named by at least three other persons.
    (3) Named by more than three other persons.

C. Material Resources
    a. Access to Funds
        (1) Bills paid by trustee or kinsperson who controls funds or by vendor payment.
        (2) Public assistance check only or Social Security check plus public assistance check requiring signature, or funds managed by kinsperson or friend who is also an attentive visitor as defined above under Ba(3).
        (3) Pays own bills from adequate personal resources or with Social Security check requiring signature and exceeding the amount of board (unsupplemented by public assistance).
    b. Facility
        (1) No resources that can be shared.
        (2) Occasional assets that can be shared—such as snacks, soda, excursions provided by family or friends.
        (3) Desirable equipment that can be shared on a regular basis (for example, a color TV).

D. Special Resource
    Has any one of the following:
    Membership in the sectarian home's sponsoring body (Mountainside)
    A significant medical connection (is a retired physician, has a close relative who is a practicing physician, or has been a registered nurse)
    Private duty nurse (Countryside)

Caseworker from the Santa Claus Society
Automobile

A-C, one point for each 1, two points for each 2, and three points for each 3. Score D by allowing two points if subject meets any one of the listed conditions. (No one is to receive more than two points.)

High resources   = 38-32
Medium resources   = 31-19
Low resources   = 18-12

At the study's start, two sections of the Social Resource Inventory, Cognitive and Self-Care Skills and Social Outreach, were used to provide a rough guide to mental alertness. This was scored as

Relatively alert   = 18-12
Less alert   = 11-0

At that time, social salience also was measured by using the item, "Name five people who live here and three people who work here." Staff members were asked, "Name three residents you would miss the most." Residents were then scored according to the number of staff members and peers who named them.

Highly chosen   = 2 or more
Less highly chosen   = fewer than 2

These measures became inapplicable as the study participants made up a smaller and smaller part of the pool of the resident population. Chapter Seven, pages 151-156, utilizes these social salience scores in its discussion of peer leadership.

The Philadelphia Geriatric Morale Scale

M. Lawton Powell's Philadelphia Geriatric Morale Scale proved to be both durable and productive. Initially it consisted of twenty-four items. Since the twenty-one-item version used in this study, the scale has been reduced to seventeen, but many of the items dropped were the very ones that stimulated the richest flow of comment by Mountainside and Countryside residents. For further discussion of the test, see Liang and Bollen (1983), Sauer and Warland (1982), Kane and Kane (1981), and Lawton (1972).

The version used here is available in a chapter by its author, M.

Powell Lawton (1973) in *Readings in Gerontology*, edited by Brantl and Brown.

In this study, 21-17 was high, 16-10 was medium, and 9-10 was low.

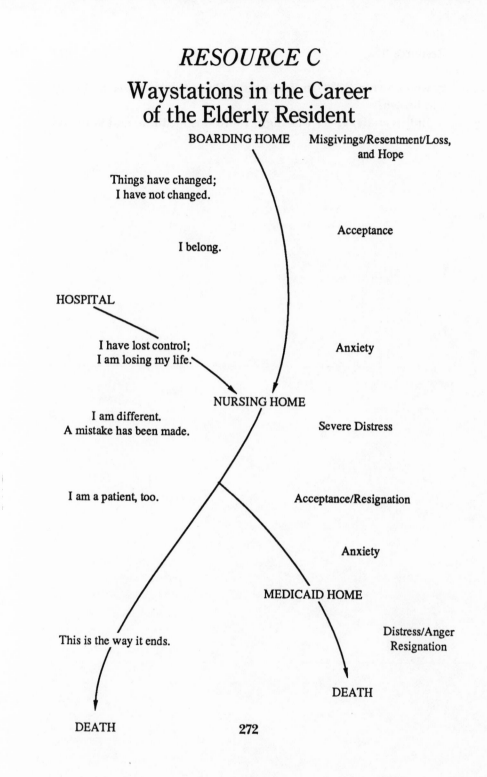

RESOURCE C

Waystations in the Career of the Elderly Resident

BOARDING HOME   Misgivings/Resentment/Loss, and Hope

Things have changed;
I have not changed.

Acceptance

I belong.

HOSPITAL

I have lost control;
I am losing my life.

Anxiety

NURSING HOME

I am different.
A mistake has been made.

Severe Distress

I am a patient, too.

Acceptance/Resignation

Anxiety

MEDICAID HOME

This is the way it ends.

Distress/Anger
Resignation

DEATH

DEATH

References

Aldrich, C. K., and Mendkoff, E. "Relocation of the Aged and Disabled: A Mortality Study." In B. Neugarten (ed.), *Middle Age and Aging*. Chicago: University of Chicago Press, 1968.

Antonucci, T. C. "Personal Characteristics, Social Support, and Social Behavior." In R. H. Binstock and E. Shanas (eds.), *Handbook of Aging and the Social Sciences*. (2nd ed.) New York: Van Nostrand Reinhold, 1985. (Antonucci credits David Plath, *Aging and Social Support: A Presentation on Work and Personality in the Middle Years*, Social Science Research Council, 1975, for the first use of the term *convoys of support*.)

Arling, G. "Aging, Failure and the Concept of a Moral Career." Paper presented at the 32nd annual meeting of the Gerontological Society of America, Washington, D.C., Nov. 1979.

Arling, G., Nordquist, R. H., and Capitman, J. A. "Nursing Home Cost and Ownership Type: Evidence of Interaction Effects." *Health Services Research*, 1987, *22* (1) 255–275.

Atchley, R. D. "A Continuity Theory of Normal Aging." *The Gerontologist*, 1989, *29* (2), 183–190.

Balcerzak, S. J. "Update: The New Long-Term Care Survey Process." *The Journal of Long-Term Care Administration*, 1985, *13* (4), 106–108.

Barusch, A. S. "Power Dynamics in the Aging Family: A Preliminary Statement." *Journal of Gerontological Social Work*, 1987,
11 (3/4), 43–56.

Bearon, Lucille B. (ed.). "Quality of Life in Long-Term Care Settings." *Journal of Applied Social Work*, 1988, 7 (3), 275–419 (special issue).

Becker, G., and Kaufman, S. "Old Age, Rehabilitation, and Research: A Review of the Issues." *The Gerontologist*, 1988, *28* (4),
459–468.

Bennett, R. G. "The Meaning of Institutional Life." *The Gerontologist*, 1963, *3* (3), 117–125.

Blau, P. W. *Exchange and Power in Social Life*. New York: Wiley,
1964.

Blenkner, M. "Social Work and Family Relationships in Later Life
with Some Thoughts on Filial Maturity." In E. Shanas and G.
E. Streib (eds.), *Social Structure and the Family*. Englewood
Cliffs, N.J.: Prentice-Hall, 1965.

Blenkner, M. "Environmental Change and the Aging Individual."
The Gerontologist, 1967, 7 (2), 101–105.

Bogdan, R., and Taylor, S. J. "Relationships with Severely Disabled
People: The Social Construction of Humanness." *Social Problems*, 1989, *36* (2), 135–148.

Borup, J. H. "Relocation: Attitudes, Information, Network, and
Problems Encountered." *The Gerontologist*, 1981, *21* (5), 501–
511.

Borup, J. H. "The Effects of Varying Degrees of Interinstitutional
Environmental Change on Long-Term Care Patients." *The Gerontologist*, 1982, *22* (4), 409–417.

Borup, J. H. "Relocation Mortality Research: Assessment, Reply,
and the Need to Refocus the Issues." *The Gerontologist*, 1983, *23*
(3), 235–242.

Bowker, L. H. *Humanizing Institutions for the Aged*. Lexington,
Mass.: Heath, 1982.

Brody, E. M. "Follow-Up Study of Applicants and Non-Applicants
to a Voluntary Home." *The Gerontologist*, 1969, *9* (3), 187–196.

Brody, E. M. "The Social Aspects of Nursing Home Care." In E.
L. Schneider and others (eds.), *The Teaching Nursing Home: A*

New Approach to Geriatric Research, Education, and Geriatric Care. New York: Raven Press, 1985a.

Brody, E. M. "Parent Care as a Normative Family Stress." *The Gerontologist,* 1985b, *25* (1), 19–29.

Brody, E. M., Kleban, M. H., Lawton, M. P., and Silverman, H. A. "Excess Disabilities of Mentally Impaired Aged: Impact of Individualized Treatment." *The Gerontologist,* 1971, *2* (2), 124–133.

Buckholdt, D. R., and Gubrium, J. F. "Practicing Accountability in Human Service Institutions." *Urban Life,* 1983, *12* (3), 249–268.

Bultena, G. L., and Oyler, R. "Effects of Health on Disengagement and Morale." *The International Journal of Aging and Human Development,* 1971, *2* (2), 142–148.

Burgio, K. L., Whitehead, W. E., and Engel, B. T. "Urinary Incontinence in the Elderly: Bladder-Sphincter Biofeedback and Toileting Skills Training." *Annals of Internal Medicine. 103* (4), 507–515.

Burton, J. R. "Managing Urinary Incontinence—A Common Geriatric Problem." *Geriatrics,* 1984, *39* (10), 46–51, 54, 59, 62.

Cath, S. H. "Some Dynamics of Middle and Later Years: A Study in Depletion and Restitution." In M. A. Berezin and S. H. Cath (eds.), *Geriatric Psychiatry: Grief, Loss and Emotional Disorders in the Aging Process.* New York: International Universities Press, 1965.

Cath, S. H. "The Orchestration of Disengagement." *International Journal of Aging and Human Development,* 1975, *6* (3), 199–213.

Charmaz, K. "Struggling for a Self: Identity Levels of the Chronically Ill." In J. A. Roth and P. Conrad (eds.), *Researching the Sociology of Health Care: The Experience and Management of Chronic Illness.* Vol. 6. Greenwich, Conn.: JAI Press, 1987.

Cherry, D. L., and Rafkin, M. J. "Adapting Day Care to the Needs of Adults with Dementia." *The Gerontologist,* 1988, *28* (1), 116–120.

Coffman, T. L. "Relocation and Survival of Institutionalized Aged: A Re-examination of the Evidence." *The Gerontologist,* 1981, *21* (5), 483–500.

Cohen, E. S. "The Elderly Mystique: Constraints on the Autonomy of the Elderly with Disabilities." *The Gerontologist*, 1988, *28*, 24–31 (supplement).

Cohen, M. A., Tell, E. J., and Wallack, S. S. "Client-Related Risk Factors of Nursing Home Entry Among Elderly Adults." *Journal of Gerontology*, 1986, *41* (6), 785–792.

Cohen, M. A., and others. "Patterns of Nursing Home Use in a Prepaid Managed Care Retirement Community." *The Gerontologist*, 1989, *29* (1), 74–80.

Cohen-Mansfield, J. "Absenteeism of Nursing Staff in a Nursing Home." Paper presented at the 34th annual meeting of American Society on Aging, San Diego, Calif., Mar. 21, 1988.

Comments from the Floor at the International Congress on Gerontology, New York, 1985.

Commitee on Nursing Home Regulation, Institute of Medicine. *Improving the Quality of Care in Nursing Homes.* Washington, D.C.: National Academy Press, 1986.

Cook, K. S., and Emerson, R. M. "Exchange Networks and the Analysis of Complex Organizations." In S. B. Bacharach and E. J. Lawler (eds.), *Research in the Sociology of Organizations.* Vol. 1. Greenwich, Conn.: JAI Press, 1984.

Cook, K. S., Emerson, R. M., Gillmore, M. R., and Yamagishi, T. "The Distribution of Power in Exchange Networks: Theory and Experimental Results." *American Journal of Sociology*, 1983, *89* (2), 275–305.

Cooney, T. J., Schaie, K. W., and Willis, S. L. "The Relationship Between Prior Functioning on Cognitive and Personality Dimensions and Subject Attrition in Longitudinal Research." *Journal of Gerontology*, 1988, *43* (1), 12–17.

Corbin, J. M., and Strauss, A. *Unending Work and Care: Managing Chronic Illness at Home.* San Francisco: Jossey-Bass. 1988.

Coulton, C. J., Dunkle, R. E., Goode, R. A., and MacKintoch, J. "Discharge Planning and Decision Making." *Health and Social Work*, 1982, 7 (4), 253–261.

Coulton, C. J., and others. "Dimensions of Post-Hospital Care Decision-Making: A Factor Analytic Study." *The Gerontologist*, 1988, *28* (2), 218–223.

Cumming, E. "Engagement with an Old Theory." *International Journal of Aging and Human Development*, 1975, *6* (3), 187–191.

Cumming, E., and Henry, W. E. *Growing Old: The Process of Disengagement.* New York: Basic Books, 1961.

Day, P., and Klein, R. "The Regulation of Nursing Homes: A Comparative Perspective." *The Milbank Quarterly,* 1987, *65* (3), 303–347.

Devitt, M., and Checkoway, B. "Participation in Nursing Home Resident Councils: Promise and Practice." *The Gerontologist,* 1982, *22* (1), 49–53.

Dowd, J. J. *Stratification Among the Aged.* Monterey, Calif.: Brooks/Cole, 1980.

Dunkle, R. E. "The Effects of Elders' Household Contributions on Their Depression." *Journal of Gerontology,* 1983, *38* (6), 732–737.

Edelson, J. S., and Lyons, W. H. *Institutional Care of the Mentally Impaired Elderly.* New York: Van Nostrand Reinhold, 1985.

Elwell, F. "The Effects of Ownership on Institutional Services." *The Gerontologist,* 1984, *24* (24), 77–83.

Emerson, R. M. "Power-Dependence Relations." *American Sociological Review,* 1962, *27* (1), 31–41.

Emerson, R. M., and Messenger, S. "The Micro-Politics of Trouble." *Social Problems,* 1977, *25* (2), 121–134.

Emerson, R. M., and Warren, C. A. B. "Trouble and the Politics of Contemporary Social Control Institutions." *Urban Life,* 1983, *12* (3), 243–247.

Engel, G. I. "A Life Setting Conducive to Illness: The Giving-Up, Given-Up Syndrome." *Annals of Internal Medicine,* 1968, *69* (2), 293–300.

Evans, L. K., and Stumpf, N. E. "Tying Down the Elderly: A Review of the Literature on Physical Restraint." *The Journal of the American Geriatrics Society,* 1989, *37* (1), 65–74.

Fottler, M. D., Smith, H. L., and James, W. L. "Profits and Patient Care Quality in Nursing Homes: Are They Compatible?" *The Gerontologist,* 1981, *21* (5), 532–538.

Garabaldi, R. A., Brodine, S., and Matsumiya, S. "Infection among Patients in Nursing Homes: Policies, Prevalence, and Problems." *Journal of the American Medical Association,* 1981, *305* (13), 731–735.

Gilford, R. "Contrasts in Marital Satisfaction Throughout Old

Age: An Exchange Theory Analysis." *Journal of Gerontology,* 1984, *39* (3), 325-333.

Glaser, B. G., and Strauss, A. L. *Awareness of Dying.* Chicago: Aldine, 1965.

Glaser, B. G., and Strauss, A. L. *Status Passage.* Chicago: Aldine-Atherton, 1971.

Goffman, E. *Asylums: Essays on the Social Situation of Mental Patients and Other Inmates.* Garden City, N.Y.: Doubleday, 1961.

Goode, W. J. "The Place of Force in Human Society." *American Sociological Review,* 1972, *37,* 507-519.

Gordon, J. B. "A Disengaged Look at Disengagement." *International Journal of Aging and Human Development,* 1975, *6* (3), 215-227.

Gubrium, J. F. "The Social Preservation of Mind: The Alzheimer's Disease Experience." *Symbolic Interaction,* 1986, *9* (1), 37-51.

Gustafson, E. "Dying: The Career of the Nursing Home Patient." *Journal of Health and Social Behavior,* 1972, *13* (3), 226-236.

Health Care Financing Administration. *State Operations Manual Issuance: Survey Procedures, Forms, Worksheets and Interpretative Guidelines.* Washington, D.C.: Department of Health and Human Services, 1989. (Advance copy circulated by the National Citizens' Coalition for Nursing Home Reform.)

Hochschild, A. R. "Disengagement Theory: A Critique and Proposal." *American Sociological Review,* 1975, *40* (5), 553-569.

Hofland, B. F. (ed.). "Autonomy and Long-Term Care." *The Gerontologist,* 1988, *28,* 1-96 (supplement).

Horowitz, M. J., and Schulz, R. "The Relocation Controversy: Criticism and Commentary on Five Recent Studies." *The Gerontologist,* 1983, *23* (3), 229-234.

Jackson, M. E., and others. "Prevalence and Correlates of Disruptive Behavior in the Nursing Home." *Aging & Health,* 1989, *1* (3), 349-369.

Jenike, M. A. "Alzheimer's Disease: Clinical Care and Management." *Psychosomatics,* 1986, *27* (6), 407-416.

Johnson, C. L., and Catalano, D. J. "Childless Elderly and Their Family Supports." *The Gerontologist,* 1981, *21* (6), 610-618.

Jones, E., and others. *Social Stigma: The Psychology of Marked Relationships.* New York: Freeman, 1984.

Jones, K., and Fowles, A. J. *Ideas on Institutions: Analyzing the Literature on Long-Term Care and Custody.* London: Routledge & Kegan Paul, 1984.

Kahn, R. L. "Aging and Social Support." In M. W. Riley (ed.), *Aging from Birth to Death: Interdisciplinary Perspectives.* Boulder, Colo.: Westview Press, 1979.

Kane, R. A., and Kane, R. L. *Assessing the Elderly: A Practical Guide to Measurement.* Lexington, Mass.: Heath, 1981.

Kane, R. L. Remarks on a panel at the International Congress on Gerontology, New York, July 14, 1985.

Katzman, R. "Alzheimer's Disease." *The New England Journal of Medicine,* 1986, *314* (15), 964-973.

Kaufman, A. "Social Policy and Long-Term Care of the Aged." *Social Work,* 1980, *25* (2), 133-137.

Kaufman, S. R. *The Ageless Self: Sources of Meaning in Late Life.* Madison: University of Wisconsin Press, 1986.

Kaufman, S. R. "Stroke Rehabilitation and the Negotiation of Identity." In S. Reinharz and G. D. Rowles (eds.), *Qualitative Gerontology.* New York: Springer, 1987.

Kayser-Jones, J. *Old, Alone and Neglected: Care of the Aged in Scotland and the United States.* Berkeley: University of California Press, 1981.

Kerschner, P. A. "The $3.75 an Hour Factor: Hard Realities Facing Nurse Aides." *Perspective on Aging,* 1987, *26* (6), 15-17.

Kingson, E. R., Hirshorn, B. A., and Cornman, J. M. *Ties That Bind: The Interdependence of Generations.* A Report of the Gerontological Society of America. Washington, D.C.: Seven Locks Press, 1986.

Kleemeier, R. W. "Attitudes Toward Special Settings for the Aged." In R. H. Williams and W. Donahue (eds.), *Processes of Aging: Social and Perspectives II.* New York: Atherton Press, 1963.

Kowalski, N. C. "Institutional Relocation: Current Programs and Applied Approaches." *The Gerontologist,* 1981, *21* (5), 512-519.

Kuhn, A., and Beam, R. D. *The Logic of Organization: A System-Based Social Science Framework for Organization.* San Francisco: Jossey-Bass, 1982.

Lawton, M. P. "The Dimensions of Morale." In D. Kent, R. Kastenbaum, and S. Sherwood (eds.), *Research, Planning and Action for the Elderly*. New York: Behavioral Publications, 1972.

Lawton, M. P. "The Functional Assessment of Elderly People." In V. Brantl and M. R. Brown (eds.), *Readings in Gerontology*. St. Louis, Mo.: Mosby, 1973.

Lawton, M. P. "Sensory Deprivation and the Effect of Environment on Management of the Patient with Senile Dementia." In N. E. Miller and G. D. Cohen (eds.), *Clinical Aspects of Alzheimer's Disease and Senile Dementia*. New York: Raven Press, 1981.

Lawton, M. P. "The Elderly in Context: Perspectives from Environment and Gerontology." *Environment and Behavior*, 1985, *17* (4), 501-509.

Lawton, M. P., and Nahemow, L. "Ecology and the Aging Process." In C. Eisdorfer and M. P. Lawton (eds.), *The Psychology of Adult Development and Aging*. Washington, D.C.: American Psychological Association, 1973.

Lawton, M. P. "Behavior-Relevant Ecological Factors." In W. W. Schaie and C. Schooler (eds.), *Social Structure and Aging: Psychological Processes*. Hillsdale, N.J.: Lawrence Erlbaum Associates, 1989.

Liang, J., and Bollen, K. A. "The Structure of the Philadelphia Geriatric Morale Scale: A Reinterpretation." *Journal of Gerontology*, 1983, *38* (2), 181-189.

Lieberman, M. A. "Adaptive Processes in Late Life." In N. Datan and L. H. Ginsberg (eds.), *Lifespan Developmental Psychology: Normative Life Crises*. New York: Academic Press, 1975.

Lieberman, M. A., and Tobin, S. S. *The Experience of Old Age: Stress, Coping, and Survival*. New York: Basic Books, 1983.

Litwak, E. *Helping the Elderly: The Complementary Roles of Informal Networks and Formal Systems*. New York: Guilford, 1985.

Locker, R. "Elderly Couples and the Institution." *Social Work*, 1976, *21* (2), 149-151.

Markson, E. "Disengagement Theory Revisited." *International Journal of Aging and Human Development*, 1975, *6* (3), 183-186.

Martin, J. D. "Power, Dependence, and the Complaints of the Elderly: A Social Exchange Perspective." *Aging and Human Development*, 1971, *2* (2), 108-112.

Mitteness, L. S. "So What Do You Expect When You're 85?" In J. A. Roth and P. Conrad (eds.), *Research in the Sociology of Health Care: The Experience and Management of Chronic Illness.* Vol. 6. Greenwich, Conn.: JAI Press, 1987.

Montgomery, R. J. A. "Respite Care: Lessons from a Controlled Design Study." *Health Care Financing Review,* 1988, 133–138 (annual supplement).

Morford, T. G. "Nursing Home Regulation: History and Expectations." *Health Care Financing Review,* 1988, 129–132 (annual supplement).

Morgan, D. L. "Failing Health and the Desire for Independence: Two Conflicting Aspects of Health Care in Old Age." *Social Problems,* 1982, *30* (1), 40–50.

Moss, M. S., and Kurland, P. "Family Visiting with Institutionalized Mentally Impaired Aged." *Journal of Gerontological Social Work,* 1979, *1* (4), 271–278.

National Center for Health Statistics, and Hing, E. "Use of Nursing Homes by the Elderly, Preliminary Data from the 1985 National Nursing Home Survey." *Advance Data from Vital and Health Statistics,* no. 135. DHHS pub. no. (PHS) 87–1250. Hyattsville, Md.: Public Health Service, May 14, 1987.

National Center for Health Statistics, and Hing, E., Sekscenski, E., and Strahan, G. "The National Nursing Home Survey: 1985 Summary for the United States." *Vital and Health Statistics,* series 13, no. 97. DHHS pub. no. (PHS) 89–1758, Washington, D.C.: U.S. Government Printing Office, January, 1989.

National Center for Health Statistics, and Sirrocco, A. "Nursing and Related Care Homes as Reported from the 1986 Inventory of Long-Term Care Places." *Advance Data from Vital and Health Statistics,* no. 147. DHHS pub. no. (PHS) 88–1250. Hyattsville, Md.: Public Health Service, 1988.

National Center for Health Statistics, and Strahan, G. W. *Trends in Nursing and Related Care Homes and Hospitals: United States, Selected Years 1969–80,* no. 30. DHHS pub. no. (PHS) 84–1825. Washington, D.C.: U.S. Government Printing Office, March 1984.

National Center for Health Statistics, and Strahan, G. W. "Nursing Home Characteristics, Preliminary Data from the 1985 National

Nursing Home Survey." *Advance Data from Vital and Health Statistics*, no. 131. DHHS pub. no. (PHS) 87-1250. Hyattsville, Md.: March, 1987.

National Institute on Aging Task Force. "Senility Reconsidered: Treatment Possibilities for Mental Impairment in the Elderly." *Journal of the American Medical Association*, 1980, *244* (3), 259-263.

Neugarten, B., and Havighurst, R. J. "Disengagement Reconsidered in a Cross-National Context." In R. J. Havighurst and others (eds.), *Adjustment to Retirement: A Cross-National Study.* Assen, The Netherlands: 1969.

O'Brien, J., Saxberg, B. O., and Smith, H. L. "For-Profit or Not-for-Profit Nursing Homes: Does It Matter?" *The Gerontologist*, 1983, *23* (4), 341-348.

Ouslander, J. G., Kane, R. L., and Abrass, I. B. "Urinary Incontinence in Elderly Nursing Home Patients." *Journal of the American Medical Association*, 1982, *248* (10), 1194-1198.

Ouslander, J. G., and Uman, G. C., "Urinary Incontinence: Opportunities for Research, Education, and Improvements in Medical Care in the Nursing Home Setting." In E. L. Schneider and others (eds.), *The Teaching Nursing Home: A New Approach to Geriatric Research, Education, and Geriatric Care.* New York: Raven Press, 1985.

Pablo, R. Y. "Intra-Institutional Relocation: Its Impact on Long-Term Care Patients." *The Gerontologist*, 1977, *17* (5), 426-435.

Parsons, T. *Social Structure and Personality.* New York: Free Press, 1970.

Pillemar, K., and Moore, D. W. "Abuse of Patients in Nursing Homes: Findings from a Survey of Staff." *The Gerontologist*, 1989, *29* (3), 314-320.

Raven, B. H., and Kruglanski, A. W. "Conflict and Power." In P. Swingle (ed.), *The Structure of Conflict.* New York: Academic Press, 1970.

Reisberg, B., and Ferris, S. H. "Diagnosis and Assessment of the Older Patient." *Hospital & Community Psychiatry*, 1982, *32* (2), 104-118.

Resnick, N. M., and Yalla, S. V. "Management of Urinary Incontinence." *New England Journal of Medicine,* 1985, *313* (13), 800–805.

Resnick, N. M., Yalla, S. V., and Laurino, E. L. "The Psychophysiology of Urinary Incontinence Among Institutionalized Elderly Persons." *New England Journal of Medicine,* 1989, *320* (1), 1–7.

Restinas, J., and Garrity, P. "Nursing Home Friendships." *The Gerontologist,* 1985, *25* (4), 376–381.

Rodin, J., Timko, C., and Harris, S. "The Construct of Control: Biological and Psychosocial Correlates." In M. P. Lawton and G. L. Maddox (eds.), *Annual Review of Gerontology and Geriatrics.* Vol. 5. New York: Springer, 1985.

Rogers, M. F. "Instrumental and Infra-Resources: The Bases of Power." *American Journal of Sociology,* 1974, *79* (6), 1418–1433.

Roth, J. *Timetables: Structuring the Passage of Time in Hospital Treatment and Other Careers.* Indianapolis, Ind.: Bobbs-Merrill, 1963.

Rovner, B. W., and Rabins, P. V. "Practical Geriatrics: Mental Illness Among Nursing Home Patients." *Hospital & Community Psychiatry,* 1985, *36* (2), 119–120, 129.

Rowe, J. W. "Health Care of the Elderly." *New England Journal of Medicine,* 1985, *312* (13), 827–835.

Sauer, W. J., and Warland, R. "Morale and Life Satisfaction." In D. J. Mangen and W. A. Peterson, (eds.), *Clinical and Social Psychology I.* Minneapolis: University of Minnesota Press, 1982.

Scanlon, W. J. "A Perspective on Long-Term Care for the Elderly." *Health Care Financing Review,* 1988, 7–15 (annual supplement).

Schmidt, M. G. "Patterns of Norm Conformity, Social Resources and Morale in Residential Settings for the Aged." Unpublished doctoral dissertation, The Graduate School, Rutgers, the State University of New Jersey, 1975.

Schmidt, M. G. "Exchange and Power in Special Settings for the Aged." *International Journal of Aging and Human Development,* 1981–82, 157–166.

Schmidt, M. G. "The Patient's Partner: The Spouse in Residential Care." *Health and Social Work,* 1987, *12* (3), 206–212.

Schnelle, J. F., V. A. Sowell, T. W. Hu, and B. Traugher. "Reduction of Urinary Incontinence in Nursing Homes: Does It Reduce or Increase Costs?" *Journal of the American Geriatrics Society,* 1988, *36* (1), 34–39.

Schur, E. M. *The Politics of Deviance.* Englewood Cliffs, N.J.: Prentice-Hall, 1980.

Senn, B. J., and Steiner, J. R. " 'Don't Tread on Me': Ethological Perspectives on Institutionalization." *International Journal of Aging and Human Development,* 1978–1979, *9* (2), 177–185.

Shaughnessy, P. W., and Kramer, A. M. "The Increased Needs of Patients in Nursing Homes and Patients Receiving Home Care." *New England Journal of Medicine,* 1990, *322* (1), 21–27.

Shifflett, P. A., and Blieszner, R. "Stigma and Alzheimer's Disease: Behavioral Consequences for Support Groups." *The Journal of Applied Gerontology,* 1988, *7* (2), 147–160.

Smyer, M. A., and Frysinger, M. "Mental Health Intervention in the Nursing Home Community." In M. P. Lawton and G. L. Maddox (eds.), *Annual Review of Gerontology and Geriatrics.* New York: Springer, 1985.

Snyder, L. H., and others. "Wandering." *The Gerontologist,* 1978, *18* (3), 272–280.

Spence, D. L. "The Meaning of Engagement." *International Journal of Aging and Human Development,* 1975, *6* (3), 193–198.

Spence, D. L. "Some Contributions of Symbolic Interaction to the Study of Growing Old." In V. W. Marshall (ed.), *Later Life: The Social Psychology of Aging.* Beverly Hills: Sage, 1986.

Stanndard, C. I. "Old Folks and Dirty Work: The Social Conditions for Patient Abuse in a Nursing Home." *Social Problems,* 1973, *20* (3), 329–342.

Starer, P., and Libow, L. S. "Obscuring Urinary Incontinence: Diapering of the Elderly." *Journal of the American Geriatrics Society,* 1985, *22* (12), 842–846.

Stoesz, D. "The Grey Market: Social Consequences of For-Profit Eldercare." *Journal of Gerontological Social Work,* 1989, *14* (3/4), 19–33.

Stone, R., Cafferata, G. L., and Sangl, J. *Caregivers of the Frail Elderly: A National Profile.* National Center for Health Services Research, Care for the Aging. Washington, D.C.: U.S. Government Printing Office, 1987.

Strauss, A. *Negotiations: Varieties, Contexts, Processes, and Social Order.* San Francisco: Jossey-Bass, 1978.

Strauss, A., and Corbin, J. M. *Shaping a New Health Care System: The Explosion of Chronic Illness as a Catalyst for Change.* San Francisco: Jossey-Bass, 1988.

Streib, G. F., Folts, W. E., and LaGreca, A. J. "Autonomy, Power, and Decision-Making in Thirty-Six Retirement Communities." *The Gerontologist,* 1985, *25* (4), 403–409.

Suzman, R., and Riley, M. W. "Introducing the 'Oldest Old.'" *Milbank Memorial Quarterly: Health and Society,* 1985, *63* (2), 177–186.

Swann, W. B., Jr. "Identity Negotiation: Where Two Roads Meet." *Journal of Personality and Social Psychology,* 1987, *53* (6), 1038–1051.

Tellis-Nayak, V., and Tellis-Nayak, M. "Quality of Care and the Burden of Two Cultures: When the World of the Nurse's Aide Enters the World of the Nursing Home." *The Gerontologist,* 1989, *29* (3), 307–313.

Tideiksaar, R. "Geriatric Falls: Assessing the Cause, Preventing Recurrence." *Geriatrics, 44* (7), 1989, 57–61, 64.

Tinetti, M. E., and Speechley, M. "Prevention of Falls Among the Elderly." *The New England Journal of Medicine,* 1989, *320* (16), 1055–1059.

Tobin, S. S., and Lieberman, M. A. *Last Home for the Aged: Critical Implications of Institutionalization.* San Francisco: Jossey-Bass, 1976.

Tolstoy, L. *The Death of Ivan Ilyich.* New York: Bantam Books, 1981. (Originally published 1886.)

Troll, L. E. "Kinship Networks." In L. E. Troll (ed.), *Family Issues in Current Gerontology.* New York: Springer, 1986.

U.S. Congress, Office of Technology Assessment. *Technology and Aging in America.* OTA-BA-264. Washington, D.C.: U.S. Government Printing Office, 1985.

U.S. Congress, Office of Technology Assessment. *Losing a Million Minds: Confronting the Tragedy of Alzheimer's Disease and Other Dementias.* OTA-BA-323. Washington, D.C.: U.S. Government Printing Office, 1987.

U.S. Department of Health and Human Services, National Institutes of Health. "Urinary Incontinence in Adults." *Consensus Development Conference Statement,* 1988, 7 (5), 1–11.

U.S. Department of Health and Human Services, Health Care Financing Administration. "Medicare and Medicaid; Requirements for Long Term Care Facilities." *Federal Register,* February 2, 1989, *54* (21), 5316–5373.

U.S. Senate, Special Committee on Aging, Subcommittee on Long-Term Care. *Nursing Home Care in the United States: Failure in Public Policy.* Washington, D.C.: U.S. Government Printing Office, 1974.

U.S. Senate, Special Committee on Aging. *Developments in Aging: 1987. The Long-Term Challenge.* Vol. 3. Washington, D.C.: U.S. Government Printing Office, 1988.

U.S. Senate, Special Committee on Aging, and E. Vierck. *Aging America; Trends and Projections.* Washington, D.C.: U.S. Government Printing Office, 1990.

Vladeck, B. C. *Unloving Care: The Nursing Home Tragedy.* New York: Basic Books, 1980.

Volland, P. J. "The Changing Health Care Environment." In P. J. Volland, (ed.), *Discharge Planning: An Interdisciplinary Approach to Continuity of Care.* Owings Mills, Md.: National Health Publishing, 1988.

Waxman, H. M., Carner, E. A., and Berkenstock, G. "Job Turnover and Job Satisfaction Among Nursing Home Aides." *The Gerontologist,* 1984, *24* (5), 503–509.

Webster, M., Jr., and Driskell, J. E., Jr. "Status Generalization." In J. Berger and M. Zelditch, Jr. (eds.), *Status, Rewards, and Influence: How Expectations Organize Behavior.* San Francisco: Jossey-Bass, 1985.

Wiener, C. L., and Kayser-Jones, J. "Defensive Work in Nursing Homes: Accountability Gone Amok." *Social Science and Medicine,* 1989, *28* (1), 37–44.

Wiener, C. L., and Kayser-Jones, J. "The Uneasy Fate of Nursing Home Residents: An Organizational-Interaction Perspective." *Sociology of Health & Illness,* 1990, *12* (1), 84–103.

Willington, F. L. "Urinary Incontinence: A Practical Approach." *Geriatrics* June 1980, *35* (6), 41–47.

Wingard, D. L., Jones, D. W., and Kaplan, R. M. "Institutional Care Utilization by the Elderly: A Critical Review." *The Gerontologist*, 1987, *27* (2), 156–163.

Wolins, M., and Wozner, Y. *Revitalizing Residential Settings: Problems and Potential in Education, Health, Rehabilitation, and Social Service.* San Francisco: Jossey-Bass, 1982.

Index